HYPOCRISY AND HUMAN RIGHTS

HYPOCRISY AND HUMAN RIGHTS

Resisting Accountability for Mass Atrocities

Kate Cronin-Furman

CORNELL UNIVERSITY PRESS   **ITHACA AND LONDON**

First published 2022 by Cornell University Press

Librarians: A CIP catalog record for this book is available from the Library of Congress.

ISBN 978-1-5017-6357-1 (hardcover)
ISBN 978-1-5017-6509-4 (paperback)
ISBN 978-1-5017-6510-0 (pdf)
ISBN 978-1-5017-6715-9 (epub)

Contents

Acknowledgments

I often feel like I learn just as much from the acknowledgment sections of academic books as from the body of the text. Even at their most anodyne, acknowledgments reveal so much about intellectual lineages and the replication of privilege in the academy. But the best ones are their own ethnographies, pulling back the curtain on the connections, practices, and communities that enable and ultimately define our work.

This book would not have been possible without the contributions of an enormous network of people, starting with my PhD advisors. Tonya Putnam invested in my work like it was her own but never tried to take credit or control. I am profoundly grateful to her for the hours she spent explaining political science to me in the early years and drinking whisky with me in the later ones. Michael Doyle has provided guidance and support for nearly two decades. His example and encouragement are why I chose to study political science. He also introduced me to Kofi Annan, which was a pretty big deal for a twenty-three-year-old aspiring human rights lawyer. Jack Snyder has offered a constant supply of wisdom on matters large and small since I first set foot in his office as an admitted PhD student in March 2009. Having him on my side has made every step of the dissertation, academic job market, and book writing processes easier and more enjoyable.

I was lucky enough to go to grad school with Pavi Suryanarayan, Steph Schwartz, Mira Rapp-Hooper, Erica Borghard, and Jon Blake, all of whom have provided critical assists with my research and general well-being dating back to my dissertation's embryonic stage. I didn't go to grad school with Anjali Dayal, Terry Peterson, or Morgan Kaplan, but they've all made invaluable contributions at various points in the life of the project. Pablo de Greiff guest starred on my dissertation committee and has been a much-appreciated early adopter of the term "quasi-compliance." Golriz Ghahraman, intrepid travel companion, made several of my research trips more fun; I don't know why I ever go anywhere without her. She and Fedelma Claire Smith have provided indispensable distance cheerleading and emotional and professional support since we first met in The Hague over a decade ago.

The members of more seminars and workshops than I can list at Columbia, Stanford, Harvard, and elsewhere provided enormously helpful feedback during the roughly six hundred years I was writing this book. Varsha Venkatasubramanian and Miriam Hornsby performed heroic feats of citation checking and indexing. And my colleagues in the Department of Political Science at University College London have offered edits and encouragement as I struggled to push this manuscript over the finish line amidst a global pandemic and the shift to online teaching.

I'm sure my parents and sisters often wonder why I do the things I do, but they never seem to question the importance of doing them. I am grateful to them for this, and to my ex-husband Peter Tsapatsaris for the years of support and enthusiasm that made this book possible—and for our five-year-old, Jamie, who after initial skepticism on being informed I was writing a book ("don't you mean READING a book?") got wholeheartedly on board.

I have the rare luck of not having felt alone in the world since sometime in late 1995, shortly before I met my best friend, Amanda Taub. Her unshakable faith in me is occasionally terrifying, but always sustaining. And like so much of my personal and professional life, this book has been profoundly influenced by our friendship.

I know it's customary to use this space to thank people for their contributions to a book project, but honestly, I'm more grateful to the book for bringing several friends, coauthors, and kindred spirits into my life. Milli Lake and Roxani Krystalli have made my life better in so many ways, providing bourbon, brownies, and unfaltering models of feminist refusal. Nimmi Gowrinathan is a consistently inspiring example of graceful resistance to rationalizing hegemonies of all kinds and there's no one I'd rather go to war with. Mario Arulthas has talked through every thought I've had in the last five years and read every word I've written (except the ones about regressions), some of them five or six times. Maybe I could have done this without him, but I wouldn't want to find out.

The argument I offer here, about how repressive states respond to human rights pressure when they can't afford to completely ignore international audiences, is enough of a theoretical innovation to get me published in prestigious outlets. But at the same time, it's old news to the survivors of human rights violations, who know in their bones that international pressure can't override the exigencies of domestic politics. It's an understatement to say that this book wouldn't exist without the hundreds of people around the world who spoke with me about their experiences seeking justice in the aftermath of atrocities. The people quoted in these pages aren't research subjects; they're the intended audience for this book and the theorists of human rights behavior with whom I hope to be in conversation.

Abbreviations

CAT   Convention against Torture
ECCC   Extraordinary Chambers in the Courts of Cambodia
ICC   International Criminal Court
ICCPR   International Covenant on Civil and Political Rights
ICESCR   International Covenant on Economic Social and Cultural Rights
ICJ   International Court of Justice
ICTR   International Criminal Tribunal for Rwanda
ICTY   International Criminal Tribunal for the former Yugoslavia
LLRC   Lessons Learnt and Reconciliation Commission
NGO   nongovernmental organization
UDHR   Universal Declaration of Human Rights
UNDP   United Nations Development Programme
UNHRC   UN Human Rights Council

HYPOCRISY AND HUMAN RIGHTS

INTRODUCTION

A reporter once asked me something that has stuck with me: "If the international community can't make states abide by their human rights obligations, what's the point of invoking them?" It's a good question. Both common sense and the academic literature tell us that international human rights pressure is much too weak a stick to compel states to change behavior they're invested in. So why bother with, for example, the performative demand that a state whose military is actively committing genocide do more to protect the rights of its marginalized minorities?

There are two answers I give to this question, which is often voiced—in far more indignant tones—by my students as well. The first is a moral argument: even if it accomplishes nothing, it's important to identify and protest violations of human rights. But the second is: "shit's complicated." This is not a fatalistic shrug; it's a position statement about the complexity of the international system and the central role that unintended consequences and unexpected audiences play in driving human rights outcomes.

This is a book about what human rights pressure does when it doesn't "work." It takes as its starting point the observation that many states facing the prospect of international censure choose a middle path between caving to human rights pressure or ignoring it. Because even if pressure doesn't succeed in convincing violator states to remedy breaches of human rights, that doesn't mean it has no effect on their behavior. Quite the contrary. Repressive states with absolutely no intention of complying with their human rights obligations often change course dramatically in response to international pressure. They create toothless commissions, permit

1

but then obstruct international observers' visits, and pass showpiece legislation while simultaneously bolstering their repressive capacity.

An example: In early 2011, amidst the Arab Spring's wave of prodemocracy uprisings, two hundred thousand Bahrainis—approximately 40 percent of the country's citizens at the time—poured into the streets to protest their government. The response was ugly. Military and civilian security forces used deadly force, arbitrary arrests, and torture in an attempt to suppress the protests. Unable to quell the uprising on its own, Bahrain's government declared a state of emergency and requested backup from neighboring countries.

In the weeks that followed, the regime pursued a vicious campaign of retaliation against suspected dissidents. Hundreds of public and private sector employees were fired from their jobs, students lost their places at universities, and popular athletes were publicly shamed and suspended from the national teams for participation in peaceful protests.[1] Medical professionals who treated wounded protesters were arrested; twenty were convicted of antigovernment activity and handed lengthy prison sentences.[2]

By June 2011, the crackdown had largely succeeded. Hundreds of people remained in incommunicado detention. Four people had died in custody, and many of those who had been released reported being tortured in an attempt to coerce confessions.[3] These abuses further enraged a domestic public that was already mobilized to demand political change. Bahrain faced growing criticism from international human rights organizations and UN officials.[4] Human Rights First warned that "the situation on the ground is still dire for those calling for democratic reforms,"[5] while the International Crisis Group noted that "none of the worst excesses—the lengthy prison sentences for political offences, job dismissals based on participation in peaceful protests, mosque destruction—have been reversed."[6]

With its legitimacy in crisis both domestically and internationally, the regime ended the state of emergency, asked the foreign troops to go home, and announced the creation of the Bahrain Independent Commission of Inquiry (BICI). Made up of foreign legal experts, the BICI was mandated to "investigate and report on the events occurring in Bahrain in February/March 2011."[7] The commissioners were tasked with determining what, if any, human rights violations had occurred and with making recommendations for responding to them.

The format of the BICI was chosen with the resuscitation of Bahrain's international reputation in mind. In the words of Bahrain's foreign minister, "King Hamad wanted to clarify the facts about what happened through a mechanism that the international community would understand and accept."[8] And, indeed, international audiences initially responded with enthusiasm. The US State Department welcomed the BICI as a "significant and positive" step toward political accommodation and reconciliation, and Human Rights Watch described the move as "promising."[9]

The BICI's report, issued in November 2011, ran nearly five hundred pages and described a culture of impunity as well as systematic violations of human rights by the Bahraini security sector and judiciary.[10] The commissioners made twenty-six recommendations to promote accountability for, and nonrecurrence of, the violations. In response, Bahrain created a national commission to oversee implementation of these recommendations, as well as a "follow-up unit" in the Ministry of Justice.[11] In March 2012, the national commission released its report, along with a press release stating that "unprecedented progress has been made in the implementation of the recommendations of the Bahrain Independent Commission of Inquiry."[12] The commission pointed to the recent establishment of a special investigations unit within the Public Prosecution Office and an ombudsman within the Ministry of the Interior as evidence of this "unprecedented progress."[13]

But international observers found Bahrain's implementation of the BICI's recommendations disappointing. In a press release titled "Bahrain: Vital Reform Commitments Unmet," Human Rights Watch criticized the national commission's conclusions, saying that "serious concerns, like accountability for crimes such as torture and relief for people wrongly imprisoned, were not adequately addressed."[14] Likewise, critics noted that the much-touted Detainees Rights Commission lacked institutional independence and that a number of its members were "from the same judicial and public prosecution office responsible for the sentencing of prisoners of conscience."[15] Meanwhile, the regime took a number of well-documented steps to enhance its ability to repress, including passing harsher laws against dissent and protest.[16]

At the June 2012 United Nations Human Rights Council session in Geneva, twenty-eight countries joined to issue a declaration condemning ongoing human rights violations in Bahrain and calling on the government to implement the BICI's recommendations.[17] Although the United States (along with the United Kingdom) declined to support the initiative, in congressional testimony a month later, the assistant secretary of state for democracy, human rights, and labor described "continuing reprisals against Bahraini citizens who attempt to exercise their universal rights to free expression and assembly."[18]

What this brief example shows is that Bahrain engaged in significant activity responding to international pressure, without actually halting the repression international audiences were condemning. Bahrain's lack of progress on its commitments was not indicative of capacity issues. Even as it insisted it was implementing the BICI's recommendations, the government imprisoned opposition leaders and adopted legislation permitting the revocation of Bahraini citizenship from anyone convicted of terrorism (an offense defined to include "disrupting public order" and "damaging national unity").[19] Over time, it walked back even the minimal progress it had made, including restoring the National Security Agency's arrest powers, which had been revoked in line with the BICI's recommendations in 2011.[20]

In the following chapters, I argue that states like Bahrain are gambling on doing just enough to escape punishment. I situate my argument within social science literature on human rights and compliance with international law and introduce the term "quasi-compliance" to describe behavior that is clearly motivated by pressure to comply with a rule but is not undertaken with the intent of actually satisfying the rule's requirements.[21] This concept addresses what initially appears to be a puzzle—why do governments facing human rights pressure go to the trouble of creating institutions that obviously fail to satisfy international demands? I suggest that this behavior is a product of the limitations on human rights enforcement in the international system and that repressive states deploy it strategically to preempt penalties for noncompliance.

I argue that these efforts often look deeply unconvincing because they don't necessarily rely on persuading anyone of their sincerity. The strategy instead aims to exploit the uneven patterns of pressure and censure created by the profound structural limitations on human rights enforcement in the international system. The number of human rights crises ongoing at any given time far outstrips the international community's available attention span and commitment to dealing with them. And in the absence of sustained political will or any hierarchical enforcement mechanism, a wide range of actors are potential veto points on decisions to censure human rights violators. Each represents an opportunity for a repressive state to protect itself from international action.

As a consequence, repressive states that fear that international pressure might escalate into enforcement action have clear incentives to mimic the outward forms of compliance, to a lesser or greater degree of plausibility depending on whom they hope to convince. And even if domestic political or resource constraints mean they can't manage a response credible enough to persuade human rights nongovernmental organizations (NGOs) or engaged foreign governments to dial back the pressure, there are still plenty of benefits to be gained by noncredible efforts. They may be enough to convince other members of the international community whose support would be needed to translate pressure into penalties for noncompliance.

In the case of Bahrain, domestic and international activists were quick to call out the cynicism of showcasing the BICI while continuing to violate human rights. "By establishing an independent commission of inquiry with the purported intention of noncompliance, the Government of Bahrain has strung along the international community while shielding itself from criticism," wrote the executive director of Americans for Democracy and Human Rights in Bahrain.[22] But the reaction elsewhere was quite different. As Amnesty International colorfully put it: "British ministers have acted like overexcited cheerleaders for Bahrain's woefully inadequate human rights reforms."[23]

The BICI process, disappointing as it was, provided Bahrain and its allies with something to point to as evidence that the country was working on its human rights record and should not be censured. Indeed, the BICI's report for years remained the focus of conversations about human rights in Bahrain, both at the domestic level and in international fora, where "international organizations and human rights NGOs also dealt with the BICI's recommendations as an essential element of the standard according to which Bahrain's human rights record and its efforts to institute political reforms were evaluated."[24]

This example suggests that quasi-compliance can be a useful strategy in a repressive state's arsenal for avoiding international enforcement of its human rights obligations. If nothing else, it can effectively delay international censure; a real benefit for a state that may simply need time to complete a crackdown.

The case of Bahrain also offers some insight into when we're likely to see states do this. Bahrain could not outright ignore the international protests over its actions or bear the reputational costs of being designated a human rights abuser, but was at the same time unwilling to tolerate the threat to regime survival that ceasing repression of dissent could pose. This is a position in which many less powerful states, particularly those dependent on international aid, are likely to find themselves.

To flesh out the mechanisms that drive quasi-compliance and its impact, I focus on an area of human rights where international pressure is consistently strong, and where there are often very significant domestic political imperatives not to buckle to this pressure: accountability for mass atrocities. Decisions about what to do in the aftermath of atrocities are politically fraught and carry with them severe potential consequences ranging from the fall of a government to the outbreak of civil war. The issue area has a high likelihood of the sort of confrontations between domestic political imperatives and international pressure that would incentivize quasi-compliance for states that can't afford to tell the international community to get lost.

One of the most striking changes wrought by the post–Cold War human rights project is that news of mass atrocities now quickly prompts demands for those responsible to be prosecuted and punished. These demands often originate with members of the victim community, but they are picked up by activists overseas, and by international civil society organizations like Human Rights Watch, the International Center for Transitional Justice, and Amnesty International. Failures to provide accountability become the focus of statements by UN officials, including special rapporteurs and the UN high commissioner for human rights, and of debates at the UN Human Rights Council. They also become sticking points in bilateral relationships, potentially leading to reductions in aid, trade, and military cooperation.

The range of possible responses to calls for accountability is broad. After mass atrocities, some states undertake massive programs of domestic prosecutions, convicting hundreds or even thousands of perpetrators. Others focus on a handful of leaders or target only low-level "trigger-pullers." A number of postatrocity governments have chosen to outsource the pursuit of accountability to international courts, while others have opted to cooperate with the international community in the creation of hybrid tribunals. Some choose to create truth commissions operating alone or in tandem with prosecutions. Many choose denial, the suppression of evidence, and additional violence against victim communities to silence their demands for justice. But others do things that seem strikingly similar to Bahrain's behavior described above.

Consider an example from 2004, when international headlines blared that seventy thousand civilians had been killed in Darfur in a matter of months. Traumatized refugees fled across the border into Chad, following devastating violence unleashed against ethnic minorities by the Sudanese government and *janjaweed* militias. As the death toll mounted, the world began to wonder if it was watching "another Rwanda" unfold. In an impassioned *New York Times* op-ed, Samantha Power, who would later become Barack Obama's ambassador to the United Nations, called on the international community not to allow another mass slaughter to go unchecked. An "emergency summit" of activists launched the Save Darfur Coalition in New York in July 2004, dedicating themselves to "mobiliz[ing] a massive response to the atrocities."[25]

Activists and human rights advocates quickly called for the prosecution of those most responsible for international crimes. Writing in November of 2003, Amnesty International exhorted the Sudanese government to "hold the perpetrators of human rights abuses . . . accountable, by bringing them to justice in fair trials."[26] Six months later, in its first report on the crisis, Human Rights Watch also demanded that the Sudanese government "prosecute alleged perpetrators in accordance with international fair trial standards" and requested that the United Nations Security Council create "an impartial Commission of Experts" to investigate the crimes.[27]

Western governments soon echoed these calls. On July 22, 2004, the US House of Representatives unanimously passed a resolution stating that the United States should "ensure the prompt prosecution and adjudication in a competent international court of justice or the United States–proposed Sudan Tribunal of individuals responsible for war crimes, crimes against humanity, and genocide."[28]

The European Union pressed for trials at the recently established International Criminal Court (ICC).[29]

Sudan's government initially denied everything and lashed out furiously at Western diplomats, demanding that they "moderate their hostile attitude."[30] But as pressure continued to build, President Omar Hassan al-Bashir empaneled a commission of inquiry. Its mandate was ostensibly to investigate the truth of allegations of atrocities, but its members were put "under enormous pressure" to exonerate the government.[31] In early 2005, they announced that while violations of international law had occurred in Darfur, there was no evidence of crimes against humanity or genocide.

International audiences did not take these findings very seriously. Days after the Sudanese commission released its findings, an international investigation empaneled by UN Secretary-General Kofi Annan announced that it had found compelling evidence of serious violations of international humanitarian law in Darfur.[32] Ultimately, these findings formed the basis of the United Nations Security Council decision to refer the situation to the ICC. Five years later, the ICC's prosecutor would charge President Bashir with war crimes and crimes against humanity, then genocide.[33]

Sudan's efforts to preempt international action were unsuccessful. But it was far from unique in making this attempt, and other states have had more success with the strategy. In the following chapters, I show that when postatrocity governments whose domestic politics strongly disfavor accountability are subjected to significant international pressure to pursue justice, they often instead create kangaroo courts, weak commissions, and sham inquiries. I argue that quasi-compliance does not necessarily target those who are exerting human rights pressure, but instead exploits the fact that there is a range of relevant actors with decision-making power, in order to successfully disrupt international efforts to censure states that have failed to provide accountability.

The argument proceeds as follows:

In chapter 1, I look at what we know about when and how human rights pressure works. I present my theory of quasi-compliant human rights behavior and focus on how the inconsistency of enforcement incentivizes efforts to game the system. I explain this behavior as a reasonable gamble on escaping punishment for noncompliance, while still avoiding the full costs of meeting human rights obligations. We should expect to see it anywhere that enforcement is unpredictable, subject to politics, and costly. This is likely to be true, and to trigger efforts to gain the benefits of compliance without paying its costs, throughout the international human rights regime. I argue that pursuing quasi-compliance in response to international human rights pressure can be a successful strategy even when it doesn't satisfy those supplying the pressure. It works by simultaneously persuading other, less engaged states that can act as veto points on multilateral action to give their support *and* by offering them the political cover to do so. Quasi-compliance should therefore be understood less as an attempt at convincingly feigning compliance, and more as a convenient fiction that lets a sympathetic audience avoid the appearance of siding with a human rights violator. This argument intervenes in a growing literature on how repressive states push back against the international human rights project. It theorizes a new audience for human rights behavior as well as a novel role for hypocrisy in international relations: protecting an audience's reputation.

Chapter 2 lays out the context for international pressure to seek accountability, tracing the origins of the perception that accountability for mass atrocities is a legal obligation as well as the emergence of international justice advocacy and its importance on the world stage. The obligation to hold accountable those most responsible for the most serious international crimes is generally traced to the post–World War II efforts to hold the Nazi regime accountable for its crimes at Nuremberg. But despite changes to the international legal architecture that created a duty to prosecute the perpetrators of genocide, crimes against humanity, and war crimes, a global commitment to accountability failed to develop until decades later. I argue here that the eventual emergence of the norm in the 1990s was a by-product of the timing of the international community's reach to the Nuremberg precedent to justify the creation of the ad hoc international criminal tribunals for the former Yugoslavia and Rwanda, which coincided with the transitional justice explosion in Latin America. The international community's *right* to prosecute international crimes and individual states' *duty* to prosecute human rights violations within their territory, previously separate concepts, were tied together, a development I document through an analysis of Human Rights Watch's reporting on atrocity crimes in the late 1980s through mid-1990s.

Once this link had been made, it provided a persuasive rationale for international jurisdiction over an ever-increasing number of situations. As the norm entrenched, international pressure to provide accountability became virtually automatic in the aftermath of mass atrocities. At the same time, enforcing the norm is difficult and costly for international audiences. The issue of accountability for mass atrocities is therefore characterized by the exact combination of consistent pressure and uncertainty of enforcement that we would expect to trigger quasi-compliant responses to human rights pressure.

Chapter 3 establishes that accountability for mass atrocities also has the kind of high domestic political stakes that could motivate states to undertake quasi-compliant responses. It shows that postatrocity governments face a complex balancing act of competing motivations—to break with the past, to settle scores, to consolidate power, to placate survivors, to promote peace—before international

pressure even enters the picture. Once it does, things become even more complicated. International audiences aren't just an additional source of demands for
justice, they are also partners in the pursuit of accountability. Alongside political obstacles, capacity and resource challenges can have a devastating impact on
a transitional justice process's ability to meet its goals. For some postatrocity governments, these concerns make the idea of commencing a domestic process
completely unthinkable, even where there are persuasive political reasons to pursue transitional justice. In those cases, they may seek assistance from outside
actors to create accountability mechanisms. But while that choice may solve an
otherwise inescapable resource dilemma, it also layers additional complexity
onto the already complicated politics of accountability. International actors have
their own set of preferences about what justice should look like, which may clash
with a postatrocity government's incentives. This creates a fraught power dynamic that can lead to overt contestation over control of accountability processes between domestic and international actors.

In chapter 4, I build on the insights developed in chapter 3 that governments
are looking to their political survival when they make decisions about whether
and how to pursue accountability for mass atrocities. I argue that this explains not
only whether justice is provided but, critically, variation in what accountability
and impunity look like across cases. The many excellent existing studies on justice
for mass atrocities mostly explain the "positive" cases, theorizing the creation of
international tribunals or the normative shifts that have enabled domestic prosecutions of systemic violations of human rights.[34] These accounts illuminate
groundbreaking changes in the international system, but they shed little light on
the negative cases (which are numerous, given that most mass atrocities are never
prosecuted). In order to contribute a fuller understanding of the range of things
states do in response to calls for justice, I take a quantitative look at accountability
outcomes, using an original data set of ninety mass atrocity events.

The main empirical takeaway of this analysis is that postatrocity governments'
reactions to calls for justice depend on where those calls are coming from. Con-
firming the expectations derived from the examples presented in chapter 3, the
data presented in chapter 4 suggest that we should only expect to see prosecutions of those most responsible for mass atrocities when the perpetrators have
been removed from power and where victims are electorally relevant. International pressure, no matter how strong, *cannot* produce robust accountability
when those domestic political conditions are not met. Instead, we see postatrocity governments under these conditions creating underpowered mechanisms
that do not qualify as legitimate prosecutions or truth commissions.

Chapter 5 demonstrates that the theory of quasi-compliance presented in chapter 1 is a useful framework for understanding postatrocity governments' reactions

to international pressure for accountability. Using case studies of the Democratic Republic of the Congo (DRC) and Burma, I examine interactions between international audiences and postatrocity governments over accountability for mass atrocities. Together, the two case studies illuminate the potential payoffs of quasi-compliance. In the case of DRC, deeply flawed accountability measures were accepted by relevant international audiences as good faith efforts to address conflict-related sexual violence. By contrast, Burma's repeated creation of commissions of inquiry and court martials to investigate crimes against the Rohingya were met with almost uniform derision from the members of the international community who had been calling for justice.

Chapter 6 returns to the idea that the intended audience for quasi-compliance is not necessarily the Western governments and NGOs who are pushing for accountability. Using a detailed case study of postwar Sri Lanka, I show that postatrocity governments can deploy quasi-compliance as coalition-blocking behavior to prevent the mobilization of cohesive international pressure and censure. Sri Lanka is well suited to explore these dynamics because it has faced strong international pressure to provide accountability for mass atrocities and strong domestic political incentives in favor of impunity. It is in exactly the position in which we would expect a state to engage in quasi-compliance. Indeed, Sri Lanka took a number of expensive, politically unpalatable actions that failed to prevent ongoing censure.

The case is also significant for human rights theory and practice. Tens of thousands of civilians are believed to have been killed by government forces in the final days of Sri Lanka's civil war. Countless others were tortured, raped, and disappeared. This is a mass atrocity that ranks behind only Syria, Darfur, and Burma as some of the worst government-perpetrated violence against civilians in the twenty-first century. Yet because Sri Lanka is not a member of the International Criminal Court and has been protected from UN Security Council action by China, pursuing justice for these abuses requires costly coordination among international actors. It is therefore an excellent exemplar of how international efforts to enforce human rights play out in hard cases.

The conclusion summarizes the book's arguments and their broader relevance for human rights theory and practice. I emphasize the complicated, and often unintended, effects of international pressure on repressive states' behavior and its extremely limited ability to actually elicit compliance. I close with a discussion of the implications of my findings for victim communities seeking accountability for mass atrocities and a reflection on the challenge of pursuing justice in the face of extreme adversity.

The evidence I present in the following chapters shows that accountability for mass atrocities is rare, that it is deeply beholden to domestic politics, and that international pressure is unlikely to achieve its aims. This is a potentially dispiriting message for survivors and other activists to receive because it suggests that there's little room to effect change. But if justice for mass atrocities is contingent, it isn't random. And that means there are practical lessons that can be extracted from careful consideration of past successes and failures. Two critical implications of the theory of quasi-compliance presented in this book are that international pressure on repressive states' behavior has complicated unintended consequences, and that third-party audiences play an important role in producing human rights outcomes.

Illuminating the windows of opportunity for impact for victim communities pursuing justice in the face of extreme adversity was a primary goal of this book project—because, along with the analytical reasons identified above for examining quasi-compliance in the aftermath of mass atrocities, I have a personal attachment to the issue area. My academic origin story is an unconventional one. I began my career as a human rights lawyer, motivated by a desire to fight impunity for genocide and other mass atrocities. But my early experiences working in the field quickly highlighted an uncomfortable truth: The victims of some atrocities get justice. Many others never do. The barriers to accountability are vast, and even when atrocities are punished, the path to justice can be long and idiosyncratic.

In my first job as a law school graduate, I sat in a hotel banquet room full of survivors of the Khmer Rouge in rural Cambodia. The tribunal set up to try members of the regime was conducting an information session about its activities. Up on the dais, the court's international staff struggled to explain through interpreters how prosecuting decades-old crimes would "combat the culture of impunity" and "instill respect for the rule of law" in present-day Cambodia. Then they invited the audience to ask questions, almost all of which boiled down to: "Why now? Where were you in 1977? Did the UN know what was happening to us?"

The disconnect between what the international lawyers thought they were doing and how the affected population understood and articulated its needs was glaring. I imagined myself in an auditorium filled with survivors of the North Korean regime twenty, thirty, or forty years in the future, hearing the same questions: "Did you know what was happening to us?" "Why didn't the UN help us?" And I began to wonder why we thought that prosecutions at a hybrid tribunal of the type being set up in Cambodia would help survivors in any real way.

I went looking for evidence for the claim that rule of law might "trickle down" into the domestic justice system and found very little. Data on the ability of atrocity prosecutions to deter future crimes was nonexistent at the time. And the findings on the impact of transitional justice processes on atrocity survivors' mental health and well-being were mixed. Frustrated, I decided I would learn to do research and start looking for answers myself. Out of this frustration was born a PhD dissertation. It was motivated by the question of whether and how international justice can contribute to improved human rights outcomes in deeply divided societies, but after being introduced to research design and the scientific method in my first year of graduate school, I quickly realized that there were important prior questions to be answered first: Why are the perpetrators of some mass atrocities tried and convicted, while others walk free? Why do some victims have to fight for decades for accountability for the crimes committed against them?

My research for the PhD, much of which made it into this book, took me back to the courtrooms of the Extraordinary Chambers in the Courts of Cambodia, to the halls of the Palais des Nations in Geneva, and to the MONUSCO offices in Goma, Democratic Republic of the Congo. In each of these places I spoke to people doing the hard work of pursuing justice for mass atrocities—constructing criminal cases, lobbying for UN resolutions, protecting victims and witnesses. Nowhere did the questions that brought me to graduate school feel more urgent than on the A9 highway in northern Sri Lanka, passing victory monument after victory monument and military base after military base, all heavily fenced and guarded, inaccessible to the people on whose stolen land they were built.

The word "impunity" is deceptively sterile. It evokes a negative space, a lack of action. But for the victims of mass atrocities, impunity isn't an absence; it's an intrusive and ubiquitous presence in their lives. For Tamil survivors of Sri Lanka's civil war, impunity is a picture-perfect beach still strewn with the possessions of the tens of thousands of civilians who sheltered there from aerial bombardment in 2009. Impunity is the soldiers who killed them building luxury resorts overlooking that beach, and other sites of horrific violence. Impunity is the signs they erected that say: "No Future Without Forgiveness."

This is a book about state behavior. The questions it explores are, at heart, questions about how international human rights pressure affects what states do, and about when and how they choose to pursue justice for mass atrocities. It's also an academic book. It has more than five hundred footnotes, makes arguments supported in part by logistic regressions, and engages arcane debates about compliance with international law. But it's also an attempt to take seriously the lived experiences of communities that have survived mass atrocities. And because I came to these research questions from a background as a human rights worker, it felt important to me to ground my analysis and arguments in these survivors' experiences of life in the aftermath of atrocities, and, hopefully, to provide them with something of value.

THE POLITICS OF PRESSURE

When Egyptian NGO workers Karim Ennarah, Mohammed Basheer, and Gasser Abdel-Razek were arrested in November 2020, their friends and colleagues got to work immediately, sounding the alarm and trying to attract as much attention as possible to what had happened. The news spread quickly through international activist and journalist networks. I have never worked in or on Egypt, but within hours of Karim's arrest on November 18, a friend of his in London had messaged me on WhatsApp asking me to tweet about it.

By the next morning, the story had been picked up widely. Media outlets all over the world reported on the arrests and interviewed other staff members at the Egyptian Initiative for Personal Rights (EIPR), the NGO where the three activists worked. Karim's wife Jess Kelly, a British citizen, started a change.org petition asking the UK's foreign secretary to take action. She also wrote a *New York Times* op-ed asking the incoming Biden administration to take a hard line against Egyptian human rights abuses.[1] Prominent political figures and celebrities from around the world shared the story on social media and called for the EIPR staffers' release.

After two weeks of sustained international outcry—including a viral video by Scarlett Johansson—Karim, Mohammed, and Gasser were let out on bail. This was "naming and shaming," the international human rights movement's best-known tactic, in action. In its simplest form, the logic of drawing attention to human rights violations is that it signals to the perpetrator government that the international community is watching, that their actions are visible to an audience, and that if they don't want to be branded a human rights abuser, they should cut it out. In other words, the hope is that by being called out (named), they are shamed into changing their behavior.

Of course, many human rights–violating states don't particularly care what anyone thinks about them. That's why the second goal of calling out human rights abuses is to make enough noise to convince other states that it is in their interests to spend a little political capital to put pressure on the violator state. Because while human rights NGOs and media organizations can name and shame, potentially inflicting reputational damage on human rights abusers, it's only other governments that can impose more concrete costs, whether that's in the form of aid and trade reductions, targeted sanctions on individual leaders, or the creation of intrusive UN inquiries to investigate the abuses. Political scientists Margaret Keck and Kathryn Sikkink named this the Boomerang, providing a handy visual for the process by which domestic activists facing an intransigent, rights-abusing government send a call for help out to citizens of other countries who can then lobby their own governments to direct pressure back on the violator state.[2]

In this case, we don't know whether Egypt was sufficiently embarrassed by global condemnation to reverse course, or whether foreign governments threatened serious consequences in bilateral conversations behind closed doors. One or both of these mechanisms did the trick, though, illustrating exactly how international human rights pressure is supposed to work.

But only up to a point. Because although the EIPR staff were released, the court didn't unfreeze their assets, and the restrictive laws that permitted their arrests remained in place. Meanwhile, one of EIPR's researchers, Patrick Zaki, was held in pretrial detention from February 8, 2020, until December 9, 2021. The organization's founder, Hossam Baghat, is still under the travel ban that has prevented him leaving Egypt since 2016. And the treatment of EIPR is not unique. Rather, it is a particularly high-profile example of a broader pattern. Egypt routinely abuses counterterrorism measures to subject human rights defenders to unjust detentions, prosecutions, travel bans, and asset freezes, and in January 2021 passed a restrictive new law that prohibits NGOs from engaging in "political" work.[3]

So while international attention and advocacy succeeded in securing the three activists' freedom in December 2020, it seems to have had limited impact beyond that. This also matches with what we know about how human rights pressure works, which is that its capacity to effect change is tightly constrained by politics. As Emilie Hafner-Burton and a coauthor put it, summing up a diverse range of findings in the literature: "International rights promotion can help a bit when domestic conditions are right, but it rarely initiates reform on its own."[4]

What, exactly, the "right" domestic conditions are is not entirely clear. A large body of research suggests, fairly intuitively, that the success of international human rights pressure requires a target state that is democratic, has reasonably independent courts and robust domestic civil society, and is well integrated into the international system.[5] For example, Amanda Murdie and David Davis tie the success of international pressure to the presence of human rights NGOs, while James Franklin shows that human rights criticism is more likely to have a positive impact when the repressive government has strong economic ties to other states.[6]

However, other research challenges this characterization of the "easy" cases for international human rights promotion. Cullen Hendrix and Wendy Wong, for instance, find that naming and shaming may have a stronger positive impact on autocracies because international publicity creates more of a splash when repression has meant that domestic civil society has been unable or unwilling to draw attention to abuses.[7] And Rochelle Terman and Eric Voeten suggest that when it comes to human rights pressure between states, relationships matter more than any characteristic of the target government.[8]

Complicating matters further, as the Egyptian example shows, even when human rights pressure achieves its immediate goals, it's not all good news. "Successes" may produce negative externalities. As Emilie Hafner-Burton points out: "some abusive leaders adjust their methods of abuse in economical ways in reply to the spotlight."[9] Jacqueline DeMeritt and Courtenay Conrad identify an explicit substitution effect, observing that "in the face of an international campaign shaming specific repressive tactics, leaders face incentives to reduce use of the shamed tactic to avoid international condemnation and increase the use of other repressive tactics to counter domestic threats."[10]

Bearing out these intuitions, Caroline Payne and M. Rodwan Abouharb find that in the face of international attention to extrajudicial killings, repressive governments commit more forced disappearances.[11] The logic is grim but compelling: You can't be held accountable for murders if there aren't any bodies. Similarly, Darius Rejali locates the emergence of torture tactics that leave less visible scars (like waterboarding) in democratic governments' desire to avoid international censure as the antitorture norm gained traction.[12] And Kristin Bakke, Neil Mitchell, and Hannah Smidt show that repressive governments often respond to international attention to human rights violations by increasing restrictions on domestic civil society—preventing the evidence of abuses getting to international audiences, rather than stopping the abuses.[13]

These examples demonstrate that the question of whether international human rights pressure changes repressive states' behavior is far more complex than "did it work?" This complexity reflects the fact that rules, and pressure to comply with them, affect behavior in a variety of ways. Consider an example from the domestic legal context: state statutes criminalizing the possession of marijuana. A simplistic assessment of these rules' impact might conclude: "People still smoke weed. These laws don't work." But that isn't a full account of the statutes' effects.

For one thing, they almost certainly deter some people who might otherwise purchase and use marijuana. But more importantly for the analogy to international human rights: among those who do not comply, their behavior is surely different than it would be in the absence of the laws. They don't smoke openly on the street, they take steps to hide their drug use from their employers, they avoid coming into contact with police while high. An analysis of these laws' effect that focused only on whether or not people comply would miss an enormous amount of rule-motivated behavioral change.

It's particularly important to be attentive to behavior that is prompted by, but doesn't abide by, rules in contexts where enforcement is lacking and full compliance may consequently be rare except among those whose preferences already match the rule's dictates. Human rights is exactly this kind of context. Policing of compliance with international law obligations in general is piecemeal, formalized through the monitoring and adjudication arrangements of individual treaties, and often depends on fellow members of a treaty pursuing enforcement. In the human rights arena, treaty members' motivation to do so is limited. Unlike the case of a trade treaty, the signatories to a human rights convention do not materially benefit from each other's commitments. They aren't injured by another party's noncompliance and have no obvious incentives to police each other's performance.

International oversight bodies and NGOs substitute for some of the task of monitoring members' compliance, but they (generally) cannot penalize infractions. Their role is to document and publicize abuses, which may or may not prompt peer states to confront human rights abusers. Peer states can act through public condemnations, reductions in aid or trade, sponsorship of UN resolutions, or even military intervention. But all of these options incur costs, making enforcement relatively infrequent.

One of the most noticeable impacts of the rarity of enforcement is the prevalence of insincere commitments. As Emilie Hafner-Burton and Kiyoteru Tsutsui explain it, the weakness of global human rights regimes creates "strong incentives to ratify human rights treaties as a matter of window dressing rather than a serious commitment to implement respect for human rights in practice."[14] Knowing that the risks of punishment for noncompliance are low, states sign onto treaties they have no intention of implementing for instrumental reasons like getting so-called signing benefits from the international community, or temporarily placating a domestic audience.[15]

But insincere commitments can sometimes have unintended consequences, leading states to deliver more on human rights and pay greater costs than they would like by empowering domestic constituencies or providing leverage to external audiences.[16] Heather Smith-Cannoy documents how post-Soviet governments granted citizens the right to individually petition UN treaty bodies in an attempt to cheaply "temporarily boost democratic credentials before a global audience," only to find that domestic civil society was able to use these supposedly empty commitments to focus attention on rights violations and push for change, ultimately improving compliance with treaty obligations.[17]

Thomas Risse, Stephen Ropp, and Kathryn Sikkink's "spiral model" suggests that in response to naming and shaming, states that are vulnerable to external pressure may make "tactical concessions" including ratifying treaties or even enacting domestic human rights policies.[18] Although these measures are undertaken disingenuously, over time they become habitual, contributing to the internalization and institutionalization of human rights norms. The result is that, as Beth Simmons puts it, even seemingly "inconsequential policy actions" can "end up entrapping repressive governments" into compliance.[19]

Recognizing the complex relationship between commitment and compliance, scholarship on the impact of international laws and norms increasingly focuses not on whether states comply but on how their behavior changes in response to rules,[20] because, as Sonia Cardenas puts it, "a state responding to international pressure faces a panoply of compliance choices beyond simply deciding whether to comply."[21] Understanding this fact has meant nuancing the concept of compliance to accommodate high and low values, multiple dimensions, or partial and full performance.[22] With respect to human rights specifically, it has meant "analytically delinking internalization and compliance," recognizing that even full compliance may be insincere, and understanding that states' adherence to their rights commitments might differ enormously depending on *whose* rights are being discussed.[23]

Most relevantly for the questions motivating this book, it has also meant paying closer attention to the varied strategies that repressive states use to resist the constraints of international human rights law, which, as Alexander Cooley and Matthew Schaaf note, "extend well beyond just noncompliance."[24] Saskia Nauenberg Dunkell, for instance, observes that they may "selectively adopt some aspects of a global model to demonstrate their commitment to a norm, while rejecting and revising other parts in response to national pressures."[25] Jelena Subotić shows that under conditions of strong international pressure to comply with a norm and low domestic interest, elites may "manipulate or hijack the international norm by fulfilling its institutional requirements while ignoring the norm's substance."[26]

In other instances, governments reject international human rights norms outright. In her discussion of "backlash politics," Leslie Vinjamuri explains the role that overt anti-international justice rhetoric played in Kenya's 2013 election, which brought to office as president and vice president two individuals who were currently facing charges at the International Criminal Court. Once in power, "they continued to pursue a range of strategies to block the advance of the ICC."[27]

Often, however, governments are a bit slyer about their efforts to flout international human rights. Consider Australia's cynical definition of its "migration zone"—the parts of its territory where people arriving without visas are protected by the Migration Act of 1958 and are permitted to apply for asylum in Australia and then remain there while their claims are processed.

In 2001, after 433 asylum seekers were rescued from a sinking boat and brought to Christmas Island by a passing Norwegian freighter, Australia excised a number of its offshore territories in the Indian Ocean (including Christmas Island) from the migration zone.[28] Anyone arriving by boat to these excised territories would no longer have the right to apply for asylum in Australia, but could instead be sent to offshore detention centers on the territory of third-party countries, where their claims to refugee status could be processed.[29] Along with a law granting broader border protection powers, these measures were defined as the "Pacific Solution" and were explicitly aimed at reducing the number of asylum seekers who could claim protection in Australia. But asylum seekers continued to arrive, and in 2012, the Australian government took the seemingly nonsensical step of excising the Australian *mainland* from the migration zone. Now no one arriving by boat anywhere on Australian territory could claim asylum.

The motivation for this legal maneuvering is that Australia is a member of the 1951 Refugee Convention, which imposes on its state parties an obligation not to return ("refouler") any refugee to a country "where his life or freedom would be threatened on account of his race, religion, nationality, membership of a particular social group or political opinion."[30] Critically, ensuring that they do not violate this non-refoulement rule requires that state parties have a process in place for determining whether any asylum seeker who arrives on their territory is or is not a refugee. Under Article 31 of the convention, state parties may not impose penalties on any asylum seeker for "illegal entry or presence" as long as they claim asylum immediately on arrival.[31]

Because Australia has defined its domestic law in such a way that arrivals by boat are never permitted to set foot on Australian territory, it is able to argue that it is technically not in violation of these provisions of the Refugee Convention. But it is clearly doing its damnedest to avoid upholding refugee rights and cannot be said to be "complying" with its treaty obligations in any real way. Zoltán Búzás offers the concept of "evasion" to describe behavior like Australia's that charts an intentional path of "following the letter of the law but violating its purpose."[32] Its goal, he explains, is "to minimize inconvenient legal obligations in an arguably legal fashion," thereby avoiding penalties for noncompliance.[33]

Jennifer Dixon describes a related strategy in her account of Turkish responses to international calls for recognition of the Armenian genocide. She suggests that under certain circumstances, faced with pressure to comply with an international human rights norm, states attempt to reinterpret the rule, focusing on "a norm's prescriptions or proscriptions, or on the conditions under which a norm applies."[34] In the Turkish case, this meant efforts to define genocide as closely as possible to the specific characteristics of the Holocaust in order to draw distinctions with the treatment of the Armenians. For Dixon, this is one of a menu of strategies that she calls "rhetorical adaptation," in which states that will not or cannot comply instead "shape their rhetoric in response to understandings of an international norm in order to avoid charges of norm violation or to resist pressures for compliance."[35]

What both Búzás and Dixon are describing are efforts to escape punishment for violating human rights norms without actually complying. In any reasonably functional domestic system, a criminal can't deflect legal consequences by hiding behind the fact that others have offended more egregiously. But for international human rights violators, this is a feasible strategy. The profound limitations on enforcement mean that there may be less of an incentive to comply than to look less bad than the worst offenders, thereby avoiding selection as one of the rare targets of enforcement.

The reactions to human rights pressure I explain in this book fit into the same category of behavior. But rather than efforts to exploit ambiguities in the law or attempts to reinterpret a norm's requirements, I am most interested in the creation of institutions that approximate compliant behavior closely enough to avoid penalty without actually meeting human rights obligations.

I call this strategy "quasi-compliance" because of its "as if" character. "Quasi" is Latin for "as if" or "as though"; in law, it is used to identify something that has a resemblance to, but lacks important components of, the term that follows the hyphen. Critically, it also identifies something that will be treated *as if it were the thing it isn't*. In other words, those things or actions that are "quasi" are "not exactly or fully what they might appear but have to be treated 'as if' they were."[36] A quasi-contract, for instance, exists when a court recognizes an as-if-contractual obligation between two parties even when the technical requirements for a contract are not met.[37]

By setting up institutions that bear superficial similarities to those that are required by human rights norms or demanded by international actors applying pressure, repressive states are engaging in a performance of "as if." The aim is to secure the benefits of compliance with behavior that resembles it but lacks its substantive characteristics: quasi-compliance.

These efforts are facilitated by the fact that compliance with international human rights obligations can be quite difficult.[38] A new state signatory to the

Convention against Torture might institute severe penalties for violations and even expend resources to retrain its security sector to respect bodily integrity rights, but the entrenched practices of decades may be hard to eradicate. If, despite these efforts, some officers continue to use prohibited interrogation techniques, is this compliance or noncompliance?

The fraught question of the boundary between compliance and noncompliance further complicates things. As Wayne Sandholtz and Kendall Stiles point out, norms are in constant flux due to ongoing interactions between rules and behavior: "Events or actions trigger disputes over the meaning and application of norms. Actors argue, seeking to challenge or expand existing norms or to invoke competing norms. These arguments inevitably modify the rules."[39]

In fact, ambiguity to what is required to be in compliance may be a feature, rather than a bug, of international norms.[40] Mona Lena Krook and Jacqui True suggest that "norms diffuse precisely because—rather than despite the fact that—they may encompass different meanings, fit in with a variety of contexts, and be subject to framing by diverse actors."[41] The upshot is that, as Búzás puts it, "compliance is not an intrinsic feature of behavior."[42] Instead, states' actions "are constructed as compliance or violation through a process of legal definition, interaction, justification, and interpretation, a process that, in turn, shapes the meaning of compliance."[43] The fact that benchmarks for compliance are therefore moving targets introduces further ambiguity that repressive states can exploit.

We should expect to see states undertake quasi-compliant strategies in response to international pressure when full compliance is politically untenable domestically due to the presence of what Sonia Cardenas terms "pro-violation constituencies."[44] This is most likely to be true in contexts where remedying human rights violations would contradict a core political value or anger a key constituency. For example, international pressure to treat migrants better is unlikely to produce full compliance from a government that was elected on a hardline xenophobic platform. And although under certain circumstances, as Jelena Subotić describes, governments facing strong international pressure and weak domestic demand will have incentives to insincerely comply in order to "use international institutions to resolve domestic political fights," generally, they will be choosing among noncompliant strategies.[45]

Unlike outright noncompliance or rhetorical ("cheap talk") strategies, quasi-compliance carries clear costs up front. The institutions Bahrain created in response to international pressure over the 2011 crackdown cost millions of dollars against a total annual government budget of less than USD 10 billion.[46] The strategy also carries political risks. The creation of new institutions with a mandate to monitor human rights or investigate abuses represents a potential threat to powerful actors in society. Therefore, it's unlikely a government would undertake expensive quasi-compliant efforts to avoid, for instance, a public statement by the UN high commissioner for human rights that they are not protecting their citizens' right to bathroom breaks on the job. By contrast, the prospect of a military or development aid cut in response to reports of widespread torture by state security forces should be expected to trigger action. All else being equal, the greater the threat posed by enforcement, the more resources states should be willing to expend on quasi-compliance. This also means that states that are structurally more vulnerable to punishment by international audiences will be more likely to undertake quasi-compliant strategies.

Quasi-compliance's viability as a strategy stems from the unevenness of enforcement of international human rights obligations. Perfect compliance with human rights obligations is rare, and noncompliance is not reliably punished. While especially widespread or shocking violations may generate public outcry sufficient to prompt members of the international community to take action against a violator state, this only happens in a minority of cases. Consequently, the strength and focus of international pressure to comply, and the threat of enforcement, is unpredictable and strongly influenced by the vagaries of international politics. Knowing that only a small proportion of human rights abusers will ever face real penalties, some repressive states gamble that they can approximate the performance of compliance well enough to be removed from the group of likely targets of punishment.[47]

Because it is costly, states are less likely to engage strongly on others' human rights malfeasance in the absence of a compelling reason to do so: a historical association with the target state, a relationship to the victim group, or a strong commitment to and bureaucratic apparatus for promoting human rights abroad. Even where one or more of these motivators exist, it may be trumped by political exigencies. And because punishing human rights deficits often presages a role in remedying them, even strongly engaged states prefer to act multilaterally. This preference opens opportunities for strategic behavior on the part of violator states.

Consider a simplified scenario: In a crackdown following an alleged coup attempt, a repressive regime detains two thousand suspected plotters and dissidents without trial. Six months later, some have been permitted sporadic visits from their families, but the fates of others are unknown. None have been granted their right to counsel, and there are credible reports of widespread torture during interrogations in the immediate aftermath of the attempt. The violator state is a signatory to both the International Covenant on Civil and Political Rights (ICCPR) and the Convention against Torture (CAT) and is in direct contravention of its obligations thereto. Several Western states have raised this issue in their officials' public statements and indicated they will introduce the matter at the next UN Human Rights Council meeting.

The violator state, which strongly prefers to keep the alleged coup plotters in detention where they can't threaten the regime's hold on power and fears that transparency about the crackdown could cause widespread unrest, now has three options: it can continue to do nothing, it can attempt to satisfy the activist states' demands that it meet its ICCPR obligations, *or* it can try to convince the other voting members of the Human Rights Council to side with it against the activist states calling for action.

While satisfying the activist states' demands would likely involve the release of detainees and the provision of restitution for those killed or tortured in custody and/or filing charges and proceeding to speedy trial of alleged coup plotters, the violator state might reasonably expect that taking the third option would require it to do considerably less; perhaps filing charges against a handful of high-profile detainees and a promise to review the cases of the others over a three-month period. These measures would still carry resource costs and domestic political risks, but to a lesser extent than full compliance. And they might be enough to convince an audience of swing states, with their own reasons to be cautious about muscular human rights enforcement, that they will not suffer reputational damage if they resist the activists' states calls for an international condemnation or inquiry.

Faced with activist states condemning human rights abuses and strong domestic political incentives not to rectify them, violator states have good reason to gamble on a middle path between doing nothing and full compliance. As the stylized example above indicates, the success of this strategy doesn't rely on convincing human rights advocates or activist states. It can succeed by swaying another audience: the states these activist states must convince to join for multilateral action.

The presence of multiple relevant audiences for human rights behavior means that there are a variety of mechanisms by which quasi-compliance might help repressive states avoid (or limit) penalties for noncompliance. In the best-case scenario, quasi-compliance might be enough to convince international human rights NGOs or UN human rights officials to ease up on pressure, and to welcome efforts in the direction of compliance. It might also convince human rights–engaged governments not to lead a push for action (i.e., sponsoring UN resolutions or calling on other states to impose sanctions) or to deprioritize human rights in their bilateral relations. Finally, it might give peer states (those who are not particularly committed to promoting human rights globally) an excuse to push back against the West and refuse to join resolutions empaneling a commission of inquiry or otherwise censuring.

Of the potential audiences for quasi-compliance, only the NGOs and UN human rights infrastructure actually need to be persuaded of anything. But they don't need to be convinced that the quasi-compliant state is meeting its human right obligations, simply that it is moving in an acceptable direction. These actors are oversubscribed and operating with limited resources, so they have to triage where to focus their attention and leverage. An indication that a repressive state is changing its ways and making an effort may often be enough to move it off of the list of urgent targets for pressure.

For quasi-compliance to affect Western government policy, it may not be necessary that foreign policy officials be persuaded of real progress in the direction of compliance. Even obviously weak efforts can impact internal foreign policy bureaucracy debates over setting priorities, improving the odds of outcomes more favorable to the quasi-compliant state. For instance, where a Western government's defense officials wish to expand military cooperation with a repressive state, that state's decision to set up a weak torture commission or gesture in the direction of security sector reform, especially if accompanied by rhetoric signaling sincerity, can provide those officials with leverage to push back against their government's own human rights officials who are arguing that continued pressure should be a cornerstone of the bilateral relationship.

Finally, for peer states that are less informed or less engaged, or who have domestic political incentives to reject robust human rights action, quasi-compliance can simply act as a convenient fiction, giving them cover to avoid appearing to be protecting a human rights violator. For this mechanism to work, demonstrations of sincerity may be less valuable than framing quasi-compliance as authentically responsive to domestic political dynamics and/or as resistance to neoimperialist human rights pressure.

Depending on their sensitivity to the threat of human rights enforcement and their political or resource constraints, quasi-compliant states might hope to impact the behavior of all of these audiences. But even if they only affect the peer state audience, it's still useful. Those engaged in policing human rights must convince others to support them and these "swing" states can potentially block multilateral action on human rights.[48]

The example above discusses potential action by the UN Human Rights Council because its institutional profile makes it a logical and common site of lobbying for multilateral human rights engagement. But these dynamics exist more broadly, even outside the institutions that formally require multilateral action. Human rights–promoting states must convince others to go along with their enforcement efforts if they don't want to bear the costs alone. Targeting these others, who may be less informed, less engaged, or less willing to support robust human rights enforcement, can be a successful strategy to buy a violator state a reprieve from international human rights pressure. In effect, this is coalition-blocking behavior.

Critically, the success of this strategy does not require that violator states convince this third-party audience of the rightness of their actions. As Ronald

Krebs and Patrick Jackson note, "persuasion does not exhaust the ways through which rhetoric might shape political contest." Violator states can recruit peer states' support by framing their conflict with human rights–promoting actors in a way that is consistent with those peer states' existing normative commitments.[49] As Michael Barnett explains, frames "fix meanings, organize experience, alert others that their interests and possibly their identities are at stake, and propose solutions to ongoing problems."[50] But actors' willingness to accept particular frames may depend less on their persuasiveness than their resonance with material interests.[51]

In a setting like the Human Rights Council, where action requires a coalition of willing participants and no state has a veto, disputes over how states' human rights behavior should be characterized have particularly high stakes. Successful targeting of peer state audiences is likely to tap into existing framing controversies in human rights fora (i.e., debates about rights as a universal versus Western imperialist project), pitting rhetorical themes like sovereignty and Global South solidarity against the human rights norm-focused arguments deployed by Western human rights–promoting actors.

The logic presented here differs fundamentally from existing theories in its account of the role of hypocrisy. Hypocrisy, the practice of "proclaiming adherence to rules while busily violating them," is common in the international system, where rules are often honored in the breach.[52] It can "undermine[] trust and credible commitments" and trigger backlash against norms.[53] However, some scholars suggest that it may also act as a "civilizing force";[54] actors are refraining from violations of norms, even if they are doing so disingenuously. The "slipperiness" of the slope that Risse, Ropp, and Sikkink describe in the spiral model relies on the fact that disingenuous behavior can become habitual and internalized over time, and that hypocrisy can therefore be a force for positive change. In contrast with tactical concessions, which tend to be accompanied by norm-reinforcing rhetoric, quasi-compliance often involves explicit resistance to demands for full compliance. While inadvertent habituation and norm internalization is plausible following half-hearted tactical concessions, it is far less likely when the actor has undertaken quasi-compliance while violently protesting international human rights pressure.

We usually understand hypocrites' motivation as the desire not to be seen to be a bad actor or suffer the reputational consequences. Although some studies note that the audiences for hypocritical action may have incentives to collude in hypocrisy to avoid the costs of challenging it, the impetus is still the protection of the hypocritical actor's reputation.[55] By contrast, I suggest that repressive states may deploy quasi-compliance in a strategy calculated less to protect their own reputation than their audience's. This is not to say that they don't also seek to preserve their own reputation; however, they are acting to prevent a significantly worse outcome than reputational loss.

States that choose this strategy are doing so because domestic politics prevents them from undertaking a response to pressure that would approximate compliance closely enough to preserve their reputation as a human rights–abiding actor. Their primary motivation is therefore to avoid more stringent penalties (for instance, sanctions or an international inquiry) by blocking the formation of a coalition that would support punitive action. Of course, they would prefer to convince those putting pressure on them that they are compliant and thereby avoid reputational damage as well, but they know that quasi-compliance that significantly undershoots the mark is unlikely to be successful in this goal. These efforts are therefore best understood not as a serious attempt at convincingly feigning compliance, but as a convenient fiction, intended to give a sympathetic audience cover to avoid appearing to be protecting a human rights violator.

Because international audiences generally do not respond to quasi-compliance with aggressive enforcement action, it is possible for multiple rounds of quasi-compliant behavior to ensue. Recalcitrant governments may edge incrementally closer to meeting their obligations as successive quasi-compliant efforts are met with increased pressure from international audiences. In this way, although domestic demand and resistance determine preferences about compliance, ultimately outcomes emerge as a product of bargaining with international audiences.

Repressive states undertake quasi-compliance in response to international pressure when full compliance is politically untenable domestically. In these contexts, the path to compliance is not slippery; it is obstructed. The "best-case scenario" is therefore that quasi-compliance is a sort of one-way ratchet, establishing a new floor for the state's performance on the human rights obligation in question. In other words: while international human rights pressure *can* measurably impact repressive states' behavior, it *cannot* elicit compliance with international standards in the absence of domestic motivations to comply.

There are several empirical implications of the theory presented here. We should expect to see states engaging in quasi-compliance when they face serious potential consequences for failing to meet their human rights obligations but have strong domestic political incentives not to comply. In other words, states that engage in quasi-compliance have similar preferences to outright noncompliers; they just worry more about the risk of punishment. This behavior will be distinguishable from "cheap talk" because it will incur significant resource and/or political costs; it's an affirmative choice to engage in costly, but circumscribed, human rights behavior, not an inadvertent consequence of empty gestures that become binding. Quasi-compliance will also be distinct from the creation of institutions that are noncompliant with international norms but responsive to domestic pressure because it will go against observable domestic preferences. Finally, quasi-compliance targeting a peer state audience will be distinguishable from inadequate good faith efforts to comply because it will be accompanied by clear efforts to resist human rights pressure. Most critically, it should be accompanied by clear signaling to swing state audiences in the form of sovereignty rhetoric, invocations of developing world solidarity, and emphasis on resisting Western conceptions of human rights.

While the relevance of such coalition-blocking behavior is particularly clear in the context of framing competitions over how human rights behavior should be characterized, it extends to other areas of international relations in which the enforcement of international rules requires other states to act in the absence of a self-interested motivation to do so. In issue areas ranging from international environmental law to anticorruption efforts, the absence of reciprocal benefits from other states' compliance means states have little incentive to monitor and enforce international rules. The result is that enforcement often requires multilateral action, opening opportunities for violator states to deploy quasi-compliant strategies in an attempt to block the formation of coalitions.

THE OBLIGATION TO SEEK JUSTICE

I was a law clerk at the International Court of Justice in 2009 when an unusual filing came in. Belgium was suing Senegal for its failure to prosecute Hissène Habré, the deposed dictator of Chad, for the systematic torture of civilians during the 1980s. According to Belgium, this violated Senegal's obligations under the Convention against Torture, a human rights treaty to which both states were party.

Habré fled to Senegal after his 1990 overthrow. From that moment, survivors of his regime's abuses and their advocates worked tirelessly to ensure he would not evade justice, calling on the Senegalese authorities to arrest and prosecute him. They hit a roadblock in 2001, when the Senegalese court of appeal ruled that the country's laws would not permit trying someone for torture committed elsewhere. But survivors living in Belgium had set in motion an investigation under that country's universal jurisdiction law and in 2005 the Brussels district court issued a warrant for Habré's arrest and requested his extradition to Belgium to stand trial.[1]

In response to the warrant, Senegalese authorities placed Habré under house arrest. But they balked at extraditing a former head of state. Instead, they announced that they would defer to the African Union on the question of who should prosecute Habré. They didn't much like the African Union's response, which was to formally call on Senegal to "prosecute and ensure that Hissène Habré is tried, on behalf of Africa, by a competent Senegalese court with guarantees for fair trial."[2] Meanwhile, the Committee against Torture (which monitors violations of the Convention against Torture) handed down a decision saying that Senegal's failure to prosecute or extradite Habré breached its obligations under the treaty.[3]

But Senegal took no action. In 2009, Belgium brought the case to the International Court of Justice (ICJ). Ultimately, the ICJ ruled in Belgium's favor: Senegal must prosecute Habré or extradite him to Belgium.[4] Fortuitously, when the ruling came down, a new government had just come to power in Senegal. More concerned about its international image than its predecessor, President Macky Sall's administration took the ICJ seriously. In cooperation with the African Union, Senegal created the Extraordinary African Chambers to try international crimes committed in Chad from June 7, 1982, to December 1, 1990. Habré's trial opened in July 2015 and less than a year later, he was convicted of crimes against humanity, war crimes, and torture.[5] He is now serving a life sentence in a Senegalese prison. Without Belgium's intervention, it's not clear that he ever would have been prosecuted.

It was unprecedented for one country to attempt to force another to provide accountability for atrocities committed on a third country's territory. Historically, impunity has been the rule, supported by a strong norm of noninterference by sovereign states in each other's affairs. Sovereignty and its privileges protected states and their officials from facing too many questions over massive violations of their citizens' human rights, let alone accountability.

In the last three decades, however, international criminal courts have prosecuted former leaders and indicted sitting heads of state. Domestic judicial systems in countries from Bangladesh to Guatemala have commenced criminal trials against former regime members for atrocities of the past. And 123 states have joined the International Criminal Court, whose founding treaty, the Rome Statute, formalizes "the duty of every State to exercise its criminal jurisdiction over those responsible for international crimes."[6] The widespread accession to the Rome Statute suggests that most states now agree, at least in principle, with human rights activists that the large-scale violation of certain rights can and must be treated as criminally culpable conduct. This belief that the authors of atrocities must be brought to justice has been variously referred to as the "nonimpunity norm," the "justice norm," the "transitional justice norm," and the "accountability norm."[7] Because this last term appears slightly more commonly in the literature, that is what I use in this book.

Norms are generally understood as "standard[s] of appropriate behavior for actors with a given identity."[8] In the case of the accountability norm, the accepted standard is that members in good standing of the international community should pursue individual criminal liability for those most responsible for the most serious international crimes. But the emergence of this norm and the rapid growth of an international institutional architecture dedicated to monitoring and enforcing it are puzzling developments given the threat to state sovereignty posed by an obligation to provide individual criminal accountability for acts of mass atrocity. The rest of this chapter documents how this happened.

I show that although an "on paper" requirement to prosecute mass atrocities has existed since the codification of genocide and crimes against humanity as international crimes immediately after World War I, the perception of the obligation as binding lagged significantly behind its codification into law.[9] I suggest that the norm's eventual entrenchment was the product of an accident in timing in which the post–Cold War reanimation of international criminal law coincided with early transitional justice efforts. And the establishment of the International Criminal Court both reflected and strengthened a growing international conviction that prosecutions are the only acceptable response to mass atrocity. As a consequence of these developments, it has become increasingly likely that when the occurrence of a mass atrocity becomes public knowledge, the state where it occurred will be beset by calls to bring those responsible to justice, leading to conflict between international audiences and postatrocity states who do not want to provide accountability.

Sovereignty, defined as a state's possession of supreme and independent authority within its territory, is *the* bedrock principle of international relations. Short of invasion, there are few acts more threatening to a state's sovereignty than a foreign entity sitting in judgment over that state's official acts. It not only usurps the state's most fundamental role of policing the monopoly of violence within its territory; it also sets up an authority superior to the state.

The creation of an International Criminal Court with the power to try sitting heads of state therefore represents a significant break with centuries of international relations tradition. The impetus for such an institution dates back at least to 1919, when the Treaty of Versailles mandated trials of ranking members of the losing powers accused of violating international law. Nine alleged German war criminals were ultimately prosecuted at the Leipzig war crimes trials. However, although the idea of using courts to punish defeated enemies for war crimes already recognized in domestic legal systems—such as abuse of prisoners of war (POWs), use of a prohibited weapon, or the targeting of civilian populations—was clearly familiar during the interwar period, the League of Nations rejected proposals to add a criminal chamber to the existing Permanent Court of International Justice because "there was not then in existence any generally recognized international criminal law."[10]

The "birth" of international criminal law is generally dated to the post–World War II Nuremberg trials. In 1945–1946, high-ranking members of the Nazi regime were tried for war crimes, aggression, crimes against the peace, and crimes against humanity before a tribunal created by the United States, the USSR, the UK, and France.[11] Ten of them were executed. Over the following three years, nearly two hundred lower-ranking regime members and affiliates were also tried.

Often described as "victors' justice," the Nuremberg trials were motivated by a desire to punish the Nazi regime for embroiling Europe in a devastating war. They were as much an exercise in vengeance against a defeated enemy as justice. Their legal validity is undermined by the retroactive nature of many of the charges ("crimes against the peace," "aggressive war," and "crimes against humanity" did not exist as defined crimes prior to 1945), and by the fact that the judges refused to hear potentially exculpatory evidence.

Despite these failings, the Nuremberg trials have come to stand for the proposition that no individual, no matter how powerful, stands above the law. They pioneered what Ruti Teitel describes as the "radical innovation" of "reaching beyond the state and its responsibility to that of the individual."[12] Although Nuremberg's highly public precedent of individual liability for the criminal actions of government is pathbreaking, its establishment of "crimes against humanity" as an international crime is at least as important a legacy.[13] Nuremberg was not the first international trial for war crimes, but it was the first time that atrocities committed by a government against its own citizens, rather than against enemy combatants or enemy civilians, were treated as violations of international law.

Ironically, the crimes against humanity charges at Nuremberg were an afterthought, secondary to the Allies' concern with holding the Nazis accountable for their initiation of an aggressive war, and their abuses of Allied POWs. Gary Bass describes their inclusion as a concession to the American Jewish lobby, angry that Holocaust victims were being ignored in the push for justice.[14]

However, if the criminal charge was a novelty, the phrase "crimes against humanity" was not new. Examining the history of the term, William Schabas finds evidence that it was in widespread use from the mid-1700s.[15] Frequently used to describe the depredations of slavery and colonialism, the phrase can be found in the writings of Voltaire, Cesare Beccaria, Henry Wheaton, and Roger Casement. Its most prominent pre-Nuremberg usage was the reaction of European powers to the 1915 slaughter of Armenians in Turkey, including condemnations by the British, who later attempted to prosecute Ottoman Turk commanders for the atrocities. Had they not fallen apart, these trials would have served as an early precedent for the law on crimes against humanity. Consequently, as Schabas explains, by 1945, "the idea that certain atrocities went beyond the sovereign authority of states, and attracted international condemnation, had been well anchored for many years."[16]

Although they may not have initially intended to hold the Nazi regime accountable for the Holocaust, the drafters of the International Military Tribunal's charter and their contemporaries recognized the importance of their decision to include crimes against humanity charges. At the time, international lawyer and scholar Hersch Lauterpacht, who proposed using the term "crimes against humanity" as a catch-all to describe the "atrocities, persecutions, and deportations" of the Nazi regime against its own citizenry, wrote that "this is an innovation which the outraged conscience of the world and an enlightened conception of the true purposes of the law of nations impel [the framers] to make immediately operative."[17]

The legal innovations of the trials at Nuremberg were codified in 1950 by the International Law Commission's Nuremberg principles, which established that war crimes and crimes against humanity were unambiguously subject to international criminal jurisdiction. The 1948 Genocide Convention similarly established genocide as an international crime triggering international jurisdiction. In addition to the jurisdictional basis for prosecuting, the Genocide Convention also codified an obligation to punish genocide.[18] A 1971 resolution of the United Nations General Assembly confirmed that an equivalent obligation existed, incumbent on all states, to either prosecute or extradite individuals accused of war crimes and crimes against humanity.[19]

Consequently, by 1971, and probably as early as the 1950s, the legal architecture supporting international jurisdiction over genocide, war crimes, and crimes against humanity was in place. Critically, it was accompanied by the idea that the impermissibility of impunity for these crimes imposed on all states an obligation to prosecute.

The decades immediately following World War II saw numerous mass atrocities similar in type, if not equivalent in scale, to Nazi crimes. In the 1950s and 1960s, hundreds of thousands of civilians were slaughtered in the USSR, in Algeria, and in Indonesia. In the 1970s, Pakistan's attempt to prevent Bangladeshi independence and the Khmer Rouge's brutal overthrow of Cambodian society produced death tolls estimated as high as three million.[20]

Despite these events, for several decades international criminal law was only invoked to prevent former members of the Nazi regime from eluding justice. In 1968, the Convention on the Non-Applicability of Statutory Limitations to War Crimes and Crimes Against Humanity was drafted to ensure that escaped Nazi war criminals could still be tried if discovered after decades in hiding. Early examples of the application of international criminal law by states all involve prosecutions of this sort. The 1961 Israeli trial of Adolf Eichmann, Bolivia's 1983 extradition of Klaus Barbie to France, and the United States' 1986 extradition of John Demjanjuk to Israel are prominent among the handful of cases affirming states' commitment to the existence of international criminal jurisdiction and the nonapplicability of statutes of limitations to these crimes. It was not until the 1990s that anyone other than former Nazis was tried for violations of international criminal law.

The narrow focus that state practice accorded to international criminal law in the 1950s to 1980s appears to reflect public opinion of the time. A search of the ProQuest News and Newspapers database for the phrase "international criminal law" yields just thirty substantive references to international criminal law in English-language newspapers between 1950 and 1989.[21] In only three was it suggested that international criminal law be applied to then-current abuses against civilians: a 1961 tongue-in-cheek suggestion by the *Chicago Daily Tribune* that UN Secretary General U Thant be tried for war crimes for civilian deaths during UN deployment in Katanga; a 1972 report in the *Times of India* that international law experts believed there should be trials for Pakistani atrocities in Bangladesh; and a 1979 letter to the editor in the *Chicago Tribune* arguing that Vietnamese treatment of ethnic Chinese amounted to the crime of genocide.[22]

Clearly, international criminal law was not a widely covered topic during most of the second half of the twentieth century (compare with 1,058 hits for the same search in the first decade of the twenty-first century). To the extent that international criminal law was raised in public discourse, it was not to advocate for accountability for mass abuses against civilians, but to decry aggression against other (state) members of the international system, or as a solution to transnational problems like terrorism.

The absence of an association between international criminal law and ongoing atrocities ended in the 1990s. By 1992, newspaper op-eds were calling for the application of the "Nuremberg precedent" to Serb atrocities in Bosnia.[23] The shift followed a separate, but related, development in international law: the 1980s-era move by the adjudicatory bodies of the nascent international human rights regime to give teeth to the duties to protect and ensure the rights guaranteed by the various international conventions (for example, the International Covenant on Civil and Political Rights and the Convention against Torture). The developing understanding of governments' human rights obligations as requiring not only that they refrain from infringing on rights, but that they affirmatively provide redress for violations, offered a frame with which the preexisting legal duty to prosecute the architects of atrocity crimes resonated.[24]

The need for a legal framework codifying the human rights obligations of states had been raised in the immediate aftermath of World War II and the Holocaust. However, imposing legal obligations on states regarding the treatment of their own citizens was a significant change to the international system, and one that took time to achieve. The 1948 Universal Declaration of Human Rights (UDHR), envisioned as an "international bill of rights," was explicitly nonbinding. Its drafters emphasized that it was intended to serve as a "guide" to the human rights that states undertook to protect, but not as a set of legal obligations.[25]

The legalization of the rights "declared" by the UDHR was a decades-long process. The drafts of the International Covenant on Civil and Political Rights (ICCPR) and the International Covenant on Economic Social and Cultural Rights (ICESCR) were submitted to the General Assembly in 1954 but not adopted until twelve years later. Finally accumulating enough ratifications to come into force in 1976, the two conventions were "the inaugural salvo" of a barrage of international human rights treaties creating legal obligations on states vis-à-vis their citizens.[26]

Although the duties imposed by these treaties are legally binding, enforcement of human rights obligations has always been difficult to achieve. Because there is no higher authority and no reliable mechanism of reciprocal enforcement, states themselves are the ultimate guarantors of human rights within their territories. Consequently, the conventions have been written not only to impose a negative obligation (to refrain from violating rights), but also as an affirmative obligation (to ensure the full exercise of rights). This is apparent in the inclusion of a commitment to provide a remedy for serious violations. Since early in its efforts interpreting the ICCPR, the Human Rights Committee (the body established to monitor compliance with the covenant) has emphasized the need to investigate and punish violations.

The regional human rights bodies rapidly made this obligation explicit with regard to the regional conventions, and by the mid-1980s had held that in some cases the obligation to provide a remedy could require the prosecution of those responsible for the violation. In the landmark 1988 *Velásquez Rodríguez* case, the Inter-American Court of Human Rights interpreted the American Convention on Human Rights to include a duty to "prevent, investigate and punish any violation of the rights recognized by this convention" that survived the fall of the regime on whose watch the violation had occurred.[27]

This issue of the responsibility of successor regimes regarding past abuses loomed large in Latin America during the 1980s. Between 1977 and 1994, fifteen countries in the region transitioned from authoritarian to democratic regimes. In many instances, the military regimes that were overthrown had committed widespread and systematic violations of human rights. Democratically elected governments in the region were voted into power on a platform of accountability and change. Their efforts to meet this demand became known as "transitional justice."[28]

In the groundbreaking 1985 "Trial of the Juntas," the Argentine courts prosecuted military leaders for the torture, forced disappearance, and murder of thousands of civilians during the 1976–1983 dictatorship. Although it was hailed as the first time that officials of an abusive government were held criminally liable for mistreatment of civilians since Nuremberg,[29] it's important to note what this trial was not. It was *not* an exercise of international criminal jurisdiction, nor was it an application of international criminal law. Former junta leaders were tried by Argentine courts under Argentine law. The Trial of the Juntas was a profoundly domestic exercise born out of local demand for justice.

Nevertheless, observing the trials in Argentina and the developing practice of empaneling truth commissions (the earliest among them in Argentina, Chile, and Uganda) to uncover the specifics of past abuses throughout the region, scholars and activists began to draw a link between domestic vindication of human rights and international legal duties. Writing in 1990, Naomi Roht-Arriaza argued that the presence of a requirement "to investigate grave human rights violations and take actions against those responsible" in "almost every major human rights-related instrument" suggested that the obligation to prosecute egregious human rights abuses of previous regimes rose to the level of customary international law.[30] In her much-cited 1991 *Yale Law Journal* article on the subject, Diane Orentlicher suggested that the existence of such a duty was grounded not only in the growing body of human rights treaty provisions requiring the investigation of allegations of disappearances, extrajudicial killings, and torture, but also in the Nuremberg precedent of requiring individual criminal liability for egregious acts of state.[31] The conclusion reached by both Roht-Arriaza and Orentlicher was that states' obligations under international law did not permit "wholesale impunity for atrocious crimes" and that successor regimes must therefore act to prevent it.[32]

At the time, the link between transitional justice and international legal duties was controversial. Responding to Orentlicher, Argentine jurist Carlos Nino suggested that the lack of enforcement of an obligation to prosecute past regime crimes undermined claims of its existence. Nino's skepticism references the fact that, in the absence of formal treaty law, the existence of international legal obligations is identified through an inquiry into the "settled practice of states" born out of the belief that the practice is obligatory (*opinio juris*).[33] The widespread prevalence of impunity shows that there was no "settled practice" of providing accountability for past regime crimes. Crucially, there was also no practice of pressuring other states to provide accountability, suggesting the absence of *opinio juris* as well.[34] For instance, there was clear evidence that the Khmer Rouge atrocities amounted to crimes against humanity on an enormous scale and, in some cases, genocide. However, despite the heavy involvement of international actors in Cambodia's transition, there was no international pressure on the new regime in the late 1980s or early 1990s to prosecute those responsible.[35]

But despite states' disinterest in enforcing an accountability obligation on successor regimes, human rights organizations began to pressure newly elected democratic governments not to allow impunity for the crimes of the past. Human Rights Watch's 1992 *World Report* stated that "A key measure of a country's evolution toward democracy is its capacity to hold past gross abusers of human rights accountable for their misdeeds."[36] This observation reflected a policy statement adopted three years previously regarding legacies of gross abuses in transitioning states, in which the organization committed to "oppose[] amnesties for such abuses" and "seek[] prosecution particularly of those with the highest degree of responsibility for the most severe abuses."[37]

It is not clear that, at the time, Human Rights Watch thought of this as advocacy for the fulfillment of an international legal obligation. Writing in the *New York Review of Books* in 1990, Aryeh Neier (then the executive director of Human Rights Watch) discussed a variety of approaches to dealing with past regime crimes, and suggested that in many cases the pursuit of truth should supercede the pursuit of justice.[38] The Human Rights Watch reports of the early 1990s did not attempt to frame their calls for justice in the language of states' international legal duties, but rather in terms of respect for victims. For instance, a 1991 report on Ethiopia following the fall of the oppressive Mengistu regime calls for accountability and notes that "it is a right of victims of human rights abuse that those responsible for committing the abuses be brought to justice."[39] A 1993 report on Somalia post–Siad Barre calls for "accountability for the many crimes of the recent past" on the grounds that "the victims of Somalia's war must be reassured that their suffering will not be forgotten."[40]

Global attention to transitional justice also prompted a flurry of activity at various United Nations human rights bodies in the early 1990s, all of which reflected a growing consensus among scholars, activists, and UN officials that impunity for past regimes' crimes was impermissible. The Human Rights Committee, analyzing the ICCPR's prohibition on torture in 1992, found that allowing amnesties would violate states' obligation to investigate. A special rapporteur's report on the rights of victims of gross violations of human rights, requested in 1989 by the UN Sub-Commission on the Prevention of Discrimination and Protection of Minorities, identified a "duty to prosecute and punish perpetrators" in cases of "certain gross violations of human rights."[41] The Vienna Declaration and Programme of Action adopted at the 1993 World Human Rights Conference confirmed this duty, resolving that states should prosecute the perpetrators of torture and extrajudicial killings and "abrogate legislation leading to impunity for those responsible for grave violations of human rights."

In the early 1990s, the breakup of Yugoslavia led to the worst atrocities Europe had seen since World War II. More than one hundred thousand people died, many of them civilian victims of vicious ethnic targeting. Journalists and human rights activists were quick to compare Serbian crimes to the horrors of the Holocaust.[42] In response, the newly unfettered post–Cold War Security Council authorized the first exercise of international criminal jurisdiction since Nuremberg. The ad hoc International Criminal Tribunal for the former Yugoslavia (ICTY) was established in 1993 to try "serious violations of international humanitarian law." Although the first defendants at the ICTY and at the International Criminal Tribunal for Rwanda (ICTR, established in 1994) challenged the applicability of international criminal jurisdiction to non-international conflicts, both courts held that violations of the laws of war constituted crimes that the international community had a right to prosecute regardless of the context in which they were committed.[43]

As Aryeh Neier has observed, allowing "international prosecution of those committing crimes in the internal armed conflicts so pervasive in our era" was a dramatic move to "rewrite international law."[44] The creation of the two ad hoc tribunals reflected a post–Cold War shift toward viewing the protection of human rights within a state's boundaries as a matter of obvious global concern, part of a "transition from a culture of sovereign impunity to a culture of national and international accountability."[45]

This shift also offered a nexus to the developing trend of transitional justice in Latin America. None of the formulations of the obligation to combat impunity restricted its applicability to successor regimes. Legally, atrocities in the absence of political transition might trigger it as easily as inaction in response to past regime crimes. At the same time, the abuses of past regimes might be not only violations of states' human rights obligations and domestic law; they might be international crimes. A UN special rapporteur's report on the obligation to combat impunity drafted in 1993 (and published in 1996) made no distinction between past and present regime crimes, but simply emphasized the duty of states to ensure the prosecution of the perpetrators. It also suggested a role for the international community through "the subsidiary jurisdiction of a foreign court or concurrent jurisdiction of an international court" when national courts are not competent to provide justice.[46]

Evidence of this newly forged link between transitional and international justice can be observed in a change in human rights advocacy on accountability during the early 1990s. Within a handful of years, advocates moved from no mention of accountability to emphasizing the need for accountability in transitional contexts to (following the creation of the ad hocs) calling for accountability in all cases where international crimes had been committed. They also began to include appeals to members of the international community to ensure accountability. This association of international justice and transitional justice, emphasized by advocates in the aftermath of the international community's in-augural efforts at prosecuting ongoing atrocities, raised the possibility that the precedent of the ad hocs might apply to an unlimited number of situations. Those states for whom human rights was a priority, and who were likely to be on the hook for the ballooning costs of international justice, began to think seriously about a permanent institution.

In the 1980s, when reporting on the commission of atrocities that clearly qualified as international crimes, the recommendations of the constituent organ-izations of Human Rights Watch generally comprised demands for the cessa-tion of the violence and admonitions that members of the international community should stop supporting perpetrator states. So, for instance, Ameri-cas Watch's reporting on the slaughter of indigenous Mayans during the civil war in Guatemala during the early 1980s condemned the atrocities as a viola-tion of Guatemala's human rights treaty obligations but made no mention of the need to bring the perpetrators to justice.[47]

As mentioned above, with the onset of the third wave of democratization and the examples of Latin American transitional justice, Human Rights Watch be-gan to demand accountability in posttransitional settings. However, during the early 1990s, these calls were not included in reports on atrocities committed in nontransitional contexts.[48] A report on Ethiopia drafted only one year before the one mentioned above (but before the transition to a new regime) conclusively identifies the aerial bombardment of civilian targets as a war crime, but does not raise the issue of accountability.[49] Similarly, an Africa Watch report exhaus-tively documenting the crimes of the Siad Barre regime in Somalia before its fall does not address the question of justice.[50] Another Africa Watch report drafted a few months later catalogs the horrors occurring in Liberia's first civil war, but does not call for the perpetrators to be punished.[51]

The divergent approach to accountability for atrocities committed under a prior versus a current regime could be attributed to practical considerations. As the next two chapters show, newly elected democratic regimes are far more likely to have the political will to prosecute abusers of a prior regime in order to signal a clean break with an abusive past. If no regime change has occurred, abusers are more likely to remain in positions of power and to be able to preempt ac-countability. Additionally, in nontransitional contexts, the conflict that produced the abuses may be ongoing, calling into question the capacity of the government to provide justice.

All of these concerns supply a practical logic for calling for accountability in transitional cases and refraining in nontransitional cases. However, as the mid-1990s approached, it became clear that practical concerns were not driv-ing the decision about whether to call for justice. A 1993 Africa Watch report on state-sanctioned ethnic violence in Rwanda calls on the government to "bring to trial all persons, not just officials and soldiers, who have been accused of killings and other gross abuses of human rights."[52] But a report drafted in the same year on abuses of civilians by all parties to Sudan's prolonged civil war carefully documents responsibility for violations of the laws of war but makes no recommendation about accountability.[53] A 1993 Helsinki Watch newsletter on shelling of civilians in the Nagorno–Karabakh conflict clearly identifies the acts as violations of the Geneva Convention, but simply calls on the parties to cease the conduct and "take disciplinary action" against those responsible.[54]

Strikingly, Middle East Watch's meticulous 1993 documentation of the Anfal campaign, which clearly establishes the commission of the crime of genocide against the Kurds, speaks directly to the need for accountability, despite political will and capacity issues. The report notes that "it would be unrealistic to expect President Saddam Hussein to put himself and his closest aides and relatives on trial," and calls on the international community to ensure that the crimes not go unpunished.[55] It therefore does not appear that the earlier absence of pressure for accountability for ongoing atrocities was due to practical considerations. Rather, the change in advocacy strategy more likely reflects a changing view of what was required.

By the mid- to late 1990s, a demand for accountability appeared to be a pro forma feature of Human Rights Watch's reporting on mass atrocities, regardless of the practical likelihood that such a recommendation would be acted on. Even in cases of powerful actors in the system with no interest in complying or vulnerability to pressure, such as Russia during the First Chechen War, Human Rights Watch still called on them to "bring to justice officers and enlisted men suspected of humanitarian law violations, in open trials before independent tribunals and punish those found guilty in a manner consistent with international law."[56] In cases where both capacity and the political will to try those responsible for attacks on civilians were absent, such as for abuses committed during Cambodia's attempt to finally weed out the remnants of the Khmer Rouge in 1995 and massacres by all parties to the conflict in eastern Zaire in 1997, Human Rights Watch now demanded that the perpetrators be brought to justice.[57] In all cases, Human Rights Watch also included calls for members of the international community to insist on accountability.

If Carlos Nino was correct in the early 1990s that the prospect of "world powers" penalizing governments for failure to provide accountability for past regimes' crimes was a "complete fantasy," just a few years later it looked remarkably possible.[58] The idea for a permanent international criminal tribunal, long dormant during the Cold War, was initially revived in 1989 as a possible solution to the problem of the international drug trade. The war in the former Yugoslavia broke out shortly after the UN General Assembly asked the International Law Commission to study the feasibility of creating such a body. Amidst horrifying violence in both Europe and the Great Lakes region of central Africa, and the growing conviction that atrocities within a state's borders were a matter of international concern, the international community's focus shifted from terrorism and narcotic trafficking to the prosecution and punishment of abuses of civilians.

Former US war crimes ambassador (and negotiator at the Rome Statute deliberations) David Scheffer explains that shift as follows:

> As the atrocity crimes of the early 1990s swamped the news and as tribunal fatigue undermined the will of the U.N. Security Council to reproduce an ad hoc tribunal with every mass killing, international lawyers and governments began to get serious about what a permanent court would look like and how it would function.[59]

A "like-minded group" of European, Latin American, and other states began to push forward an agenda for the creation of a permanent international tribunal to try atrocity crimes.[60] Critically, following the successful establishment of the ICTY, the United States' position changed "from cautious skepticism to qualified support" for an international criminal court.[61] What the United States envisioned, however, was a court that would defer to powerful states' interests, requiring Security Council approval for any case to proceed. But as Nicole Deitelhoff meticulously documents, other states' efforts to frame the court's prospective effectiveness "as resulting from universal applicability" and "independence from and impartiality toward the political interests of states" pulled support away from this more conservative approach.[62]

By the time of the Rome Statute's drafting in 1995, the proposition that "the most serious crimes of concern to the international community as a whole must not go unpunished" was apparently uncontroversial, suggesting that the accountability norm had entrenched.[63] The negotiating history at Rome indicates that the state parties understood the ICC's establishment primarily as a means to improve compliance with an existing obligation under international law, rather than the enshrinement of new substantive legal duties.[64] It is not uncommon for an international treaty to formalize an obligation that already exists as a matter of custom, but in the case of the Rome Statute, there was almost no past practice of requiring accountability. As Aryeh Neier observed in 1998, "actual judicial punishment of those who committed even the most heinous violations of rights has been infrequent since the war crimes trials after World War II."[65] But the establishment of the ad hoc tribunals had been a watershed moment for international justice, and their link to the rhetoric of obligation surrounding transitional justice was apparently persuasive.

The Rome Statute, with its affirmation that "it is the duty of every State to exercise its criminal jurisdiction over those responsible for international crimes," was adopted on July 7, 1998.[66] By this time, the conversation among advocates and international legal scholars was no longer about whether an obligation to provide accountability for acts of mass atrocity existed, but about what precisely it entailed. Writing in 1996, Juan Méndez (at the time, Human Rights Watch's general counsel) noted the presence of "an emerging principle in international law that states have affirmative obligations in response to massive and systematic violations of fundamental rights."[67] Based on a survey of the Genocide Convention and the Convention against Torture's obligations to punish, the development of crimes against humanity law, and the rise of universal jurisdiction laws, he concluded that "if anything, the disagreement (or skepticism) is on the content of the obligation."[68]

Such assertions by advocates were bolstered by the ability to appeal to decisions of international courts, emphasizing the importance of prosecution and upholding the emerging principles, identified by the UN special rapporteurs, of intolerance for amnesties and impunity. In its 1998 decision in *Kurt v. Turkey*, the European Court of Human Rights held that the European Convention on Human Rights' "right to an effective remedy" specifically requires "a thorough and effective investigation capable of leading to the identification and punishment of those responsible."[69] In the same year, the ICTY held in *Furundzija* that amnesties for torture were impermissible under international law because of torture's status as a jus cogens crime requiring prosecution and punishment.[70]

The Rome Statute's entry into force, on July 1, 2002, conclusively established that the obligation to provide accountability for mass atrocities required criminal prosecution of those most responsible for the most serious international crimes. Critically, the court was designed to exercise complementary jurisdiction, which locates the primary obligation to provide accountability with the territorial state and only invokes international involvement when the state is "unable" or "unwilling" to prosecute. The court's jurisdictional regime was designed to facilitate compliance with this obligation by offering a backup option when lack of capacity or political will prevents states from pursuing justice. This underscores two things: first, that it is the responsibility of the entire international community to ensure that impunity is not permitted for international crimes, but second, that the states where they occur bear the primary obligation to prosecute them.

Michal Ben-Josef Hirsch and Jennifer Dixon argue that the strength of the accountability norm is evident in the fact that there is "a strong international expectation that individual perpetrators *should* be held accountable and *should not* get away with impunity."[71] Even though prosecution of the authors of atrocities remains rare, states that permit (or pursue) impunity are met with significant international censure. Take the case of Syria.

An estimated half a million civilians have died as a consequence of the civil war raging since 2011. In ten years of hostilities, human rights groups have repeatedly documented egregious violations of international law by government forces (and, to a lesser extent, by the rebels). The Assad regime has engaged in widespread and systematic custodial torture and extrajudicial killings of suspected regime opponents, attacks on civilian targets including hospitals and aid conveys, and the use of prohibited weapons. As evidence of these atrocities has piled up, international condemnation has been consistently paired with demands that the perpetrators be held criminally accountable. As early as 2011, human rights organizations, UN officials, and Western governments all raised the possibility of the Security Council referring the situation to the International Criminal Court.

Global power politics have insulated the Assad regime from accountability, but the ongoing bloodbath in Syria has been consistently framed by a wide variety of international actors in terms of an unacceptable state of impunity.[72] And as Beth Simmons and Hyeran Jo point out, this diversity of different actors engaged in promoting and policing the accountability norm is a component of its strength: "diversity among normative adherents helps to grant legitimacy to norms, increases their broad salience, and reduces the costs associated with defending them."[73]

Calls for justice for mass atrocities may come from members of the victim community protesting in the streets. They may come from international civil society organizations like Human Rights Watch, the International Center for Transitional Justice, and Amnesty International. They may come from the prosecutor of the International Criminal Court, the UN high commissioner for human rights, or the various special rapporteurs for human rights within the UN system. They may come from foreign governments that are trading partners or aid donors of the postatrocity state. As Rosemary Nagy explains, "the question today is not whether something should be done after atrocity, but how it should be done. And a professional body of international donors, practitioners and researchers assists or directs in figuring this out and implementing it."[74]

The consistency of condemnations of impunity and the range of actors involved reflects the accountability norm's high level of concordance, or broad acceptance of the norm as the appropriate standard of behavior, which Ben-Josef Hirsch and Dixon identify as one of two critical components of norm strength.[75] The rapid proliferation of international justice bureaucracy reflects the other: institutionalization, or the norm's codification in international law.[76] These are mutually reinforcing phenomena. As Adam Bower points out, "institutionaliza-tion has therefore played a dual role in both providing logics for challenging nonimpunity, but also in facilitating efforts by states, transnational civil soci-ety, and the court itself to counter attacks and bolster normative validity."[77]

The idea that the large-scale violation of certain human rights is not only un-acceptable to the international community but can and must be treated as criminally culpable conduct is an increasingly fundamental norm of the inter-national community. Accountability pressure is virtually guaranteed following the publicization of atrocities. But the decision about whether to pursue justice is one with extraordinarily high political stakes for postatrocity governments, as the next two chapters show. This is what sets the stage for postatrocity gov-ernments to employ quasi-compliant strategies in response to international ac-countability pressure, as detailed in chapters 5 and 6.

3

VICTIMS AND PERPETRATORS

The model of accountability for mass atrocities envisioned by international actors calling for justice looks something like this: Evidence of a massacre emerges. In the face of outcry from both domestic and international audiences, the relevant state authorities investigate. The suspects are identified and are then tried by a court applying substantive international criminal law and upholding fair trial rights. If the prosecutor presents adequate evidence, the perpetrators (both those who pulled the trigger and those who gave the order) are convicted and sentenced to lengthy prison terms.

Of course, this almost never happens.

A much more familiar story is the one that played out in Uzbekistan in 2005, when the arrest and trial of twenty-three local businessmen on spurious charges of Islamic militancy sparked a conflagration in the city of Andijan. After the verdict in the case was postponed, armed locals staged a prison break and seized control of a nearby government building. Emboldened by their actions, crowds of protesters gathered nearby calling for an end to injustice. But instead of meeting their demands, the government responded with deadly force.

According to eyewitness testimony, security forces opened fire on the protesters with no warning.[1] Unarmed civilians were killed as they attempted to flee. In the aftermath, the death toll was hotly contested. Rumors spread about mass graves outside of town and covert military operations to transport bodies away from the scene. Eventually, the Uzbek government acknowledged the deaths of

187 people, most of whom it said were "terrorists." Human rights groups put the total at over a thousand.

Some of the Andijan protesters escaped across the border into Kyrgyzstan. For those who remained, the situation was precarious. In the aftermath of the massacre, President Islam Karimov launched a vicious crackdown. Journalists who had covered the events at Andijan were forced to flee, and almost every foreign NGO found itself expelled from the country. As members of the international community called for an independent investigation into the massacre, the government pursued criminal charges against those suspected of involvement in the "uprising" and convened a window-dressing parliamentary commission to validate the official narrative of an attempted Islamist revolution.

In the months following the massacre, the Karimov regime's relationship with the West soured. Uzbekistan lost millions of dollars in aid and arms sales. Angry about Western interference, it ended its air-base agreement with the United States. But the estrangement didn't last. The European Union lifted its arms embargo in 2009, the United States in 2012. And just in time for the Andijan massacre's ten-year anniversary, the United States announced a new five-year plan for military cooperation with Uzbekistan.

The Andijan victims continue to call for justice, but so far it has eluded them. Their story, of violence at the hands of the state followed by official denials and international outcry that eventually fades into apathy, is one experienced by atrocity victims the world over. Although the entrenchment of the international accountability norm means that victims have a clear legal obligation to appeal to, as well as robust support from members of the international community, there are often equally strong factors weighing in favor of impunity.

Questions about the pursuit of accountability for atrocities touch on the most core sovereign prerogatives: the monopoly on violence and the power to adjudicate and punish. They reflect some of the deepest political dynamics within a society: Which groups can make claims on the government? Whose opinions matter? Decisions to pursue justice are therefore both contentious and highly contingent.

The rest of this book looks at how international human rights pressure affects postatrocity governments' decisions about accountability. But to understand the impact of an intervention, it's helpful to have a sense of how events might have unfolded without it. This chapter focuses on the domestic political concerns that drive governments' preferences about how to respond to mass atrocities before considering how that influences their engagement with international audiences. I begin with a detailed look at how accountability decisions unfold in the relative *absence* of international involvement through a case study of Ethiopia's transitional justice decisions following the fall of the Derg regime in 1991.

Glass shattered and red liquid splashed on the ground as the crowd in Addis Ababa's Meskel Square cheered. Shouting "death to counterrevolutionaries," Colonel Mengistu Haile Mariam symbolically destroyed the blood of the Ethiopian revolution's enemies. It was the opening salvo in a campaign of mass slaughter—the Red Terror—that would claim the lives of half a million of his countrymen and women.

Mengistu's Marxist junta, the Derg, had seized power from Ethiopia's collapsing monarchy in 1974. It rapidly purged the government of officials loyal to Emperor Haile Selassie. Sixty of them were extrajudicially executed in the early days of the new regime. The deposed emperor was quietly murdered and buried under the floor of his former palace.

But the major challenge to the Derg's consolidation of power didn't come from the remnants of imperial rule; it came from the civilian left. The revolutionary coalition had quickly fractured, with the All-Ethiopia Socialist Movement (MEISON) aligning itself with the Derg, and the Ethiopian People's Revolutionary Party (EPRP) setting itself up in opposition. Both sides were brutal in their efforts to eliminate their rivals. The EPRP launched an assassination campaign against members of the Derg, while the regime imposed the death penalty for opposition to the regime. The result was that "any Ethiopian opposed to the Dergue [sic] or 'suspected of being lukewarm to the revolution' could be branded as either an anarchist or a political murderer."[2]

In early 1977, Mengistu slaughtered his opponents within the Derg and became its undisputed leader. With the internal challenge to his power suppressed, he turned to the external threat. His speech in Meskel Square heralded the beginning of an all-out assault on the EPRP. Heavily armed civilian defense squads were sent into the streets of the capital to search out regime opponents. Those suspected of counterrevolutionary sentiments were detained, or simply killed on the spot. As survivors recounted, "The Dergue [sic] glorified the execution of those it called 'counter-revolutionaries' in chilling radio announcements. Those announcements were always preceded by a popular folksong: fiyel wotete."[3]

When the EPRP's youth committees organized a May Day protest calling for civilian rule, the Derg responded with deadly force. In the "May Day Massacre" and its immediate aftermath, over a thousand suspected EPRP supporters were gunned down; many of them were left lying in the streets. Almost all of them were young, barely out of childhood. As one journalist explains, "simply knowing how to read and write and being aged about 20 or less were enough to define the potential or active 'counter-revolutionary.'"[4] The regime famously required family members collecting their corpses to pay for the bullets used to kill them. Thousands more were arrested, some later released with the scars of torture, others never seen again.

The May Day Massacre was only the beginning—what one historian of the period described as "the dress rehearsal" for the bloodshed that followed.[5] With the EPRP in retreat, the Derg turned on its ostensible allies, rooting out those suspected of insufficient loyalty to the regime. MEISON members who had played a critical role in the first phase of the Red Terror were themselves the targets of the second phase. No one was safe:

> Mass arrests and the virtually systematic use of torture produced confessions which generated a daily quota of "suspects," themselves arrested and tortured and in turn denouncing a new wave of "counter-revolutionaries." Killer commandos roamed the towns, sometimes striking down their victims in broad daylight in sight and sound of everybody, who tried to make sure they saw and heard nothing.[6]

The killings became less public in the third and final phase of the Red Terror, but by the end of 1978, tens of thousands had been slaughtered, many more detained and tortured, and others had fled abroad. The leftist threat to the Derg had been eradicated and an entire generation broken. Those left alive were "so cowed and terrified that any expression of dissent in Addis Ababa was unthinkable for a decade."[7]

The Red Terror is the most well known of the Derg's human rights abuses, but it is emblematic of the regime's broader approach to rule. For seventeen years, the junta kept itself in power through widespread and systematic violations of the rights of its citizens. Its brutality against perceived political opponents was matched by merciless counterinsurgency tactics in the multiple campaigns the Derg fought against internal rebellions. As one of the architects of the counterinsurgency campaign in Tigray, Legesse Asfaw, put it, "to kill the fish, you have to drain the water."[8] Human rights groups documented war crimes ranging from the use of chemical weapons, to the aerial bombardment of civilian targets, to the intentional infliction of starvation on communities suspected of supporting the rebels. In 1991, Human Rights Watch estimated that the death toll "undoubtedly exceed[ed] 150,000."[9]

In the end, the Derg's brutality contributed to bringing it down. As one scholar explains, "the Derg decided to crush the insurgents, thereby adopting an all-out repressive policy. The indiscriminate nature of this repression gave people no other alternative than to support the armed groups."[10] Although Ethiopia's army was dramatically larger and better equipped than the insurgencies, it suffered devastating defeats at the hands of both the Eritrean People's Liberation Front and the Tigray People's Liberation Front in the late 1980s. The military was further weakened by the execution of twelve of its senior leadership following a failed coup attempt in 1989. When several of the rebel movements who had been fighting separate insurgencies for years joined together to form the Ethiopian People's Revolutionary Democratic Front (EPRDF), it sounded the death knell for the regime. As the EPRDF forces advanced on Addis Ababa, Mengistu fled into exile in Zimbabwe.

The Derg went out with a whimper. When the EPRDF entered Addis Ababa on May 28, 1991, Ethiopia's massive army had disintegrated, many of its troops having "fled with their weapons into Kenya, Djibouti, Somalia, and Sudan."[11] The institutions of government had collapsed, leaving a power vacuum ready to be filled.

A new state had to be built from the ground up, and it had to be one that would solve the "national question" more effectively than previous Ethiopian regimes. Long-standing tensions between the Tigrayans and Amhara threatened to boil over. Several ethnonationalist movements had joined to oust the Derg, but now faced the challenge of holding together a big-tent coalition as it took up the reins of government. The stakes were particularly high given the security threats posed by instability in neighboring Sudan and Somalia and Ethiopia's regular experience of famine. The new government also faced the immediate question of what to do with the members of the old regime.

An accountability process offered a solution to both of these problems, an opportunity to "create a decisive breach with the past and the old political order, concomitantly giving legitimacy to a new system of federal government and its ethnic policies."[12] When the transitional government took office on July 5, 1991, it moved quickly to arrest the remaining high-ranking Derg officials and created "Peace and Stability Committees" to investigate and detain suspected human rights abusers. Over the next few months, "over 2,000 central military and civilian officials were arrested."[13]

The fact that the new government had come to power after a long and bloody civil war coexisted in tension with its desire to engage in full accounting of the crimes of the Derg era. On the one hand, a truth-telling process would assist in the creation of a cohesive new Ethiopian polity bound together by a shared understanding of the past and help to entrench the new government's federalist approach to the national question. But on the other hand, a retributive approach focused on proving the guilt of Derg regime leaders would "legitimize the ethnic resistance towards the regime as justified and warranted, thus acquitting the resistance movements for their actions and violations."[14]

The result was a dual mandate. The transitional government established a special prosecutor's office (SPO) and asked it both to "establish for public knowledge and for posterity a historical record of the abuses of the Mengistu regime" *and* "bring those criminally responsible for human rights violations and/or corruption to justice."[15] It was explicitly constructed as both an instrument of retributive justice and a truth-finding process. In a letter to the United Nations, the transitional government emphasized that the trials would fulfill Ethiopia's obligations to punish violations of international law, but also "the right of the families to know the fate of their relatives and to receive restitution."[16]

As the Ethiopian case shows, the decision to pursue accountability is complicated. A number of different and potentially competing motivations were at play in the post–Derg regime's decision-making process: to signal a decisive break with the past, to settle scores with representatives of an abusive regime, to consolidate and legitimize a precarious hold on power, to placate the survivors of Derg crimes, and to preserve peace and stability in the face of simmering ethnic tensions. In the following pages, I look at each of these motivations in turn, drawing out how they have influenced the shape of transitional justice processes in a wide variety of contexts.

Breaking with the Past

Demand for accountability from victim communities can enhance a new regime's incentives to signal a break with a history of violence. When Augusto Pinochet fell from power in Chile in 1990 one of the first orders of business of the new, democratic, government was the establishment of a truth commission to probe extrajudicial killings and disappearances committed by the prior regime. This decision reflected the Chilean people's demand for a clear signal that such abuses of power would never be tolerated again as well as the desire of the new administration to firmly establish itself as a different sort of government. South Africa's famous Truth and Reconciliation Commission was designed to play a similar role: both clarifying the horror of what had happened under apartheid and allowing the country to move forward into a new political future.

But the institutions that arise out of a postatrocity government's desire to break with the past don't necessarily meet the demands of the victims. When Hissène Habré's brutal regime fell, his secret police, the Documentation and Security Directorate (DDS), stood accused of widespread torture and extrajudicial killing. Tens of thousands had been slaughtered in detention and in ethnic cleansing campaigns against Chad's minorities. Habré was replaced by his former military commander in chief, Idriss Déby, who marched into N'Djaména at the head of a rebel army in December 1990. The new government wasted little time in setting up a Commission of Inquiry into the Crimes and Misappropriations Committed by Ex-President Habré, His Accomplices and/or Accessories.

The commission faced serious difficulties in the execution of its mandate. It was underresourced, unable to compel the testimony of perpetrators, and, perhaps most damningly, forced to set up shop in a former DDS detention center, where victims were understandably reluctant to come testify.

Nevertheless, the commission took its work seriously. Its report, published in 1993, found that the Habré regime was responsible for "widespread massacres and acts of dreadful savagery" against unarmed civilians.[17] It estimated that the regime had killed more than forty thousand of its citizens and recommended that those responsible be prosecuted. It also called for memorialization of the dead as well as the creation of a national human rights commission and a purge of human rights abusers from the security forces.[18]

None of the Chadian commission of inquiry's recommendations were implemented. In fact, many of the individuals named as perpetrators remain in positions of power in the government and military today. Consequently, many observers have concluded that the Déby regime deployed the process cynically as a means of legitimizing its rule during the rocky transitional period and that there was never any intention to proceed with a justice process.[19]

Settling Scores

Signaling a break with the past can also shade into score settling. When the Sandinistas broke the Somoza family's four-decade-long grip on power in Nicaragua, they embarked on an ambitious program of legal reforms: The Statute on the Rights and Guarantees of Nicaraguans outlawed torture and arbitrary detention and put in place fair trial protections. But Nicaraguans who had suffered under the Somozas didn't just want an end to the brutality and impunity of the past. They wanted their abusers punished. The Sandinistas themselves had been viciously targeted by regime forces during the two years of rebellion that brought them to power. Their answer to calls for retribution was a massive program of trials for Somoza "war criminals."

Over the course of the first eighteen months of the Sandinista regime, nearly eight thousand Somoza officials and military personnel, including nearly every member of the former National Guard, were prosecuted in widely publicized proceedings.[20] Ultimately, nearly 80 percent of those tried were convicted and given sentences of up to thirty years. The process was deeply flawed from a fair trial perspective. Many of the 6,300 trials conducted were heard by panels lacking any professional judges (or indeed lawyers). The charges were often vague and the accused had little time or resources with which to mount a defense. But although they were heavily criticized by international human rights groups at the time, the trials satisfied the victims and arguably served their purpose of punishing and delegitimizing those associated with Somoza abuses.

Consolidating Power

When transition occurs through violence, as it did in Nicaragua, it is not only score-settling imperatives that militate for retributive justice, but also rule legitimation concerns. After driving out the perpetrators of the 1994 genocide, a minority Tutsi regime took power in Rwanda. It immediately set about eliminating the Hutu Power threat. This involved outlawing the previously ruling political party, which had presided over the genocide; pursuing the *interahamwe* militia into the refugee camps in Democratic Republic of the Congo; and commencing a massive program of prosecutions.

By the time the process wound down in 2012, the domestic courts and the *gacaca* traditional justice process had tried more than two million accused perpetrators. Approximately 65 percent of them were found guilty.[21] Given that Rwanda's total population is under twelve million, this designated more than 10 percent of its citizens as criminals. The logic of this was at least in part to justify Tutsi rule. The experience of the genocide and the guilt of the Hutu Power regime is so fundamental to the current regime's claim to power that it holds and televises annual reenactments of the genocide to keep the injury present in the minds of the public.

For the twentieth anniversary of the genocide in 2014, the Rwandan government invited dignitaries from all over the world to observe a mass commemoration at Kigali's Amahoro Stadium. Thirty thousand people crowded the stadium.[22] Reenactors dressed in white and gray lay on the ground as if dead while survivors narrated their stories. Many in the audience who had lived through the genocide found the spectacle intensely traumatic and had to be carried out for medical attention. The pageant culminated with actors in the uniforms of the Rwandan Patriotic Front (now the government) lifting the "bodies" from the ground. The message was clear and was echoed in President Paul

Kagame's concluding remarks: The ruling regime was the savior of the genocide victims and the Rwandan nation.[23]

Placating Survivors

If the Rwandan model of mass accountability reflects the precarious position of a government that came to power during cataclysmic violence in a sharply divided society, it also reflects the enormous scale of the crime. With over half a million dead, even if the new government did not view the accountability process as critical to consolidating its power and crafting a new, "post-ethnic" Rwanda, it would still be politically expedient to meet the demands of the survivors and their co-ethnics.

In Argentina in the 1980s, sustained advocacy by victims' groups pushed the new government to allow trials of the junta in civilian courts, rather than pursuing a more limited transitional justice approach in the military courts. With so many citizens affected by the crimes of the junta, and the new government's rise to power predicated in part on a commitment not to allow amnesty for regime crimes, Argentina's new leaders had obvious reasons to comply with victims' preferences.

By contrast, when survivors are a small, and/or marginalized group, their government may have little interest in their demands. Hundreds, maybe thousands, of people died on the Wagalla airstrip in early February 1984. The victims were ethnic Somalis living in Kenya's North Eastern province. Their killers were members of the Kenyan army, ostensibly investigating reports of a planned rebellion by members of the Degodia clan. Survivors say more than 5,000 people lost their lives at Wagalla and have spent decades demanding accountability for the massacre. But despite a promise from then-President Moi in 1992 that compensation would be paid to the families, the government took no action and maintained its official position that only fifty-seven people had died.

When a national truth commission was created in the aftermath of Kenya's 2007–2008 election violence, hearings were finally held into the Wagalla Massacre.[24] But the commission's credibility with victims was marred from its inception, when an official implicated in ordering the killings was appointed to lead it. Ultimately, it confirmed that the massacre had taken place, and that the death toll was far greater than previously acknowledged. It recommended an official apology and reparations for the victims. In 2015, President Uhuru Kenyatta issued a blanket apology for "past wrongs," but reparations have yet to be paid.[25]

Ethnic Somalis are a tiny minority in Kenya—some 6 percent of a national population of 45 million. And since independence-era efforts to join Kenya's North Eastern Province to Somalia, they have been persistent targets of repression and discrimination by the government. Their demands therefore had little impact on successive Kenyan governments, who neither sought their votes nor valued them as citizens.

Promoting Peace and Stability

The Kenyan case also underscores the fact that robust transitional justice processes are less likely when individuals involved in atrocities remain in positions of power. This is a broader issue than the question of perpetrators prosecuting themselves. Even where dramatic regime change has occurred, individuals implicated in abuse may still be politically powerful. When that is true, pursuing accountability too vigorously can be risky because it gives them an incentive to threaten peace deals or democratic bargains. In both the Chilean and South African examples mentioned above, victims called for a more retributive approach. However, given that these countries transitioned to democracy via a negotiated process that relied on the support of members of the perpetrator group, prosecutions were not politically feasible.

In the aftermath of junta crimes in Haiti in the 1990s, "coup victims [] incessantly demanded justice."[26] The military, and its associated paramilitary, had extrajudicially executed thousands and systematically raped and tortured to terrorize the civilian population after deposing the country's first democratically elected government. Eventually, with a US-led military intervention imminent, the junta leaders agreed to step aside in exchange for amnesty. Faced with the question of how to deal with the Cédras regime's crimes, the returning president Jean-Bertrand Aristide ordered the creation of a truth commission. In the words of one of its members, this move reflected "a tremendous feeling that Haiti had to confront the past."[27] The expectation among the victims was that the truth commission's findings would be used to pursue criminal charges against those implicated in serious abuses.

But the commission was underresourced and poorly organized, leading to delays in beginning its work and administrative challenges during its operation. Most problematically, the government lacked the capacity to protect either the commissioners or the witnesses. Members of the junta and the paramilitary had not been disarmed and were still operating freely. Although the commission's investigators managed to take testimony from nearly 5,500 witnesses and create a database of violations that could be used for statistical analysis of patterns of violence, Raoul Cédras supporters actively interfered in its work. As one commissioner reported, "we received threats, death threats and people calling and shooting the air so you can hear it through the phone."[28] These issues prevented the commission from holding public hearings and hampered their investigations. And when the truth commission's 1,200-page report documenting abuses suffered by nearly nine thousand victims was finalized in February 1996, the government opted not to make it, or the accompanying list of alleged perpetrators, public.

Imperatives to break with the past, settle scores, consolidate power, placate survivors, and protect peace and stability directly shape what transitional justice institutions look like and how they operate. The examples above underscore that the weight postatrocity governments accord to these competing imperatives depends on the relative power of victim and perpetrator groups in society. This is because postatrocity governments are looking to their own political futures when they decide whether and how to pursue accountability. But all of this is further complicated by the fact that postatrocity governments must reckon with the fact that accountability processes require significant resources and expertise.

Turning back to the case of post-Derg Ethiopia, in 1995, the *New Yorker* reported that the prosecution of Derg officials "was being spoken of as an African Nuremberg."[29] But unlike the trials at Nuremberg, the SPO was organized entirely under domestic law—applying the Ethiopian penal code and employing only Ethiopian lawyers and judges. It was a massive undertaking for a country whose institutions had been hollowed out by years of war and dictatorship. The government optimistically predicted that the process would be a crucial step in restoring the rule of law. In practice, the justice system struggled to process a charge list that initially included 5,198 military and civilian officials of the Derg.

Because most senior members of the judiciary had been dismissed in the lustration process that followed the fall of the Derg, the job of prosecuting the former regime was left to "junior and inexperienced judges."[30] Even those who had the legal competence to play this role were fatally understaffed and under-resourced. One observer writing at the time of the trials reported that:

> There is no system of consolidating laws and distributing them to judges in the country. The judges spend most of their time handling court administration, writing down the words of witnesses and oral arguments which could have been done by court clerks. The judges also conduct their own research without any assistants.[31]

The problems extended beyond the judiciary. Before 1994, Ethiopia had never had a public defenders' office.[32] The result was that while the top leadership of the Derg were represented by the country's best (and most expensive lawyers), lower-ranking members were stuck with the poorly prepared new public defenders.

On the prosecution side, an initial staff of approximately thirty prosecutors and four hundred investigators struggled to build the complex legal case against the Derg. They were operating on a shoestring budget of USD 200,000 (later supplemented by USD 1 million from the international community, along with computers, forensic experts, and other assistance).[33] Access to evidence and the ability to secure custody of suspects was complicated by the fact that "the federal and regional police were reluctant to collaborate with the SPO, under the pretext that their powers of investigation were usurped by the SPO."[34] As a consequence of these logistical and resource issues, the Red Terror trials dragged on for fourteen years, from the first indictment in 1994 to the final appeal in 2008.

Ultimately, more than a thousand individuals were convicted during this protracted effort. In the showpiece trial, *Special Prosecutor v. Colonel Mengistu Hailemariam et al.*, sixty-six high-ranking Derg officials were tried (twenty-one in absentia) on a list of charges that ran for 269 pages.[35] The court returned a genocide conviction in 2006 and sentenced the defendants to life in prison, which the Federal Supreme Court later overturned to impose the death penalty.

By any measure, the Red Terror trials were a massive transitional justice effort that held accountable a large number of those implicated in the abuses of the Derg regime. Yet the degree to which the prosecutions achieved the goals set out by the new government were limited. Despite high hopes that that the trials would send "a clear message . . . that governments should be accountable to the people and answerable before the law," they were controversial and seen by many as "victors' justice."[36] Former Derg officials argued that the Tigrayan (minority) ethnicity of the new regime undermined its legitimacy, saying "they should not be ruling. They are not competent to try us."[37] Others attacked the trials as "lip service to human rights . . . a diversion, a ploy to win approval from Western donor countries—particularly the United States."[38]

For the most part, however, despite the fact that the crimes of the Derg affected the lives of nearly all Ethiopians, there was a profound lack of public interest in the trials. This is partly due to the length of time over which the proceedings dragged. The transactional government detained approximately two thousand former regime members in 1991 when it came to power, but the SPO didn't begin operating until eighteen months later. Consequently, the process bogged down in a time-consuming flood of habeas corpus petitions that delayed the start of the trials.

Once the trials were underway, prosecutorial strategy led to further road-blocks. As one observer explained, "the SPO introduced far too many witnesses to prove certain issues. . . . It appears that the SPO, by choosing this strategy wanted to create a forum for witnesses, most of whom were affected in some way, to vent their sorrow and testify in public against leaders who were responsible for some of the most atrocious crimes."[39] Ethiopia's relationships with the donor community soured when the process had only been running for two years, leaving the SPO alienated from technical experts and advisors who might have helped develop a more efficient strategy.

The slow pacing and technical hiccups contributed to a failure to engage the attention of a population struggling to emerge from decades of abuse and conflict. As one observer put it at the time, "everyday political, social and economic challenges faced by the Ethiopian people eclipse the accounts and images of the trials."[40] Furthermore, the new government's own failings on human rights became more and more apparent as time went on. By the time the verdict against Mengistu and his top lieutenants was handed down, desire for transitional justice had been subordinated to concerns about ongoing violations. In light of the post–Derg government's abysmal human rights record, the long-running Red Terror prosecutions took on the quality of a mockery, creating the impression that they served simply as "a political ritual whose function is to legitimate the new system of governance and its rulers."[41]

Even the leadership recognized that the trials had not been a success as an act of political communication. Speaking to a reporter, Prime Minister Meles Zenawi admitted "I think we sort of swallowed more than we could chew. The judicial system in our country was not structurally capable of managing such an exercise quickly. And as time went by the exercise became more and more irrelevant."[42]

For countries emerging from devastating conflict, resource and capacity challenges often compound the political obstacles to transitional justice described above. Where governance institutions have been ravaged by war or eroded by neglect and corruption under a long-running autocracy, it can prove a staggering challenge to keep municipal power on and clear the criminal docket, let alone create new, complex institutions. Accountability processes also require expertise. Even in the United States, which has more than a million licensed attorneys, familiarity with the specialized substantive and procedural law involved in war crimes and crimes against humanity trials is rare. And it's not just lawyers and judges whose expertise is critical. Criminal prosecutions rely on investigators to gather evidence and forensic experts to interpret it. Any process involving victim and witness participation requires mental health experts and providers of social services to address the needs of individuals who may be retraumatized by engagement with legal (or quasi-legal) processes.

Given the complexity and expense of transitional justice processes, it's no surprise that some postatrocity governments find them impossible to undertake without substantial external assistance. Consider the trial of Charles Taylor.

In Liberia's 1997 presidential election, Taylor's supporters famously rallied under the slogan "He Killed My Ma, He Killed My Pa, I'll Vote for Him."[43] It was an exaggeration, but not by much. The 1989–1997 civil war, sparked by Taylor's uprising against Samuel Doe's government, had taken the lives of nearly a quarter of a million Liberians. Taylor won the presidency, propelled to office by the Faustian votes of Liberians convinced that the man who had instigated the violence was the only one who could stop it.

The fragile peace brought by Taylor's election did not last long; a new civil war broke out in 1999. By August 2003 two-thirds of the country had fallen to the rebels advancing on the capital, Monrovia. Taylor fled into exile in Nigeria, leaving Liberia with the chilling prediction, "God willing, I'll be back."[44] In his fourteen years as a militia leader and politician, he had soaked West Africa in blood. He was not only responsible for the near destruction of Liberia; his backing of a brutal insurgency in Sierra Leone facilitated the slaughter of more than fifty thousand people and the displacement of millions more.

Taylor's escape into comfortable exile in a seaside villa in Nigeria infuriated human rights advocates, who wanted him brought to justice for the atrocities committed in the Liberian and Sierra Leonean civil wars. But many survivors of the violence he had unleashed just wanted him gone. As Liberia struggled to rebuild, transitional justice efforts focused on truth seeking and security sector reform rather than on bringing those responsible to justice. But in neighboring Sierra Leone, the mood was different. In 2000, the country's president asked for UN assistance in setting up a war crimes court. The hybrid Special Court for Sierra Leone got underway in early 2002 and by the end of the following year had indicted thirteen accused war criminals. One of them was Charles Taylor.

For nearly three years, Nigeria's government resisted international pressure to hand over Taylor for prosecution. But in March 2003, in response to a request from Liberian president Ellen Johnson Sirleaf, Nigeria agreed that Taylor could be taken into custody. Two days later, he disappeared. An alert border guard apprehended him nearly six hundred miles away, attempting to cross into Cameroon in a Jeep with diplomatic plates and a trunk full of US dollars.[45] He arrived in Freetown, Sierra Leone, in handcuffs, only the second head of state since Nuremberg to be handed over to an international criminal tribunal.[46]

When Taylor was eventually convicted of war crimes and crimes against humanity, it wasn't in Freetown. Both the Sierra Leonean and Liberian governments argued that his ongoing popularity meant prosecuting him in the region posed too big a risk of renewed political instability. Instead he was quickly transferred to The Hague, where his trial was conducted in a courtroom of the International Criminal Court on loan to the Special Court for Sierra Leone. In 2012 he was sentenced to fifty years in prison, which he is serving in a maximum-security facility in the United Kingdom.

The process of trying and convicting Charles Taylor involved at least five countries (both the United States and the United Kingdom played significant roles in determining the form that the Special Court for Sierra Leone would take and in pushing both Nigeria and Liberia to ensure that Taylor would end up before the court), the UN secretary-general, the Security Council, and the International Criminal Court. This kind of extensive involvement of international actors in accountability processes has become increasingly common.

For Sierra Leone, which ended its civil war in 2002 with fewer than one hundred lawyers among its approximately 4.5 million citizens and had not yet criminalized war crimes or crimes against humanity, low capacity led to the request for UN help and the creation of the hybrid Special Court for Sierra Leone. Involving the international community (whether by operating a hybrid tribunal or by outsourcing the process entirely to an international court) can give fragile governments opportunities they would otherwise have to forgo to address victims' desire for justice and punish those most responsible for atrocities while minimizing the appearance of victors' justice or score settling. But while international assistance seems like a straightforward solution to the problems of inadequate resources or expertise to prosecute at home, cooperative efforts between postatrocity governments and international courts are rarely uncomplicated.

The establishment of the International Criminal Court in 1998 was accompanied by much fanfare about how its existence would ensure that even powerful heads of state would not escape justice. But the court's first three cases were actually self-referrals by governments asking the court to dispense justice against troublesome rebel groups operating within their borders. In each of these cases (as well as the other self-referrals), the ICC ended up issuing warrants only for non–state actors, despite credible allegations of government atrocities in most instances.

For example, after a decade and a half fighting the rebel Lord's Resistance Army (LRA), the Ugandan government decided in 2003 to refer the situation in Acholiland to the ICC. The move was controversial at the time. The conflict was still ongoing, and many observers worried that the ICC's involvement would derail delicate peace negotiations.[47] Beyond that, however, human rights advocates worried that by bringing in the ICC, the Ugandan government had ensured that state-perpetrated atrocities would be erased from the narrative of the conflict.[48] The ICC would need the government's cooperation to collect evidence of war crimes and crimes against humanity and would be unlikely to jeopardize the relationship by investigating state forces' conduct.

In fact, this is exactly what happened. In 2005, ICC Chief Prosecutor Luis Moreno-Ocampo issued warrants for five LRA commanders on war crimes and crimes against humanity charges. But despite credible evidence that the Ugandan People's Defence Forces had committed serious abuses against the civilian population in northern Uganda, there have still been no warrants issued for members of the Ugandan security forces or civilian leadership.

Likewise, after the 2011 election violence in Côte d'Ivoire, evidence emerged that serious violations of international law had been committed by supporters of both the incumbent Laurent Gbagbo (who refused to concede the election) and the democratically elected Alassane Ouattara. Yet after the Ouattara administration announced its intention to ratify the Rome Statute, in effect asking the ICC to investigate the election crisis, the prosecutor only issued indictments for the ousted Gbagbo, his wife, and one of his chief supporters. As in Uganda, the need for cooperation from the sitting government appeared to constrain the ICC's ability to act impartially.

An example from the Democratic Republic of the Congo shows just how vexed the relationship between the ICC and self-referring governments can become. In March 2013, the notorious Congolese warlord Bosco Ntaganda, also known as "The Terminator," walked into the US embassy in Kigali and asked to be surrendered to the International Criminal Court. The ICC had unsealed a warrant (issued nearly two years earlier) for Ntaganda in 2008, but prospects for his arrest had always looked dim. Although the Congolese government had self-referred the violence in eastern Democratic Republic of Congo to the court in 2006, it had later incorporated Ntaganda and the Congrès national pour la défense du peuple (CNDP) militia, of which he was chief of staff, into the national military. As a general in the Congolese army, Ntaganda was untouchable.

For several years, international media routinely ran articles marveling at his status as a "man about town" in Goma, capital of North Kivu province.[49] Despite calls from the ICC prosecutor, human rights NGOs, and Western governments to hand him over to face justice, neither the Congolese government nor the UN peacekeeping force, MONUSCO, was willing to jeopardize regional security by arresting him. But then, in April 2012, he defected from the army along with three hundred of his loyalists, forming a new rebel group, the M23. Congolese President Joseph Kabila announced that he would have Ntaganda arrested but saw no reason to transfer him to The Hague. After a yearlong insurgency during which M23 managed to seize Goma from Congolese forces, Ntaganda fell out with M23 leadership and apparently fled across the border into

Rwanda, finding his way to the US embassy. At that point, the Congolese government was only too happy to see him in ICC custody, giving an official statement that "we'd prefer to have him judged here, but if he is sent to The Hague, that's no problem either. The most important thing is that justice is served."[50]

The trajectory of the Uganda and Congo ICC investigations and prosecutions demonstrates that even when postatrocity governments ask for international assistance pursuing accountability, their cooperation is not guaranteed. International assistance may solve the problems of limited resources and expertise, but it does not produce justice free from politics. In fact, the same domestic political factors outlined above continue to influence the extent and character of their cooperation with internationalized justice efforts, both while these institutions are being set up and once they're operating.[51] Relationships with international actors may even become outright antagonistic. As Sidney Leclercq observes regarding Burundi's negotiation process with the United Nations regarding transitional justice:

> National actors used multiple strategies to slow the negotiation process and the concrete inception of TJ institutions, including not clearly identifying the national counterpart for the negotiations; slow responses to UN correspondence; drafting project laws or propositions known to be unacceptable to international norms; nonimplementation of an existing law on the establishment of a national and nonjudicial TRC; multiple lengthy technical commission processes; and recourse to "national consultations."[52]

The tortured negotiating history of the Extraordinary Chambers in the Courts of Cambodia (ECCC) underscores the degree to which cooperation with hybrid tribunals is contingent and driven by domestic politics. The ECCC was set up to provide accountability for the crimes of the Khmer Rouge, whose brutal social engineering policies and purification mania led to the deaths of more than 1.7 million Cambodians. Their Democratic Kampuchea regime was forced from power when the Vietnamese invaded Cambodia in 1979. Thirty years later, trial opened against the first person to be prosecuted by the ECCC, a hybrid tribunal operating with significant UN assistance. Kaing Guek Eav, also known as "Comrade Duch," faced war crimes and crimes against humanity charges for his role overseeing the notorious Tuol Sleng torture center, where at least twelve thousand Cambodians are believed to have been murdered.

The road to the ECCC was long and rocky. The Khmer Rouge retreated into the jungle after the fall of Democratic Kampuchea, and elements of the movement continued to fight the Vietnamese and their client Cambodia People's Party (CPP) government throughout the 1980s. Despite a 1991 peace settlement that saw the withdrawal of the Vietnamese forces and the installation of a UN transitional authority, violence persisted, with the remaining Khmer Rouge elements rejecting the results of the UN-sponsored election in 1993. But within a few years the movement began to fall apart. In 1996, senior Khmer Rouge official Ieng Sary defected to the government along with several thousand fighters. The next year, leader Pol Pot was captured by a breakaway faction and handed over to state custody.

As the Khmer Rouge disintegrated, members were offered amnesty as an enticement to defect to the government. This did not sit well with many victims of the Democratic Kampuchea era, who wanted the perpetrators of crimes against them punished. In June 1997, with the assistance of the UN human rights office in Phnom Penh, Cambodia's co–prime ministers sent a letter to UN Secretary-General Kofi Annan, citing the precedent of the ICTY and ICTR and requesting international assistance bringing the Khmer Rouge to justice. Years of wrangling followed, as each party to the negotiations tried to exert control over what the ultimate accountability mechanism would look like. When a team of international experts proposed an ad hoc tribunal sitting in a neighboring country, the Cambodian government balked.

Prime Minister Hun Sen repeatedly raised the possibility that an accountability process would disincentivize future defections and jeopardize Cambodia's progress toward peace. Meanwhile, he accepted the surrender of Khieu Samphan and Nuon Chea (respectively Democratic Kampuchea's head of state and Pol Pot's second in command) and declared the defeat of the Khmer Rouge. Once the threat posed by the movement was neutralized, Hun Sen appeared to no longer see any point to international criminal prosecutions. Local civil society concluded that he had "seen the international tribunal as an instrument to defeat the Khmer Rouge more than as a means of establishing justice."[53] He told the UN in March 1999 that "there would be no international tribunal, outside or within Cambodia and that Cambodian law did not allow for the participation of foreigners as judge or prosecutor."[54]

Faced with the UN's insistence that justice would not be served without an international tribunal, Hun Sen doubled down.[55] He allegedly told diplomats, "I do not wish a foreign woman to come to Cambodia and dress up in a Khmer dress. I want a Khmer woman to dress in a Khmer dress and for foreigners to come and help put on the make-up."[56] A novel approach was offered to resolve the stalemate: a "mixed" tribunal, in deference to both the Cambodian government's insistence that it be a Cambodian court and the need to impose international standards. But the specific form the tribunal would take remained contentious, with both sides attempting to secure ultimate control.

As John Ciorciari and Anne Heindel explain, "the question of control was linked to the Court's jurisdiction, because neither side wanted to entrust the other with the power to determine the scope of prosecution."[57] In direct contradiction with the UN's conclusion that there were at least twenty surviving individuals responsible for serious violations of international law, Hun Sen preferred to limit the scope to four or five defendants. This preference reflected the fact that former Khmer Rouge fighters now occupied high positions in his own military hierarchy and that he himself was a member of the Khmer Rouge before defecting to Vietnam.

Despite misgivings, the UN ultimately agreed to a Cambodian-majority court. But when the Cambodian legislature approved a draft implementing law that contradicted the draft framework agreement between the government and the UN, Kofi Annan withdrew the UN team from the negotiations with the support of Cambodian and international human rights advocates.

Cambodia seemed happy to let the matter rest at this point, but third-party states, including the United States, Japan, and France, pushed the UN to return to the negotiating table. In a significantly weakened bargaining position as a result of this pressure, the UN was forced to agree to most of Cambodia's proposals. Despite the emerging norm of majority-international hybrid tribunals (several of which had been empaneled in the interim), the final agreement specified that Cambodian nationals would occupy most of the key positions in the ECCC. Human rights advocates predicted that the structure would "fail the most basic test of credibility with Cambodians and the international community."[58] The ECCC's first international prosecutor later lamented that "in the end, the victims of the Khmer Rouge got the tribunal that Hun Sen and his allies, including other former Khmer Rouge throughout the regime, wanted." Meanwhile, Deputy Prime Minister Sok An gloated that the "Cambodian model" might "stand as an example for others in the future."[59]

The interaction between the United Nations and Cambodia over the setup of the Khmer Rouge Tribunal clearly demonstrates that while international assistance can solve problems of resource and capacity constraints, it cannot substitute for an absence of political will at the domestic level. As a general matter, we should therefore assume that a postatrocity government that is not willing to prosecute high-level perpetrators for their crimes domestically is also unlikely to cooperate as an international court attempts to do so. In the next chapter, I consider what other predictions we can make based on the discussion of the domestic and international politics of accountability here and then investigate how well they explain what has happened after ninety mass atrocities committed over the last half-century.

WHAT HAPPENS AFTER MASS ATROCITIES

A man in fatigues stands outside of Guatemala's Supreme Court holding a rope wrapped around the neck of a figure robed as Lady Justice. Nearby, another soldier points a gun at the neck of a kneeling peasant. They are actors, the silver paint on their clothes and skin giving them the look of living statues. Around them, people dressed in street clothes silently hold up signs: "We demand justice for the case of genocide."[1] It's May 23, 2012, and the genocide conviction of former president Efrain Rios Montt has just been overturned. The names of the victims, indigenous Ixil villagers killed by the Guatemalan military in the 1980s, lie on the ground, hand-sewn onto patches that list their ages and the last time their loved ones saw them alive.

On the other side of the world, the faces of young Sri Lankan men disappeared in the suppression of a Marxist rebellion stare out from a memorial wall. Their family members stand vigil nearby, marking an annual commemoration of the missing. They carry signs in Sinhala and English: "Compensate all the families of the disappeared!"

Another public square, thirty-five years earlier: A group of women stands across from the office of Argentina's president. They are the Madres de la Plaza de Mayo, recognizable by the white scarves covering their hair and the signs they hold showing the names and photos of their children who were disappeared by the government. Their demands appear in a daring newspaper ad: "We do not ask for anything more than the truth."[2] Three of their leaders eventually join the ranks of the disappeared, targeted by the military junta for their activism.

The victims of mass atrocities are rarely silent. Even the dead make their presence known. The echoes of their voices join those of the living survivors, calling for justice, compensation for their suffering, or simply the truth of what happened—and sometimes, all of the above. But as the previous chapter indicated, whether and how victims' demands are met depends on a complicated array of domestic and international factors. But how common *is* it? What proportion of mass atrocities are ever prosecuted by domestic courts like Ethiopia's? Who ends up before the International Criminal Court? Is the decades-long wait for accountability experienced by victims from Chad to Cambodia typical? In short: what happens after mass atrocities, and why?

Answering these questions isn't easy. By some accounts, justice for atrocities is becoming significantly more common.[3] By others, the international justice moment of the late 1990s and early 2000s was a mere blip and impunity is overwhelmingly the rule.[4] One reason that it's not immediately obvious which is the more accurate picture is that it's not actually clear what a "mass atrocity" is. The phrase conjures visions of Nazi gas chambers, of piles of skulls in Cambodia and Rwanda. But while it is colloquially understood to refer to large-scale, deliberate attacks on civilians, the term lacks a precise meaning. It has been used to describe everything from school shootings to the Armenian genocide.

Definitions given in the social science and policy literature impose casualty thresholds ranging from five thousand civilian deaths over any time period to fifty thousand intentional deaths over five years.[5] This variance results in significant disagreement over the scale implicit in the term *mass atrocities*. Additionally, definitions based on death tolls omit types of events that seem to cry out for inclusion: the mass rape of as many as fifty thousand women in Bosnia, the Assad regime's systematic use of torture against tens of thousands of Syrian civilians, the forced displacement of more than seven hundred thousand Palestinians from their homes in 1948.

In defining "mass atrocity" for the purposes of my PhD dissertation, I tried to capture all of the events that would unambiguously merit use of the term today. In search of guidance when I began the project in 2012, I first looked at the casualty figures for events under investigation by the International Criminal Court pursuant to the prosecutor's own initiative or a UN Security Council referral. My logic was that these were instances in which we know that members of the international community believed that an atrocity crime requiring accountability had occurred.

I had two reasons for using a current standard rather than a floating threshold that might more accurately represent an evolving understanding of what the term means. The first is that information on violence against civilians improves over time. We might therefore expect that casualty counts from the 1970s are far more likely to underestimate the true total than casualty counts from the 2010s. Using a more permissive definition, based on a current understanding of what constitutes a mass atrocity deserving of international outcry, therefore reduces the risk of erroneously ruling out early events that ought to be included. The second reason is that the process by which mass atrocities come to light, attract attention, become the subject of sustained accountability advocacy, and ultimately receive justice is idiosyncratic and can stretch over decades. This argues in favor of using the most expansive possible definition of mass atrocity that would apply during the period after an atrocity occurred.

Fatality counts are notoriously difficult to obtain and are subject to a variety of biases. Especially in cases of ongoing conflict, available estimates are likely to be rough and to represent the entire civilian mortality as a consequence of the violence, rather than direct, intentional deaths. Even in cases of relatively recent wars, it is hard to find figures more precise than the International Rescue Committee's controversial 2007 estimate of 5.4 million "excess deaths" caused by the Second Congo War and its aftermath.[6] These types of estimates include deaths from disease and starvation, and they rely on the accuracy of preexisting estimates of the baseline mortality within a population.

When multiple conflicts occur simultaneously within a single state's territory, the obstacles to credible fatality estimates are even more profound. For instance, both Ethiopia and Burma have fought multiple long-running, overlapping insurgencies in the postcolonial era, leading to extensive civilian death and displacement. In both cases, state forces have committed widespread violations against civilian populations, but it is very difficult to ascertain which civilian deaths are attributable to intentional acts (and whose) and which are not.

Another facet of this problem is that some mass atrocities have been minimally reported in the West. It is widely understood in Afghanistan that as many as eighty thousand civilians were disappeared by the secret police after the Communist takeover in 1978. But for whatever reason, this particular episode of brutal political repression has never made the list of well-known atrocities. Similarly, the massacres of the Algerian Civil War failed to draw the world's attention away from the cataclysm in the Balkans in the 1990s, despite the deaths of nearly two hundred thousand civilians. The result is that fatality estimates in these cases are rough and are not triangulated from multiple sources and that attribution is difficult.

An example from Libya provides an illustration of these issues. As Benghazi convulsed in February 2011, reports circulated that the Gaddafi regime had murdered more than two thousand civilians during the early days of the uprising. The chief prosecutor of the International Criminal Court at the time, Luis

Moreno Ocampo, repeated outlandish rumors that state security forces were consuming Viagra in order to fuel a program of mass rape.[7] Ultimately, investigations found no truth to the rape allegations and revealed that the death toll had been inflated by a factor of ten. But in the absence of sustained international attention to this crisis and the subsequent NATO intervention, it's likely that the original, incorrect, stories would have remained the conventional wisdom.

Similarly, Pakistan's military is often blamed for the deaths of three million civilians during the Bangladesh Liberation War in 1971. However, many Bangladeshis trace this figure to a slip of the tongue made by independence leader Sheikh Mujibur Rahman, substituting "million" for "lakh" (hundred thousand) in an early reference to the violence.[8] But despite widespread awareness that three million people cannot have been killed, it remains the most commonly cited figure.

In cases of mass rape, these problems are compounded by the potential invisibility of the crime. Rape generally only becomes apparent to external observers through the testimony of victims or the publicization of medical records. But because it may only be certain types of victims who come forward to demand justice (those who are either unusually brave, unable to hide their victimization, and/or comparatively less likely to be stigmatized by their families and communities) or to seek medical attention (those who are most severely injured, or those who live closest to a treatment facility), our understanding of mass rape events is subject to extreme reporting bias.[9]

These are hard problems to correct for; consequently, compiling a comprehensive list of mass atrocities is a fraught enterprise. Where fatality estimates are precise, it is generally due to the efforts of exactly the sort of accountability mechanisms discussed in this book. Where there has been no institutional response to mass atrocity, casualty figures are sketchy at best, especially for events that occurred before human rights organizations began systematically collecting and reporting detailed evidence of violations of international law.

As a consequence, I am deeply skeptical of my (or anyone's) ability to draw up a definitive list of mass atrocities meeting *any* definition. But because the story I am telling here is about what happens when atrocities become publicly known, I am reasonably—which is to say, only barely—comfortable using commonly accepted fatality counts to determine whether events qualify for inclusion in the list and to establish their scope. But this approach undoubtedly leaves out some events that ought to be included and is likely biased in the direction of underincluding earlier events, underincluding events in remoter (or simply less reported on) locations, and underincluding events characterized by sexual violence against vulnerable populations.[10]

With these caveats set out, the accepted fatality counts for the ICC investigations are as follows: approximately 1,200 people dead over the course of one month in Kenya's 2007–2008 postelection violence; at least eight hundred massacred in a single day in Côte D'Ivoire's 2010–2011 postelection violence; and five hundred people killed in ten days during the Libyan revolution.[11] The launch of investigations into these events suggests that members of the international community agree that events in which hundreds of civilians are killed during a brief period of time qualify as mass atrocities. Based on this, I set an initial inclusion criterion for my list of one thousand intentional noncombatant deaths or rapes within a one-month period.

This criterion for inclusion captures cases of sudden, brutal attacks on civilian populations such as the Wagalla massacre, in which Kenyan soldiers extrajudicially executed approximately five thousand Somali men in 1984, or the Andijan massacre described at the beginning of chapter 3. It also captures murderous ethnic targeting during communitarian violence, for example, India's 1984 pogroms against Sikhs, as well as violence against civilians committed during high-intensity intrastate conflicts, like the forty thousand or more civilians estimated to have been killed by indiscriminate shelling during the final months of Sri Lanka's civil war.

It would not, however, catch instances of long-running, but low-intensity, violence of the state against its citizens like the seven thousand disappeared by the Argentine junta between 1976 and 1983 or the estimated ten thousand people killed by the Gaddafi regime over the course of its forty-two years in power. To ensure that this type of violence is not left out of my analysis, I also include cases in which a threshold of five thousand intentional civilian deaths or rapes was reached over any time period.

Imposing these thresholds makes it possible to identify a discrete set of events that led to mass atrocities. However, like any threshold-applying approach, it draws arbitrary distinctions between cases of like kind. For instance, the violence of the Pinochet regime in Chile (an estimated 3,197 deaths, most in the month immediately following the 1973 coup) is included, while that of the Marcos regime in the Philippines (3,257 deaths between 1972 and 1986) is not.

Finally, I include only mass atrocities that occurred (or were ongoing) in 1970 or later. This is because it was not until the human rights conventions (the International Covenant on Civil and Political Rights and the International Covenant on Economic, Social, and Cultural Rights) came into force in the 1970s that holding individual perpetrators criminally liable for violations of international human rights became a real option. Although the requirement of accountability for international crimes has existed on paper since the 1940s, it only became practically enforceable in the 1970s. (Indeed, as chapter 2 makes clear, international actors did not make serious efforts to enforce it until the 1990s.) I therefore expect that a start date of 1970 should generously capture the entire universe of cases of interest.

To identify events for inclusion, I looked at the existing lists of mass killing events in the academic and policy literature mentioned above, the Uppsala Conflict Data Program (UCDP) data sets of civil wars and one-sided violence, and human rights reporting by Human Rights Watch and Amnesty International. I also consulted several secondary sources, including Matthew White's *Atrocities: The 100 Deadliest Episodes in Human History*, Rudolph J. Rummel's *Statistics of Democide: Genocide and Mass Murder Since 1900*, and René Lemarchand's *Forgotten Genocides: Oblivion, Denial, and Memory*. I performed a final check by googling every country's name in combination with "atrocity," "genocide," "war crimes," and "crimes against humanity," then researching any identified events to establish whether they met the criteria for inclusion.

This approach yielded ninety events occurring between 1970 and 2014 that were associated with the commission of mass atrocities.[12] The events on the list took place on the territory of fifty-seven countries.[13] Over the last half-century, mass atrocities have occurred in all regions of the world but have been most common in sub-Saharan Africa. Their scale varies widely, from the approximately one thousand dead during interethnic attacks in Nigeria, Burma, and India to the three million killed by the Khmer Rouge.

The majority of the events on the list (fifty-five of ninety) are civil wars. One-sided violence of the state against its (perceived) political opponents is also very common, comprising one-quarter of the events on the list (twenty-two). However, this type of violence trends downward over time, alongside widespread democratization during the time period covered.

A large majority (eighty-one) of the events on the list involved the perpetration of atrocities by state actors. In almost all cases, these were attacks by state forces against their own citizens, on their own territory. (There are a small handful of instances in which this was not true, e.g., Rwanda's 1996 assault on the refugee camps in Zaire and Iraq's use of prohibited weapons against Iranian civilians in the early 1980s.) But non–state actor perpetrators are also common (forty-three events).[14] Importantly for considering the question of the domestic politics of accountability for mass atrocities, one-quarter of the included events involved attacks against members of a recognized religious or ethnic minority on the basis of their identity.

Beyond the difficulty discussed above of figuring out what we're actually talking about when we talk about "mass atrocities," there's an additional challenge to definitively identifying patterns in whether, and which, victims receive justice. It can be surprisingly hard to tell what transitional justice measures governments have put in place. War crimes convictions of high-profile military commanders are easy to spot when they happen. But it can be harder to tell what's going on when a postatrocity government appoints three people to investigate reports of serious human rights violations. Is this a truth commission? A whitewash? Something else?

In considering the question of whether postatrocity governments provided accountability, I looked for any executive or legislative action to pursue prosecutions domestically, to seek the assistance of international actors in the creation of a hybrid tribunal, to refer the matter to an international court, or to set up a truth commission.

This approach necessarily excludes the trials related to some of the atrocities on the list that took place in the domestic justice systems of third-party states (for instance, Spanish prosecutions of former Guatemalan regime leaders for genocide against indigenous peoples) pursuant to universal jurisdiction laws. These trials, generally undertaken at the initiative of individual investigative judges in foreign countries, are outside this project's scope. It also excludes one-off trials initiated by victims' groups and/or conducted by crusading judges or prosecutors, such as the (twice suspended) trial of former Guatemalan dictator Rios Montt. Although these processes can be an important step on the path to accountability, they are also outside the project's scope because they are not initiated by political leaders vulnerable to electoral and international pressures.

As explained in chapter 2, the obligation to provide justice for mass atrocities is understood to require that trials target command-level (not just low-ranking) individuals, do not prosecute in absentia, and fulfill (contemporaneous) international fair trial standards.[15] I therefore do not count as domestic trials any process that fails any of these tests. I employ a similarly strict approach to identifying truth commissions because distinguishing between commissions with the capacity to uncover the truth and commissions intended to serve as window dressing is critical for tracing the political imperatives surrounding the creation of these institutions. Contrast, for example, South Africa's much-lauded 1996 Truth and Reconciliation Commission with Algeria's 2003 exercise, which met with immediate criticism from human rights groups for its narrow mandate and limited investigative powers, or Zimbabwe's 1983 investigation into the Matabeleland massacres, which never even released a report.

Fortunately, practitioner discussions of "best practices" for truth commissions identify some of the structural components necessary for these mechanisms to function effectively. One is the ability to issue subpoenas, which is an indication of an institution's ability to uncover the truth, even when powerful political actors may be inclined to suppress it. For my purposes, I consider the ability to compel testimony (through a subpoena or other measure such as the imposition of fines) sufficient "teeth" for a body to qualify as a truth commission when accompanied by witness protection measures, public hearings, and independence (including financial) from the executive.

In twenty-seven of the ninety events on the list, prosecutorial mechanisms abiding by fair trial standards tried high-level perpetrators for mass atrocities. These trials took place in domestic court systems, at international criminal courts, and at hybrid tribunals. In seven of the cases, truth commissions with the power to compel testimony attempted to establish a record of abuses.

Prosecuting mass atrocities has become slightly more common over time. Sorting on the decade in which an atrocity ended (on the theory that accountability becomes easier to provide after violence has ended, and that this is therefore the most generous test) reveals an increase from 9 to 39 percent of atrocities being prosecuted from the 1980s to the 1990s. Some atrocities eventually receive justice decades after the fact. Cambodia and Bangladesh, for instance, are both currently holding trials for 1970s-era crimes. These cases suggest that some of the cases of inaction are simply cases of no action *yet*.

We might expect that the higher the body count, the louder the outcry, and the more likely that accountability would be provided. But the record of impunity for horrific violence against civilians in Syria and Myanmar in the last decade suggests that atrocities with massive death tolls may be just as likely as smaller ones to go unpunished, even in recent years. Indeed, the data suggest no association between the scale of the violence and the likelihood that a postatrocity government will seek accountability.

There is, however, some variation over region. In Latin America, trials or truth commissions have been instituted with regard to eight of the nine mass atrocities that occurred in the region between 1970 and 2014. But a substantial majority of atrocities in Europe (including Central Asia), East and South Asia, and the Middle East and North Africa have gone completely unaddressed. In sub-Saharan Africa, the record is more mixed, reflecting the International Criminal Court's activities there over the last decade.

The patterns described here demonstrate that accountability outcomes after mass atrocities vary widely and are deeply contingent. Sometimes, prosecutions of those most responsible for serious crimes follow quickly on the commission of mass atrocities. But often, victims wait decades to see their abusers in the dock. And while some of the most severe, shocking to the conscience crimes of the modern era have gone unpunished, in other times and places postatrocity governments have swiftly sought justice for comparatively smaller abuses.

Although there are varied and complicated motivations determining the potential political benefit or detriment posed by any given accountability choice, the insights about postatrocity governments' decision calculus distilled in the previous chapter can be simplified as follows: preferences about whether and how to pursue accountability reflect domestic demand for, and resistance to, justice. These two factors, which are functions of characteristics of the victims and characteristics of the perpetrators, drive the political viability of efforts to seek accountability.

Accountability is least likely when demand is low (victims are marginalized, disorganized, or otherwise unsupported by mainstream civil society) and resistance is high (perpetrators have tight links to government or can act as spoilers to peace). It is most likely when demand is high and resistance low. These factors can be linked, as is the case, for example, in Sri Lanka, where demand for justice is low and accused perpetrators remain in power *because* they are members of the majority ethnic group and the alleged atrocities were committed against a minority perceived as a threat.

Demand for justice is driven, at least in part, by the identity of an atrocity's victims. When the victims are marginalized (for instance, a small ethnic minority living in a remote region like the Somali Kenyan victims of the Wagalla massacre), there is less likely to be a strong movement calling for accountability. By contrast, when victims represent a broad cross section of society (for instance, perceived political opponents of the Chilean junta), mass mobilization for justice is more likely.

The postatrocity government's sensitivity to domestic political pressure is also critical. In a democracy, when public opinion is cohesive and firmly against accountability, it is potential political suicide for a regime to force war crimes trials. Conversely, when there are widespread and strong demands for justice, it is politically risky to refuse to provide it. If public opinion is divided, the relevant opinion holders are those who are crucial to the regime's continued tenure: for example, coethnics, labor, city dwellers. In an autocracy, the relevant group might be even smaller: the army, or the president's clique.

When there is strong demand for justice among a postatrocity government's constituency, the political benefit should offset, to some extent, the cost to provide it. But if the relevant public is neutral or apathetic about accountability, the regime will be unlikely to be willing to pay for it. And when politically important groups oppose accountability, pursuing it adds political costs to the resource costs, making it an even less attractive option.

Resistance to accountability is likely to be lowest when perpetrators are non–state actors and highest when they are state actors who remain in power. It is a truism that the perpetrators of mass atrocities don't prosecute themselves. And when they remain in power, resistance to international involvement in accountability exercises will also be especially strong. Even when perpetrators are not formally in office, their political power may make accountability infeasible because they hold high-ranking positions in the military or command the loyalty of voters.

As the previous chapter indicated, cooperation with international actors to pursue accountability is subject to the same political constraints as domestic exercises. The presence of perpetrators in power is therefore also likely to be a strong barrier to prosecution by international courts. Criminal adjudication, as a component of policing the monopoly of violence, is a fundamental prerogative of the sovereign state. When international criminal courts exercise jurisdiction over non–state actors, they borrow this prerogative. And when they exercise jurisdiction over government conduct, they essentially commit a compound sovereignty incursion, first by usurping adjudicatory power, and second by judging sovereign actions.

In the absence of strong resistance, postatrocity governments may be willing to cooperate with internationalized justice mechanisms at lower levels of demand for accountability because of the comparatively lower resource requirement. But even when international actors share the burden, an accountability process can cost a postatrocity government tens of millions of dollars. Cambodia's contribution to the hybrid Khmer Rouge Tribunal, for instance, has totaled USD 41.1 million as of June 2021.[16] Because of the high cost, postatrocity governments are unlikely to pursue justice, even at the international level, unless they expect significant political benefits.

Taking these dynamics into account, we should expect that postatrocity governments will not be interested in providing accountability when resistance is very high or demand is very low. As demand increases in the absence of resistance, they will be willing to refer atrocities to international courts, or, when demand is very high, conduct domestic prosecutions. When demand is high but resistance is moderate, postatrocity governments will prefer to create truth commissions.

To check the usefulness of this framework for explaining accountability outcomes, I used my list of atrocities to make a data set of postatrocity country-years. This means that there is an entry in the data set for any given country in which a mass atrocity occurred for the year in which it happened and each year thereafter. So, for example, Burma has an entry for 2012 when violence in Rakhine State led to the deaths of thousands of Rohingya, and another for 2013, and another for 2014 (when the data set ends). If the data set continued to the present day, there would be additional entries for 2015, 2016, 2017, and so on. Additionally, Burma would also have a separate entry in 2017 for the Rohingya genocide, and for each subsequent year. Adding up all the postatrocity country-years for the ninety atrocities on the list totals to 2,469 entries in the data set.

The reason I did this was so that I could then identify the years in which postatrocity governments chose to undertake an accountability process. For each entry, I noted whether the postatrocity government commenced a domestic trial process, initiated cooperation with an international or hybrid court, or created a truth commission. Next, I looked for indicators of demand for and resistance to justice.

Because this is essentially a gut check on the association of demand and resistance with accountability outcomes, I use fairly rough proxies. To establish the existence of demand, I checked for the presence or absence of a domestic movement calling for justice for each atrocity in each year.[17] I did this by examining scholarly works, media coverage, and human rights reporting on each atrocity for references to formal or informal civil society organizations dedicated to pursuing justice. Where this approach did not yield any evidence of domestic mobilization, I performed an additional check using Google to search combinations of (1) the country name, (2) "civil society," "NGO," or "movement," and (3) "accountability," "post-conflict justice," or "transitional justice." For every organization I identified, I went to the website to confirm that the mandate was indeed linked to demanding justice for the relevant mass atrocity and to establish the year in which these activities began. Where websites were not available, I searched for interviews with involved domestic activists to get this information. For any given atrocity, a domestic movement is identified in the data as having been present for the earliest identified year of mobilization and every year thereafter unless there was evidence that it had announced success or become defunct.[18]

Domestic movements mobilized to demand justice for thirty-nine of the ninety atrocities in the data set and were active in a total of 662 postatrocity years. They become more common over time; domestic movements formed in response to eight of the fifteen atrocities beginning after 2000. Unsurprisingly, they are less likely to organize under conditions of autocracy. Movements were active in only 61 of 841 years under autocracy, compared with 357 of 755 years under democracy.[19]

To identify the presence or absence of resistance to justice, I check whether anyone responsible for abuses during the atrocity in question is in high office in that year.[20] My logic here is that resistance is likely to increase the closer the ties perpetrators have to the ruling government. As a rough cut on this, I look at who is occupying the executive. For postatrocity country-years in which the atrocity-committing regime remained in power, I assume that resistance to justice is high. Where power has changed hands since the commission of the atrocity, I refer to reporting (by media and human rights organizations) to ascertain whether current leaders were implicated and double-check by using Google to search their names in combination with "war crimes," "crimes against humanity," and "atrocities."

There are three caveats to this approach: First, in cases where power clearly resides elsewhere than the chief executive (as confirmed by human rights reports on the country in question) and has been occupied continuously by perpetrators, I consider resistance to justice to be high even if the chief executive has changed hands. So, for instance, in Algeria, where the intelligence director remained in office for twenty-five years and referred to himself as the "God of Algeria," I treat that as the perpetrator continuously occupying the executive.[21] Second, I focus exclusively on high-ranking perpetrators (those most responsible for the most serious violations) and therefore do not measure the presence of lower-ranking perpetrators in high office.[22] Finally, this approach does not catch cases like present-day Cambodia, where those in high office are not personally believed to have ordered mass atrocities but have protected members of their regime who are.

Perpetrators were in power in 1,173 years in the data set. There are only six atrocities in the data set in which the perpetrators were never in power (i.e., violations were committed solely by nonstate actors). As of 2014, when the data set ends, the perpetrators of twenty-five atrocities remained in power.

Unsurprisingly, the data show that justice movements are much rarer when a regime that committed atrocities remains in power.[23] Nevertheless, there are cases in which justice movements mobilize while perpetrators remain in power. For example: the Madres de la Plaza de Mayo organized while Argentina was still under junta rule to demand justice for their disappeared children.

In line with the prediction that trials and/or truth commissions will only be pursued when domestic demand is high and resistance is low, there are zero cases in the data set in which prosecutions or a truth commission were initiated while a perpetrator held high office.[24] Also bearing out expectations, the presence of a domestic movement demanding justice significantly increases the odds that postatrocity governments will initiate prosecutions (in either a domestic or international court) or a truth commission. When perpetrators were not in power, the existence of a domestic justice movement made it more than twice as likely that a postatrocity government would pursue accountability in any given year.[25]

This suggests that domestic demand and resistance do play a large role in explaining accountability decisions. The discussion of capacity constraints in chapter 3 suggests an alternative, but potentially complementary, explanation for postatrocity governments' accountability behavior: that states with higher judicial capacity will be more likely to provide accountability.[26] However, better scores on judicial independence and capacity indexes do not appear to be associated with decisions to provide accountability for mass atrocities.[27] Despite suggestions that prosecution of the authors of serious violations of human rights is becoming more common over time as the global norm of providing accountability entrenches, among the events in my data set postatrocity governments appear *no more likely* to provide accountability as time goes by.[28]

There is a positive association here between International Criminal Court membership and the creation of robust accountability institutions.[29] At first glance, this result suggests tentative support for the idea that the ICC can contribute to the provision of justice not just through its own cases but by incentivizing states to prosecute domestically in order to avoid the court's attention. (This idea is known as "positive complementarity."[30]) However, a closer look calls this interpretation into question. There are thirteen mass atrocities in the data set for which domestic prosecutions were pursued. All but three ended *before* 2002, when the ICC's jurisdiction took effect. This means that the postatrocity governments in these cases can't have undertaken these trials to preempt international action. Rather, the results suggest the opposite causal relationship: States that provide accountability domestically are more likely to sign on to the ICC because they have less to lose by committing themselves.

While the results presented above suggest that a focus on the dynamics of domestic demand and resistance gives us a pretty good sense of whether postatrocity governments will pursue justice, they also obscure something significant: namely, that postatrocity governments are not facing a binary choice between doing nothing after mass atrocities and initiating prosecutions or truth commissions. In fact, the approach to identifying trials and truth commissions described above ruled out about as many institutions as it ruled in. While total impunity is the most common response to mass atrocities (prevailing with regard to forty-eight of the ninety mass events on the list), some form of mechanism has been created in response to the other forty-two atrocities on the list. (Table 4.1. lists the sixty-three total mechanisms.) But in only twenty-two cases did these mechanisms meet the definition of a trial or a truth commission.

After twenty of the ninety atrocities on the list, governments created weak mechanisms (sometimes more than one) that did not qualify as legitimate prosecutions or truth commissions. Most often, these were investigative commissions lacking independent authority, but occasionally there were rushed trials in absentia or kangaroo courts set up expressly to try low-ranking scapegoats. Even as robust criminal prosecutions and truth-seeking exercises become more prevalent over time, so do these other mechanisms.

In fact, by the 2000s, the majority of domestic institutions created in response to mass atrocities (seventeen of thirty-two) do not meet international standards for trials or truth commissions. Updating the country-year data set to include information about *any* institution created after a mass atrocity with an ostensible mandate related to uncovering what happened reveals that governments implemented mechanisms of this sort in 35 of the 2,469 country-years. Notably,

TABLE 4.1 Accountability institutions employed in response to mass atrocities

INSTITUTION TYPE	CASES
Domestic prosecution	Colombian civil war; Pakistan v. Bengals; Dirty War (Argentina); Red Terror (Ethiopia); LRA (Uganda); al-Anfal (Iraq); Croatian independence; attacks on Marsh Arabs (Iraq); Bosnian Serbs; Libyan Civil War
International prosecution	LRA (Uganda); Croatian independence; Bosnian Serbs; Rwandan Civil War and genocide; Ituri conflict (DRC); Darfur conflict (Sudan); Kivu conflict (DRC); Kenyan election crisis; Second Ivorian Civil War; Libyan Civil War; Northern Mali conflict; Central African Republic
Hybrid prosecution	Khmer Rouge (Cambodia); Habré regime (Chad); Sierra Leone Civil War; Kosovo; East Timor referendum violence
Truth commission	Military dictatorships (South Korea); Idi Amin regime (Uganda); Habré regime (Chad); Peruvian Civil War; First Liberian Civil War; Cédras regime (Haiti); Sierra Leone Civil War; Second Liberian Civil War
Other domestic institution	Guatemalan Civil War; Hutu rebellion and genocide (Burundi); Pinochet regime (Chile); Indonesian occupation of East Timor; Lebanese Civil War; Dirty War (Argentina); Sandinista rebellion (Nicaragua); Matabeleland (Zimbabwe); Sri Lankan Civil War; Sri Lanka vs. JVP II; mass killing of Hutus (Burundi); Algerian Civil War; Bosnian Serbs; Second Burundi Civil War; Rwandan Civil War and genocide; East Timor referendum violence; Darfur conflict (Sudan); Kivu conflict (DRC); Kenyan election crisis; Second Ivorian Civil War

of the nineteen countries that have put in place at least one of these weak institutions, thirteen have done so since 2000. This pattern suggests that even as the accountability norm was entrenching, noncompliant institutions were becoming more common than compliant ones.

These institutions look something like accountability mechanisms but lack the ability to truly pursue justice for mass atrocities. They therefore potentially qualify as the sort of attempts to approximate compliant behavior closely enough to avoid the penalty envisioned by the theory of quasi-compliance proposed in chapter 1. Of course, without detailed process tracing, it would be difficult to establish whether any given weak institution is the result of a quasi-compliant impulse or simply a failure of capacity. However, we can look for patterns that might suggest there's something worth exploring qualitatively.

If the theory of quasi-compliance is a useful framework for understanding these weak accountability institutions, two things should be visible in the quantitative data: (1) the determinants of robust accountability exercises and of these underpowered institutions should be very different; and (2) postatrocity governments that create weak institutions should be more vulnerable to international interference than those that don't. In other words, we would expect that while postatrocity governments will only pursue prosecutions or truth commissions in the presence of significant domestic demand (and the absence of resistance), they should create quasi-compliant institutions when they are worried about international enforcement.

"Vulnerability to enforcement" is a pretty abstract concept. We might think of it in terms of low status in the international system or military weakness, but because enforcement of human rights norms more frequently takes the form of sanctions and aid cutoffs, I chose to proxy it with dependence on development aid from Western sources.[31]

Postatrocity governments that created weak institutions were, on average, receiving Western aid in amounts equal to 6.97 percent of the country's gross domestic product (GDP).[32] This is higher than the average across the data set (5.56 percent), and several times higher than the average for postatrocity governments launching domestic prosecutions (1.60 percent).[33] This effect remains strong even if we measure aid dependency differently.[34] Notably, there is no correlation between the *amount* of aid received from Western sources and the creation of these institutions.[35] In other words, it's not an effect of receiving large amounts of aid (which may simply indicate that the recipient state is larger, or alternately in good standing with the international community); it's about being *dependent* on aid.

Aid dependency is a stronger predictor of the creation of these institutions than any of the factors found to predict the creation of robust accountability institutions.[36] These results suggest that it is indeed plausible that what we're seeing is quasi-compliant accountability behavior driven by postatrocity governments' vulnerability to international enforcement.[37] Two other patterns in the data also lend support to the characterization of these institutions as quasi-compliant efforts: these institutions are more common when perpetrators remain in power and it's correlated with higher levels of democracy.[38] This bears out the theoretical intuition that postatrocity governments would create quasi-compliant institutions in response to international pressure when domestic resistance is high. Also, higher judicial capacity appears to be positively correlated with quasi-compliance. This makes sense; the theory assumes that creating these institutions takes effort and money.[39]

The rest of this book digs into the specifics of how governments facing low domestic demand for accountability or high resistance from perpetrator-aligned constituencies respond to international pressure for justice for mass atrocities. Building on the theory of quasi-compliance developed in chapter 1, the book explores the outcomes of attempts to do "just enough" to escape penalties for noncompliance with the global accountability norm.

DOING JUST ENOUGH?

Nearly three-quarters of a million Rohingya crossed the border into Bangladesh in the final months of 2017, driven out of their homes in Rakhine State by brutal violence at the hands of Burma's military. The rate of population displacement was remarkable, rivaled in recent memory only by the mass exoduses from Rwanda and Kosovo in the 1990s.

The Rohingya refugees carried with them stories of atrocities so horrifying that human rights workers and UN officials consistently described them as among the worst they'd ever seen.[1] Traumatized survivors told of the mass rape of women and girls, the slaughter of infants, and the deliberate starvation of trapped populations. Satellite imagery attested to the deliberate burning, then bulldozing, of Rohingya villages. From the earliest days of the crisis, human rights reporting documented "a clear and systematic pattern" to the abuses.[2]

The evidence of mass atrocities was undisputable. As the crisis escalated, numerous international actors described the Burmese military's actions as a "textbook example of ethnic cleansing."[3] Government officials from numerous countries, including France, Malaysia, Pakistan, and Turkey, all characterized the attack on the Rohingya as genocide. Human rights groups and Western governments called on Burma to end the crackdown, allow the Rohingya to return home safely, and prosecute those responsible for violations of international law.

Amidst mounting international outrage, the Burmese government consistently denied all allegations of abuses. The military insisted that its activities in Rakhine State were a legitimate counterinsurgency operation targeting Rohingya militants. Openly invoking the hate speech propagated by militant Buddhist monks, officials characterized the Rohingya as "dirty," lying, illegal immigrants. The government, including its Nobel Peace Prize laureate civilian leader Aung San Suu Kyi, made a concerted push to brand the Rohingya as Islamic militants and dismiss all claims of abuses as fabrications. It also barred Yanghee Lee, the UN special rapporteur on human rights in Burma, from entering the country to assess the situation, a decision Lee concluded "can only be viewed as a strong indication that there must be something terribly awful happening in Rakhine."[4]

Yet multiple times in late 2017 and early 2018, the Burmese government announced ostensible investigations into allegations of atrocities. These moves were at odds with the patterns presented in the previous chapter, which showed that when domestic demand for accountability is low and resistance from perpetrators high, postatrocity governments will strongly prefer impunity. But as the case of Burma shows, it's not only domestic audiences that postatrocity governments have to take into account. International audiences often make up a separate constituency demanding accountability, as they have done consistently with regard to mass atrocities committed against the Burmese Rohingya. Critically, international audiences have the capacity to punish states who refuse to provide it, or even to intervene to provide it themselves.

Governments like Burma's that have strong domestic political incentives not to provide accountability for mass atrocities are unsurprisingly deeply averse to the prospect of international action to ensure justice. For some states in the system, this is not a serious concern. None of the five permanent members of the Security Council needs to worry about their officials being tried by an international court over their objections. For others, the risk of enforcement is very real. Even those states like Burma that are protected by a veto member, that can rest assured that their patron will block a move for prosecutions, may still find themselves the subject of an intrusive international inquiry.

But as in all contexts in which enforcement is uncertain, postatrocity governments do not have perfect information about whether international audiences will bother to enforce the norm. International audiences for accountability behavior include a range of actors. A number of international nongovernmental organizations engage in advocacy on postatrocity justice. The most prominent among these are Human Rights Watch, Amnesty International, International Crisis Group, and International Center for Transitional Justice. Additionally, representatives of international governmental organizations such as the UN secretary general, the chief prosecutor of the ICC, and the UN high commissioner for human rights as well as numerous special rapporteurs for human rights within the UN system all monitor and issue public statements on states' accountability behavior.

These actors are a critical piece of the story. However, their behavior doesn't vary much across cases. Impunity for atrocities will trigger condemnation from almost all international human rights NGOs, international justice bureaucrats, and high-profile UN officials almost all of the time.[5] What does vary, however, is what happens next. When human rights groups publicize a postatrocity government's failure to bring the perpetrators of international crimes to justice, they hope to convince other governments to take up the issue, either through bilateral pressure for domestic accountability or by pushing for an international investigation that could ultimately lead to international trials or trigger domestic action.

Postatrocity governments trying to avoid enforcement of the accountability norm can reasonably conclude that robust international action is most likely in instances where impunity persists for particularly egregious violations, about which there is a high level of global public awareness, but they cannot predict with complete accuracy which cases those will be. Their uncertainty stems from the fact that (1) the domestic politics of other states informs their willingness to act, and (2) the set of interested states is not constant across cases.[6]

A foreign government might care about the absence of accountability in another state for a number of reasons. It might have a significant diaspora population of the victim group agitating for justice, as the Tamil populations in Canada, the United Kingdom, and the United States have done, leading these governments to spearhead a push for an international investigation into Sri Lankan atrocities. It might have another domestic constituency pushing for accountability, such as the Save Darfur movement, which lobbied for the United States to support a Security Council referral of the Sudanese government's crimes to the ICC. It might take a particular interest because it is the former colonial power of the postatrocity state, as Belgium has demonstrated through commencing universal jurisdiction prosecutions regarding events in Rwanda and the DRC. It might also be a major donor to the postatrocity state who is unwilling to be seen to be funding a violator of international law, an issue that arose for the United States with regard to South Sudan.

Policing postatrocity governments' compliance with the obligations to provide justice for mass atrocities can be enormously costly. A state that pushes for internationalized trials of another state's past atrocities might end up on the hook for tens of millions of dollars. For example: Japan has contributed more than $83 million to the Extraordinary Chambers in the Courts of Cambodia. Foreign governments will therefore generally prefer to pressure postatrocity governments to provide accountability domestically whenever possible.

These dynamics, in which domestic politics and international pressure push in opposite directions and international audiences are reluctant to aggressively enforce the accountability norm, set up exactly the incentives for quasi-compliance outlined in the first chapter. With the threat of enforcement of the accountability norm uncertain and the domestic political stakes so high, it's no surprise that postatrocity governments often gamble that they can preempt international action by creating institutions that look something like justice. As the theory advanced in chapter 1 suggests, the viability of a quasi-compliant accountability strategy depends in part on the fact that it not only reduces the egregiousness of the violation of the norm; it also communicates that the postatrocity government is sensitive to international pressure.[7] It suggests that the possibility of domestic accountability, which international audiences almost always prefer to externally provided justice, remains open given the application of sufficient leverage. They therefore respond by pushing for the quasi-compliant government to do better and applying pressure in the form of public statements, reductions in foreign aid, or suspension of trade benefits.

While recalcitrant states resent international pressure to provide accountability domestically, their priority is to avoid usurpation of sovereign functions through international action and to prevent potential knock-on effects such as punishment at the polls by their domestic audience. Knowing that enforcement is costly for international audiences and will only be pursued in a limited number of cases, they have a strong incentive to remove themselves from the set of most likely targets for enforcement, even if that move exposes them to more pressure to pursue justice domestically.

The more vulnerable a postatrocity government is, the more effort it is likely to expend in the direction of quasi-compliance, even when enforcement looks relatively unlikely. Note, however, that we are likely to observe quasi-compliant accountability behavior in its less robust forms even from postatrocity states that are relatively immune to international enforcement. It can help them avoid embarrassing (if relatively toothless) censure and may therefore be worth expending some effort and resources. Even the temporary diffusion of pressure can be very valuable; for instance, if a postatrocity government is able to delay the empanelment of an international inquiry, or even a statement of condemnation, past a domestic election. But if they're lucky, international audiences will accept their quasi-compliant effort as "good enough" and leave them alone.

This possibility stems from the fact that international audiences will not always be able to differentiate quasi-compliance from failed attempts at full compliance. If capacity is obviously sufficient or insufficient, even in the absence of full information about the domestic political attitudes influencing the postatrocity government's preferences about accountability, international audiences will know what they're seeing. But in borderline capacity contexts, they may not be sure if the state is capable of implementing satisfactory trials. They'll have to rely on other signals, like the postatrocity government's public statements about accountability and other human rights behavior, to differentiate quasi-compliance from inability to comply.

If a postatrocity government is able to pass off quasi-compliance as a good faith accountability effort, it can avoid signaling sensitivity to pressure. The possibility of preempting international pressure in addition to enforcement makes quasi-compliance an especially attractive strategy. Consider the case of the Democratic Republic of the Congo (DRC), where faltering progress toward accountability for sexual violence has been attributed by international audiences to the country's limited capacity rather than lack of political will, despite evidence that both factors were at play.[8]

The civilian population of the eastern DRC has borne the brunt of more than a quarter-century of instability and violence stemming from the aftermath of the Rwandan genocide. Abuses of human rights, ranging from the use of child soldiers to forced labor to torture, are endemic. But the Kivus are associated most prominently in the eyes of the global public with one type of violation: rape. Although precise numbers are unavailable, it's clear that sexual violence has been committed in the DRC on a scale rarely seen elsewhere. The perpetrators have been members of rebel groups, the state military (FARDC), ex-combatants, and civilians, motivated by logics of ethnic cleansing, terrorism, and simple opportunism. The crime has been so widespread that activists coined the term re-raped to refer to the large numbers of survivors who have been assaulted on more than one occasion. The injury of sexual violence is compounded by the limited availability of medical and psychosocial services, the stigmatization of victims who may be rejected by their families and communities, and the threat of violence to those who report the crime.

Despite headlines trumpeting the failure of the international community to address sexual violence in the DRC, the issue has been the subject of sustained international attention for years. Countless aid dollars have been spent on interventions ranging from the essential (funding and training for fistula repair) to the laughable (a 2009 US initiative to supply rape victims with video cameras). And a very high-profile awareness-raising campaign mobilized widespread support for regulation of "conflict minerals," despite overstated claims about the relationship between mining and sexual violence in the DRC.[9]

While prevention has proved unattainable in the face of ongoing conflict, focus has shifted to providing accountability for sexual violence crimes. The context is extremely challenging. Judicial capacity (as well as general governance capacity) is limited. When I visited the Ministry of Justice in North Kivu in August 2014, the electricity was out and my interlocutors had neither pens nor business cards. Notably, this followed what almost all interviewees described to me as major improvements from the conditions in 2009, when judges didn't even have access to paper.[10]

On top of the resource issues, prosecution of international crimes is hampered by interference from political authorities, the risks of pursuing powerful figures, and the challenges of arresting anyone in a war zone. Even in the rare instances where cases proceed to sentencing, the prison system is so inadequate that some convicts have been housed in facilities without locks. Prison breaks are common, and many criminals never end up serving their time.

It is clear from the foregoing that the DRC is a case in which the government has had good reason to avoid pursuing justice. And while there has been demand for accountability from the victim community, they are extremely remote from the central government, nearly a thousand miles away from the capital. But international actors have consistently pushed for the perpetrators of sexual violence crimes to be prosecuted. The DRC's rape crisis has been a fixture in Western media since late 2007, when the American playwright V, who was known as Eve Ensler at the time, made a high-profile visit to Goma. Her impassioned account of her trip catalyzed international activism on "Congo's war on women."[11] Alongside grassroots organizing in the West, high-profile advocacy campaigns by Human Rights Watch and The Enough Project demanded justice for these crimes. US Secretary of State Hillary Clinton undertook an unprecedented official trip to Goma, where she met with survivors of sexual violence and called on the Congolese government to prosecute those responsible. The DRC's dependency on development and humanitarian aid, as well as other types of foreign assistance, is extreme, making it highly sensitive to external pressure.[12] Consequently, in 2009, with significant assistance from Western governments and NGOs, the government commenced a high-profile effort to address international demands through military trials of sexual violence crimes, applying international law.

Political scientist Milli Lake identifies three levels at which international actors have intervened to facilitate accountability for sexual violence crimes in eastern DRC. At the central state level, they have pushed for updated legislation and supported the establishment of a Comité Mixte de la Justice (CMJ) that includes international stakeholders and oversees justice sector reform. At the community level, they have worked with victims and witnesses to encourage and safeguard their participation in criminal proceedings. Most notably, they have also substituted directly for the state at the level of local judicial institutions through the establishment of mobile courts. As Lake explains:

> For war crimes and crimes against humanity cases, NGOs will be alerted to mass atrocities through their own networks: usually through personal contacts, through rapid response units, from partner NGOs

in remote areas, or from the United Nations Office for Humanitarian Affairs (UN-OCHA). When organizations involved in administering mobile courts (such as ABA ROLI) learn of such incidents, they will work with Congolese justice authorities, MONUSCO and other donors and organizations, to provide a rapid legal response.[13]

This rapid legal response involves the coordination of evidence gathering, witness preparation, trial logistics, and publicity, all done with heavy involvement from international actors. The only piece of the process over which the Congolese judicial system retains exclusive authority is decision and sentencing.

The involved organizations have been present in the DRC for many years. For instance, one of the organizations I met with in 2014, Avocats sans Frontières (ASF) has been working on justice issues in eastern DRC since 2002. The American Bar Association's Rule of Law Initiative, another major sponsor of the mobile courts program, has been providing legal aid in the region since 2008. The United Nations is also heavily involved, both through the support of the United Nations Development Programme (UNDP) to the mobile courts and through the monitoring and capacity-building work of the Joint Human Rights Office, a cooperative endeavor between the MONUSCO peacekeeping mission and the Office of the High Commissioner for Human Rights established in 2008.[14] These offices are heavily funded and staffed, providing jobs for hundreds of people (both locals and internationals).

Since 2009, with the assistance of these and other international actors, the Congolese military courts have convicted more than 250 individuals for international crimes.[15] The majority of those who have been brought to trial have been low-ranking soldiers in the national army. This is partly due to the fact that responsibility for sexual violence crimes may be harder to assign when perpetrated by non–state actor armed groups who don't wear uniforms and lack a clear chain of command. But it's also the result of reluctance on the part of prosecutors to charge non–state actors "for fear that it will escalate tensions and lead to more violence."[16]

Prosecutions of high-level military commanders have also been avoided due to the obvious political risk, as well as an additional procedural complication: Members of the FARDC may only be judged by their peers or superiors. Consequently, "some of the highest-ranking officers may benefit from de facto immunity from prosecution because of the lack of military magistrates of equal or superior ranks."[17]

The prosecutions of low-ranking army members that have been carried out have suffered from serious procedural shortcomings. The high-profile Minova case, which tried thirty-nine members of FARDC for mass rape, is illustrative of some of these issues. In November 2012, FARDC suffered a humiliating defeat at the hands of the M23 rebel group. Driven out of the provincial capital of Goma, they descended on the town of Minova. Over the course of two weeks, soldiers raped more than 130 women and girls, including children as young as six. When these crimes came to light, international actors exerted significant pressure to have the perpetrators brought to justice, in part because some of the troops implicated had been trained by the United States. An investigation began in December 2012.

When the Minova trial opened on November 20, 2013, it was heralded as a watershed moment in the fight against impunity for sexual violence. But the decision handed down on May 5, 2014, was deeply disappointing to victims and their advocates. Only two of the soldiers, and none of the high-ranking officers, were convicted of rape. Another twenty-two soldiers were convicted of lesser charges, such as pillage. It transpired that the judicial investigation had not bothered to match specific perpetrators to specific victims' testimony, nor had it bothered to establish the presence of specific military units in Minova on the dates in question.[18] Evidence later emerged that the Congolese government intentionally rigged the investigation to prevent any senior commanders from being implicated.[19]

The proceedings were also concerning from a fair trial rights perspective. The unit commanders on trial did not have lawyers appointed for them until approximately two weeks before the trial and were not provided with any assistance for attorneys' fees.[20] Once assigned, the defense attorneys were not given dossiers of the charges against their clients, but instead had the choice of paying thousands of dollars for a copy or camping out in the prosecutor's office to read them in the week before the trial opened.[21]

The Minova case is a particularly egregious example, but both the deficits in political will and the challenges of collecting adequate evidence, establishing command responsibility, and conducting a fair trial are endemic in eastern DRC, given constrained resources and ongoing insecurity. The DRC's efforts in the direction of accountability have generally fallen far short of international standards of credible prosecutions of "those most responsible for the most serious crimes." Instead, they were problematic exercises that violated fair trial rights and targeted only low-level actors. Additionally, against the scale on which sexual violence crimes have been committed, they represent a drop in the bucket. Lake finds that of 332 instances in which international crimes were reported to have been committed in the Kivus between 2005 and 2012, only thirty-four were even investigated by military prosecutors, let alone brought to trial.[22]

Politics continue to be the ultimate arbiter of whether or not cases are pursued. Compare, for example, two instances of mass rape committed by the same unit of former Mai-Mai militia in the same area of South Kivu Province in 2011.

In the first, a lieutenant colonel named Mutuare Daniel Kibibi along with eight others was convicted of crimes against humanity just six weeks after the incident in the town of Fizi. But the commanding officer, Colonel Nyiragire "Kifaru" Kulimushi, was not prosecuted. Just five months later, he defected from the military with 150 of his soldiers who then raped more than 120 women in the nearby village of Nakiele.[23] This later crime remains unpunished, while Colonel Kifaru continues to enjoy good relations with military command. By contrast, the less popular Kibibi "was perceived to have been handed over to military prosecutors by the Congolese army as a 'sacrificial lamb' intended to evidence the commitment of the armed forces to promoting human rights and gender justice."[24]

Despite its flaws, this limited and problematic program of sexual violence prosecutions in the DRC was welcomed internationally as encouraging progress. Representatives of international organizations with whom I spoke in North Kivu in 2014 agreed that serious inadequacies existed with the Minova and other trials, yet they expressed optimism about what they saw as progress toward accountability. International human rights NGOs echoed this opinion, noting the extensive work still to be done, but concluding "this progress is encouraging and deserves to be recognized."[25]

The DRC shows the best-case scenario for international reception of accountability behavior that does not satisfy the norm's requirements or the demands of those calling for justice. At the other end of the spectrum is Burma, where international actors have been harshly critical of the government's claims to be pursuing accountability domestically for alleged atrocities against the Rohingya.[26]

Routinely described as one of the world's most persecuted minorities, the Rohingya have experienced decades of repression and violence at the hands of successive Burmese governments, which have claimed they are not citizens, but illegal colonial-era immigrants from Bangladesh. Acting under the pretext of counterinsurgency, the Tatmadaw (as Burma's military forces are officially known) have committed large-scale, systematic violence against the community on several occasions, most notably in 1978 and 1991, when several hundred thousand Rohingya were forced to flee across the border into Bangladesh.

Making their situation even more precarious, in 1982 the Burmese Citizenship Law formally stripped the Rohingya of their citizenship, leaving them essentially rightsless. And in 1992, the government created an interagency border security force, the Nay-Sat Kut-kwey Ye (NaSaKa), tasked with enforcing a set of discriminatory policies restricting the Rohingya's freedom of movement.[27] For decades, the Rohingya who remained in Burma or returned there after fleeing to Bangladesh lived in grinding poverty, subjected to arbitrary arrest and torture by the NaSaKa and to ever-increasing legal restrictions on their fundamental human rights, including the right to education and the right to marry and procreate freely.

In 2012, violence broke out in Rakhine State. Although the conflict was widely described as "ethnic riots" between Rakhine Buddhists and Rohingya, human rights groups and journalists have documented state involvement in the violent targeting of Rohingya, suggesting that "pogrom" may be the more appropriate classification of the violence.[28] In the aftermath, the Rohingya were put on lockdown. They were confined to camps and urban ghettos and forbidden to migrate. As a consequence of the desperate conditions in which they found themselves, many attempted to escape. In early 2015 a crisis developed when approximately twenty-five thousand Rohingya boarded rickety boats and set out to sea. Many of the neighboring countries refused to accept these boats and pushed them back out into the sea, causing enormous human suffering.

It was clear to many observers that the Rohingya were enormously vulnerable and at risk of mass atrocities. In its 2015 report, *Early Warning Signs of Genocide in Burma*, the US Holocaust Memorial Museum warned that "many preconditions for genocide are already in place" and described the Rohingya's precarious situation within Burma as "an especially alarming problem that has received inadequate international attention."[29] A Yale Law School legal analysis conducted in late 2015 went further, arguing that there was "strong evidence that genocide [was] being committed against Rohingya."[30] A study by the International State Crime Initiative claimed that the Rohingya were facing "the final stages of a genocidal process."[31]

When Rohingya militants attacked several border posts in October 2016, security forces responded with unrestrained fury. Reports emerged almost immediately that the Tatmadaw was committing extrajudicial killings, torture, and sexual violence against the civilian population in the name of counterinsurgency. By early 2017, the UN had labeled these abuses likely crimes against humanity.[32]

Despite the intensity of the violence, the atrocities being inflicted on the Rohingya did not draw much attention. That changed in August 2017, when another round of militant attacks on security posts provided the pretext for a sharp escalation to an already incredibly violent status quo. As the Tatmadaw unleashed hell on the Rohingya population, thousands fled across the border to Bangladesh each day. Soldiers systematically burned the villages they left behind and laid land mines to prevent their return, giving credence to the allegation that Burma intended to finally purge itself of the entire Rohingya population. But as the death toll mounted and reports of ever-more horrific atrocities emerged, many international observers (myself included) began to ask whether Burma was expelling the Rohingya or exterminating them.[33] The intentional targeting of teachers and religious leaders and the particular brutality inflicted on women and very young children raised the possibility that Burma was engaged in a genocidal campaign to erase Rohingya culture and prevent the survival of future generations.

Condemnation of Burmese atrocities and calls for accountability came swiftly. In response, the Tatmadaw conducted an "internal investigation" into the violence in Rakhine. On November 13, 2017, it announced its findings, absolving itself of any culpability: "Security forces did not commit shooting at innocent villagers and sexual violence and rape cases against women. They did not arrest, beat and kill the villagers."[34] In fact, there were "no deaths of innocent people" in Rakhine State at all, the report concluded. The Tatmadaw blamed the violence instead on the Rohingya militant group Arakan Rohingya Salvation Army (ARSA), which had claimed responsibility for the August 25 attacks on the security forces. Notably, the report was issued the day before Aung San Suu Kyi was due to meet US Secretary of State Rex Tillerson.

Human rights organizations dismissed the report immediately, pointing to the copious testimonial and satellite evidence of crimes against humanity. Both Amnesty International and Human Rights Watch denounced it as a "whitewash," pointing to the fact that the investigation team conducted no interviews with Rohingya who had fled across the border and referred to those Rohingya still in Rakhine State that it did interview by the derogatory term "Bengalis."[35]

Human Rights Watch Asia Director Brad Adams concluded that "the Burmese military's absurd effort to absolve itself of mass atrocities" was one more piece of evidence that the Burmese authorities "can't and won't credibly investigate themselves."[36] It was far from the first exercise of its kind; in fact, the Tatmadaw had released a similar report just six months earlier, which "uncovered no wrongdoing except in two minor incidents" in the counterinsurgency campaign that began in October 2016.[37] Meanwhile, Aung San Suu Kyi, Burma's de facto civilian leader, embarked on a propaganda campaign to undermine claims of atrocities as "fake rape" and "fabrications."[38]

But the allegations were becoming harder and harder to refute. On December 12, 2017, Wa Lone and Kyaw Soe Oo, reporters for Reuters, were arrested in a restaurant in Yangon. They had been set up. A police officer had been ordered to arrange a meeting with them and pass them "secret documents from Battalion 8," one of the paramilitary police battalions deployed in Rakhine.[39] The two Reuters journalists were on the trail of evidence of a massacre. They had photographs from Inn Din village, where, on September 2, 2017, ten men and boys were extrajudicially executed by Burmese soldiers and buried in a shallow mass grave. They had also interviewed Rohingya and Rakhine Buddhist residents of Inn Din and, critically, members of the 8th Security Police Battalion who were present at the massacre. This was what prompted the sting, and one of the officers who had spoken with them was also arrested for violations of the Police Disciplinary Act. Five Inn Din villagers who had spoken with the reporters were detained as well.

Once detained, Wa Lone and Kyaw Soe Oo were pressured to drop the story.[40] But less than a week later, the Tatmadaw announced it was conducting its own investigation into the mass grave at Inn Din.[41] In early January it released a statement conceding that "10 Bengali terrorists" had been killed by villagers and security forces "because ethnic Buddhist villagers were threatened and provoked by the terrorists."[42] The statement promised that "the army will take charge of those who are responsible for the killings and who broke the rules of engagement."[43] Aung San Suu Kyi lauded the announcement as "the first step on the road of taking responsibility" and the US envoy welcomed it as "an important step."[44] But on the same day, the two Reuters reporters were formally charged with violating Burma's Official Secrets Act, an offense carrying a prison sentence of up to fourteen years.[45]

Reuters published the report Wa Lone and Kyaw Soe Oo had been working on in February 2018.[46] It was remarkable, searing reporting and they won a Pulitzer Prize for it.[47] The Reuters report also prompted widespread calls for their release and for an "independent, credible investigation" into atrocities committed in Rakhine State.[48] The Burmese authorities cast doubt on the validity of the report even as a spokesman issued a statement that "action according to the law" would be taken against those responsible for the killings.[49] He clarified strenuously that the move was "not because of Reuters news. The investigation was being conducted even before Reuters news."[50] At a UN Human Rights Council (UNHRC) session a few weeks later, Burma's representative talked up the investigation, saying it was "a clear sign of accountability" and "a positive step forward in fight against impunity."[51] He added that "we have stated time and again that the Government shall never condone impunity and action will be taken against any perpetrators in accordance with the law if there is concrete evidence."[52]

In April 2018, the military announced that seven military personnel had been sentenced to ten years in prison with hard labor for their role in the Inn Din massacre.[53] Although international press coverage had noted that the admission of involvement in the killings and the subsequent convictions were unprecedented moves by the Burmese military, nobody was particularly impressed.[54] Amnesty International, for instance, described the entire process as "shrouded in mystery," observing that "the military has never, for example, released the names of the seven officers and soldiers who had been prosecuted and sentenced, making it impossible to independently determine if they remain in prison or not."[55] Indeed, in November 2018, seven months into the supposed ten-year prison term, the soldiers were quietly released.[56]

This became a familiar pattern: initial vehement denials of abuses, followed by defensive claims to be pursuing accountability domestically, and ultimately very little to show for it. After a rough UN Human Rights Council session in

March 2018—during which the chair of the Independent International Fact-Finding Mission on Myanmar, empaneled a year earlier by the council, reported that "the response of the Myanmar Government and military to the events and allegations has been totally inadequate and is of grave concern"—Burma announced it would launch an "independent commission of enquiry" (ICOE) to investigate allegations of human rights violations in Rakhine.[57] The ICOE would become the lynchpin of Burma's efforts to defend itself on the world stage.

Human Rights Watch spoke for much of the international community when it blasted the announcement as the Burmese government's "latest sham."[58] Indeed, it was immediately apparent that the proposed commission was not designed to pursue justice for mass atrocities at all. In a briefing paper communicating complete skepticism of the ICOE, the International Commission of Jurists laid out the standards for effective commissions of inquiry: they should "have a mandate that does not suggest a premeditated outcome; possess necessary resources; be able to provide witnesses with effective protection from intimidation and violence; be composed of members with the expertise, competence and independence to investigate effectively; and be free to report fully and publicly."[59] The ICOE, in the International Commission of Jurists' view, met none of these standards. One of the domestic commissioners (the panel comprised four members, two domestic and two international), for instance, had publicly denied ethnic cleansing.[60] As the commission prepared to begin its work, the chairperson, Filipino diplomat Rosario Manalo, stated "there will be no blaming of anybody, no finger-pointing of anybody."[61]

Meanwhile, Burma continued its "clearance operations" in Rakhine State, constructed military bases and detention centers on the land the Rohingya fled, and steadfastly refused international pressure to grant them citizenship rights if they return. Observing the evidence of disingenuousness, Human Rights Watch warned "concerned governments should treat the commission with heavy skepticism and make sure Myanmar's government doesn't use this commission to shield itself from the critical scrutiny it deserves."[62] But that's precisely what Burma tried to do.

In August 2018, when the Independent International Fact-Finding Mission released a damning report accusing the Tatmadaw of war crimes, crimes against humanity, and genocide and the UN Human Rights Council empaneled the Independent Investigative Mechanism for Myanmar, Burmese officials rejected the findings and argued that they were acting domestically.[63] "If there is any cases [sic] against human rights, just give us strong evidence, record and date so that we can undertake the investigation into it" said the president's spokesman, adding "we have already formed the Independent Commission of Enquiry to carry out the implementation process."[64]

This would be a consistent refrain. A year later, when the Security Council convened an informal meeting on "Mass Atrocity Crimes in Myanmar: Where do we stand on accountability?" Burma objected strenuously, claiming it had demonstrated that it "is addressing the issue of accountability by setting up the Independent Commission of Enquiry."[65] And in September 2019, when the Independent International Fact-Finding Mission reported to the Human Rights Council that the Rohingya were still facing a threat of genocide and that top generals should be prosecuted by an international court, Burma "categorically rejected" the findings but simultaneously insisted "we are addressing it with our national accountability mechanisms."[66] Burma's permanent representative to the UNHRC pointed to the work of the ICOE and claimed that "the Myanmar Armed Forces has also established its own Court of Inquiry."[67] Mirroring the language of the ICC's complementary jurisdiction, he told the council that "Myanmar is willing and able to address accountability issue with its national accountability mechanisms."[68] Multiple times during the UNHRC session he repeated "Myanmar strongly rejects any mechanism or any attempt to take the matter to any international judicial or legal body unless it is patently clear that national remedies have been exhausted."[69]

But by this time, several international actors had taken matters into their own hands. The Independent Investigative Mechanism for Myanmar, with its mandate to "collect, consolidate, preserve and analyse evidence of the most serious international crimes and violations of international law committed in Myanmar since 2011" became operational in August 2019.[70] Just a few weeks before, the ICC's chief prosecutor, Fatou Bensouda, had requested the court's permission to open an investigation into crimes against humanity against the Rohingya committed in part on Bangladeshi territory. It was granted in November 2019, four days after Gambia sued Burma in the International Court of Justice for violations of its obligations under the Genocide Convention.

With all of these developments drawing headlines, the Tatmadaw announced a court martial of military personnel for "weakness in following the instructions in some of the incidents at Gutabyin village."[71] The "incidents" in question were first reported by the Associated Press in February 2018 (just a week before Reuters's Inn Din story ran), following the discovery of five mass graves in and around the village of Gu Dar Pyin.[72] Based on witness testimony and video evidence collected from Rohingya refugees in Cox's Bazar, the Associated Press alleged that the military had "systematically slaughter[ed]" as many as four hundred villagers on August 27, 2017. As usual, the Burmese government denied the report, saying that nineteen "terrorists" had been killed when they attacked the military, and that they been "carefully buried."[73] But a year and a half later, they'd changed their tune.

As the court martial conducted its hearings, Aung San Suu Kyi found herself representing Burma in oral proceedings before the International Court of Justice in December 2019. Gambia had requested provisional measures, essentially asking the court to issue a temporary restraining order preventing Burma from committing any further acts of genocide while it considered the case. She denied everything, refused to say the word "Rohingya," and repeated the party line that the court's intervention was inappropriate because Burma was acting domestically. As she put it, "a rush to externalize accountability may undermine professionals in domestic criminal justice agencies. What does the appearance of competition between domestic and international accountability actors do to the public's trust in the intentions of impatient international actors?"[74]

The ICOE scrambled to submit its report, six months ahead of schedule, before the International Court of Justice handed down its decision on the provisional measures request. The commissioners' conclusion that "possible war crimes" may have occurred but that systematic mass atrocities had not been committed was not well received. In a comprehensive takedown of the ICOE's work, the Global Justice Center cited problems with the commission's independence, impartiality, and methodology, including the notable fact that the commissioners only conducted interviews in Rakhine and that victims were interviewed with security officers present.[75] Human Rights Watch again pulled no punches: "Scapegoating a few low-ranking soldiers will fool no one. The commission's report is only meaningful if the military acknowledges responsibility and agrees to an independent international justice process."[76]

On January 23, 2020, the International Court of Justice granted Gambia's provisional measures request.[77] The judges ordered Burma to protect the Rohingya from genocide and prevent the destruction of evidence of crimes that had already occurred. They also ordered Burma to report regularly on its compliance with the order. With the first such report due in May 2020, the president's office issued directives mandating compliance with the Genocide Convention and the preservation of "documents, images, videos, audio [clips] and other media related to the events that occurred in northern Rakhine State referred to in the ICOE's final report."[78] Human Rights Watch's Param-Preet Singh described the impact of these measures as "nonexistent."[79]

A month later, the Tatmadaw announced it had convicted three members of the military in the Gu Dar Pyin court martial.[80] Again, the Tatmadaw did not release their names or offer any details on their crimes. Human rights organizations criticized the lack of transparency, noting that neither members of the victim community nor international or domestic civil society observers had been permitted to be present at the hearings.[81]

At nearly every turn, Burma's claims to be pursuing accountability were met with scorn from members of the international community pushing for justice for mass atrocities. The words of Thai diplomat Kobsak Chutikul perfectly encapsulate the widespread skepticism: "This just goes on and on. Next year it will be another commission, another board. It is all for show—there is nothing real. It is a hoax."[82]

This response forms a sharp contrast with the international reception for flawed accountability measures in the DRC described above. There are of course numerous relevant differences between the DRC and Burma, including the fact that the latter case arguably involves genocidal conduct by a state actor. But from the perspective of the accountability norm, they are both instances in which horrific mass atrocities have been committed and the territorial governments have put in place flawed accountability measures that do not satisfy the norm's requirements. Yet in one case international actors have welcomed limited progress and in the other they have condemned it.

This difference may stem in part from Burma's reliance on the ICOE as the centerpiece of its supposed national accountability strategy. The disingenuous creation of commissions of inquiry to deflect pressure to investigate serious violations of human rights is a tactic well recognized by activists and advocates. As then–special rapporteur on extrajudicial, summary, or arbitrary executions Philip Alston put it in 2008, "commissions can be used very effectively by Governments for the wrong purposes: to defuse a crisis, to purport to be upholding notions of accountability and to promote impunity."[83] Indeed, as Human Rights Watch pointed out in 2018, Burma has "a long history of creating mechanisms that aimed to dilute or deflect international calls for action rather than to prosecute those responsible."[84]

But the military investigations and court martials were received equally badly. And, critically, they were assumed to be window dressing aimed at preventing international action. Rohingya lawyer and activist Tun Khin described the Gu Dar Pyin trials as "superficial actions to alleviate international pressure," while Human Rights Watch dismissed them as "the latest attempt to feign progress on accountability in an apparent attempt to influence the United Nations and international tribunals."[85] Yet from a lawyer's perspective, it is hard to argue that the DRC's military trials—where low-ranking perpetrators were scapegoated, suspects did not have the opportunity to mount a defense, and those convicted are frequently able to escape without serving their full sentences—are procedurally *that* much superior to Burma's military trials, where again low-ranking perpetrators have been scapegoated, the lack of transparency raises serious fair trial concerns and convicted perpetrators have not served out their sentences.

Notably, however, representatives of the Congolese government have repeatedly pointed to ongoing instability and limited judicial capacity as a justification for limited progress on prosecuting sexual violence crimes. For instance, in response to criticism from the Joint Human Rights Office for slow progress on accountability, the Ministry of Justice emphasized that the main obstacle to the pursuit of perpetrators was their location deep in conflict zones and consequent difficulties of identification.[86] Burma, by contrast, has displayed outright hostility to international pressure and insisted that domestic efforts are perfectly adequate. The president's spokesman even slipped up at one point and explicitly stated that the ICOE's purpose was to respond to "false allegations made by the UN Agencies and other international communities."[87]

Where Burma has kept international actors out, refusing to issue visas to the fact-finding mission and barring the special rapporteur from visiting even as it claimed to be investigating reports of atrocities, the DRC's more cooperative stance has meant that international actors have been deeply involved in efforts to pursue justice for sexual violence crimes there.[88] Consequently, they have a different relationship with the end result than they would observing a postatrocity government's effort from the outside. Not only are they intimately familiar with the constraints under which the judicial system operates, they're invested at an organizational level in the outcome. As a result, accountability behavior that might otherwise be treated as noncompliance has been accepted as a good faith effort and meaningful progress in the direction of justice for mass atrocities.

Burma illustrates how those pushing for accountability respond to efforts that fall short of the norm's requirements when they are not persuaded of good faith. But international human rights NGOs and Western governments are not the only audiences for performances of accountability behavior. In the case of Burma, for instance, China was far more receptive to its desultory gestures in the direction of accountability and persistently critiqued Western pressure, arguing that it was "actually not helpful in resolving the problem."[89] In the next chapter, I use a case study of postwar Sri Lanka to explore how profoundly unconvincing accountability efforts can successfully preempt international interference by preventing the mobilization of cohesive international pressure and censure.

CHOOSING YOUR AUDIENCE

"Our troops went to the battlefield carrying a gun in one hand and a copy of the Human Rights charter in the other": so then-President Mahinda Rajapaksa insisted on multiple occasions following the end of Sri Lanka's decades-long civil war. But the evidence that the security forces committed massive violations of human rights and international humanitarian law has long been incontrovertible. A dozen years later, perhaps as many as 150,000 people remain unaccounted for.[1] Despite increasingly insistent calls for accountability from survivors and members of the international community, successive Sri Lankan governments have flatly refused to investigate or prosecute the authors of these atrocities.

Nevertheless, during its tenure in power after winning the war, the administration of President Mahinda Rajapaksa created a spate of institutions with mandates tangentially related to accountability, none of which were actually tasked with investigating alleged violations of the laws of war. And while transitional justice institutions that fail to meet international standards often deviate from "best practices" because they are responding to domestic political imperatives, it was obvious in the case of Sri Lanka that domestic politics militated against the creation of any accountability mechanism whatsoever. Indeed, these institutions met with criticism from the government's staunchly nationalistic domestic constituency.

As the following pages will show, these institutions were created at moments of acute international pressure, in line with the theory of quasi-compliance presented in chapter 1. Each and every one of them was met with skepticism from those calling for justice, exemplifying the seeming puzzle of quasi-compliance:

Why would a state that strongly prefers impunity go to the trouble of creating costly human rights institutions that do not satisfy those pushing for action?

But as the theory outlined in chapter 1 suggests, the intended audience for states engaging in quasi-compliance is not always the Western governments and international NGOs that promote and monitor human rights. Those engaged in policing human rights must convince others to support them. And these others—states that are less informed and less engaged and may have domestic incentives against robust human rights action—can make up a potentially receptive audience for quasi-compliance.

The account of contestation over postwar justice in Sri Lanka that I present here is based on a combination of interviews, participant observation, field observation, and primary source research undertaken over the course of six trips to Sri Lanka.[2] The sensitive nature of the subject matter—unacknowledged mass atrocities—called for a careful approach, focused on developing the contextual knowledge necessary to assess and interpret contradictory claims about profoundly politicized events. As Sarah Parkinson points out, this kind of approach has "a marked advantage over work based solely on formal interviews" when researching sensitive subjects.[3] It allows the researcher to analyze what Lee Ann Fujii called the "meta-data" of an interview—"informants' spoken and unspoken thoughts and feelings which they do not always articulate in their stories or interview responses, but which emerge in other ways."[4] This is particularly important in repressive environments like postwar Sri Lanka where silences on sensitive topics can convey as much information as what is said.

This fieldwork presented some challenges. On my first visit to Sri Lanka, the phrase *war crimes* was rarely heard in public. Discussions about mass atrocities were conducted in whispers with eyes peeled for listeners. Activists and members of civil society who advocated for accountability were labeled traitors and threatened with violence. International organizations and foreign governments that raised the issue of abuses by the military were derided as terrorist sympathizers. Meanwhile, the government engaged in extensive monitoring and surveillance (both electronic and physical) of individuals critical of the regime.

Despite the precautions required by these dynamics, I was able to travel all over the country, including to seven of the eight districts in the former war zone, and speak with people from all walks of life about justice for war crimes. In total, I conducted more than seventy-five formal interviews on the domestic politics of accountability with involved individuals ranging from members of the victim community, to domestic human rights activists, to former Sri Lankan military leaders, to representatives of international civil society.[5] I conducted additional interviews about the international politics of accountability in New York, Washington, DC, London, Geneva, and Chennai. The interview data are

supplemented by hundreds of hours of off-the-record conversations and participant observation at meetings on Sri Lanka at the US State Department and the
UK Parliament, at the 25th Session of the UN Human Rights Council in
March 2014, and at conferences, meetings, and social events with activists in Sri
Lanka and abroad.[6] In combination, these methods yielded detailed and comprehensive data about five years of back and forth between Sri Lanka and the
international community on the issue of postwar justice. They paint a picture
of the deliberate creation of quasi-compliant institutions as part of a strategy to
disrupt the formation of a coalition on the UN Human Rights Council that
would support an international investigation into state crimes.

Sri Lanka's fight against the Liberation Tigers of Tamil Eelam (LTTE) came to a
bloody end in May 2009. State-perpetrated abuses of human rights had been
common throughout the decades-long conflict, but civilian loss of life escalated
shockingly in the final days. As government forces advanced across the Vanni
region of northeastern Sri Lanka, the hundreds of thousands of civilians living
under LTTE control were caught between them and their target. Repeatedly dis-
placed as the army pushed forward, the panicked civilians ended up trapped on
a narrow stretch of land between the Bay of Bengal and the Nandikadal Lagoon.
The war's final battle took place there, near the village of Mullivaikkal. In the
days leading up to it, an estimated forty thousand civilians lost their lives, many
to government shelling of hospitals and so-called no fire zones.[7]

The LTTE was utterly defeated. Thousands of fighters had been killed in the final phase of the war, and thousands more taken into government custody. Some of
these prisoners of war would be tortured, raped, or summarily executed, their brutal fates recorded in grainy cell phone videos taken by the giddy victorious army.
Others landed in "rehabilitation" camps. Many never made it home to their families.[8] The civilians who emerged from Mullivaikkal were also detained, impounded
in a vast network of camps where conditions were grim and abuses rampant. Meanwhile, the Sri Lankan government declared its "humanitarian operation" a success
and prepared to celebrate "Victory Day," a newly declared public holiday.

For Sinhalese citizens in southern Sri Lanka, a nightmare had ended. The
ever-present fear of a suicide attack finally lifted. Many in the south had never
met any Tamils, believed the LTTE to be monsters, and felt only relief that the
leaders of the rebellion had been slaughtered en masse. They did not doubt the
government's assurances that the final push had been conducted with the utmost
care for civilian safety. They had no desire to question the official story.

As the war ground to a close, journalists and aid workers had no access to
the battlefield.[9] However, doctors operating inside the siege area were able to ra-

dio information out regarding casualty numbers. Together with testimony from escaping civilians and the eyewitness account of a UN official, these numbers painted a picture of indiscriminate bombardment of civilian populations as well as targeting of hospitals and no fire zones.

As information about the dire plight of civilians began to emerge, Sri Lanka vehemently denied the reports. At a special session of the UN Human Rights Council, Western governments called for an international inquiry into abuses committed by both sides. But on May 27, 2009, the Rajapaksa regime scored a diplomatic victory. It pushed through the Human Rights Council a resolution welcoming "the liberation by the Government of Sri Lanka of tens of thousands of its citizens that were kept by the Liberation Tigers of Tamil Eelam against their will as hostages."[10] No mention was made of violations of international law or the need for accountability.

If a majority of Human Rights Council members was willing to accept Sri Lanka's portrayal of the brutal last days of the war as a hostage rescue, many Western governments were not. Intransigence over human rights issues in the aftermath of the war profoundly affected Sri Lanka's relationships with the West. When the US State Department released a report detailing extensive violations of international law during the final phase of the war,[11] Sri Lanka rejected the findings as an attempt "to bring the government of Sri Lanka into disrepute, through fabricated allegations and concocted stories."[12] It addressed the report with a two-pronged line of argument that would become a persistent refrain: First, "the Sri Lanka Armed Forces were scrupulous in affording protection to the civilians and safeguarding their welfare"; and second, "Sri Lankas [sic] domestic jurisprudence provides all the necessary scope for those perceiving themselves subjected to a violation of their human rights."[13]

Bilateral relations with the United States, traditionally warm, had already begun to decline in 2007 when Congress reduced economic assistance and suspended military aid and arms sales to Sri Lanka over concerns about human rights violations by the security forces. In 2010, Congress halted all nonhumanitarian aid following a screening on Capitol Hill of the Channel 4 documentary *Sri Lanka's Killing Fields*, which showed clear evidence of war crimes. In 2013, humanitarian assistance was reduced from an $8 million allocation to $6 million.[14]

Sri Lanka's relationship with other major aid donors suffered similarly. In 2010 the European Union suspended the Generalised Scheme of Preferences Plus (GSP+) trade benefit and many European countries curtailed their bilateral development aid. Over the 2009–2012 period, disbursements from "traditional development partners" (the United States, Japan, and Europe, along with the international development banks) decreased from 48.76 percent to 29.30 percent of foreign development finance.[15]

These penalties failed to induce the Sri Lankan government to change course. Sri Lanka took no action as the evidence mounted. When a year had passed with no sign of a domestic response, UN Secretary-General Ban Ki-moon yielded to Western pressure and created a Panel of Experts on Accountability in Sri Lanka. This body would ultimately conclude that the final push to defeat the LTTE was a "grave assault on the entire regime of international law" and call for a full international investigation.[16] But from the beginning, Sri Lanka resisted its work, calling it "an unwarranted and unnecessary interference with a sovereign nation."[17]

At the same time, Sri Lanka created its own mechanism: The Lessons Learnt and Reconciliation Commission (LLRC). The move was surprising, given the regime's furious insistence that Sri Lanka had no human rights issues in need of investigation. What's more, it faced allegations from political opponents that it was caving to international pressure. But, as the director of one Colombo civil society organization explained, the government "could see the signs of the U.N. mobilizing" and "fear[ed] a war crimes tribunal."[18]

It quickly became clear that the LLRC would not deliver anything like justice. As an individual involved in the LLRC's work pointed out, its role was "not projected as an accountability mechanism as such" but rather "to promote reconciliation."[19] The mandate was to investigate the failure of the 2002 ceasefire and to make recommendations to avoid a recurrence of communitarian violence. Notably, "each sitting was preceded by a general statement from a commissioner . . . describing the work of the commission to encourage peaceful coexistence."[20] This, the government apparently felt, came close enough to dealing with alleged to war crimes "to be a counterpoise to international action."[21] Members of the activist community spoke harshly of the LLRC's mandate, characterizing it as window dressing on the government's refusal to investigate the alleged atrocities. As one victims' advocate put it: "Their task was to sweep it under the carpet."[22]

Many members of both domestic and international civil society declined to participate in the LLRC's work out of concerns about its "inadequate mandate, insufficient guarantees of independence, and lack of witness protection."[23] Nevertheless, the members of the LLRC spent eighteen months taking testimony from thousands of Sri Lankans. Apparently, they were shocked by what victims and witnesses told them. A member of the LLRC staff confided that the testimony was "very, very difficult to hear."[24]

In late 2011, the LLRC released its report, including a comprehensive treatment of interethnic relations by which members of Colombo civil society pronounced themselves "pleasantly surprised."[25] Among its recommendations, the LLRC called for the establishment of a database of those detained by the government along with other measures aimed at "bringing a sense of closure."[26] But its members resisted the conclusion that the stories they had heard were the result of the security forces' intentional actions. The LLRC's most publicized finding was that the Sri Lankan military "had not deliberately targeted civilians in the N[o] F[ire] Z[one]s."[27] In other words, it avoided the issue of accountability for atrocities entirely.

As the March 2012 session of the UN Human Rights Council approached, Tamil voices from within Sri Lanka and from the diaspora lobbied for the international investigation envisioned by the Panel of Experts report. The regime pushed back hard on the diplomatic front, emphasizing its rights as a sovereign state and the supremacy of domestic remedies. "We have the capability and the will to solve our own problems," said the foreign minister.[28] The government pointed to the LLRC as evidence that it was handling the matter domestically, and as the Human Rights Council meeting drew closer, attempted to double down on this strategy. While still denying the validity of all allegations of war crimes, the Ministry of Defence disclosed for the first time in August 2011 that its claims of a "zero civilian casualty rate" were inaccurate.

This admission enabled Sri Lanka, one month before the Human Rights Council met, to announce that an "army court of inquiry" had been convened to investigate allegations of war crimes and that a court martial would try anyone for whom the court found prima facie evidence of involvement in violations of international law.[29] But when the Human Rights Council session passed without an international investigation being empaneled, the army court of inquiry quietly closed up shop. Months later, it announced that the military was *not* responsible for any civilian casualties during the final phase of the war. Notably, it stated that:

> At all stages of the Humanitarian Operation, the Sri Lanka Army behaved as a well-disciplined military force observing the International Humanitarian Law (IHL) and the law of war.[30]

In May 2013, UN High Commissioner for Human Rights Navi Pillay announced she would conduct a visit to Sri Lanka. The announcement coincided with increased attention to Sri Lanka's human rights failures as a result of its selection as the host of the November 2013 Commonwealth Heads of Government Meeting (CHOGM). In the run-up to the meeting, the Canadian government, which boycotted the meeting, and others drew attention to Sri Lanka's abysmal human rights performance. Impunity for war crimes was the primary focus and an addendum to all allegations about current abuses. Amidst the outcry, with Navi Pillay's visit around the corner, President Rajapaksa announced the creation of a new commission to investigate wartime disappearances in July 2013.[31]

Activists on the ground pointed out that creating institutions in response to international pressure had become par for the course for Sri Lanka, but that "they're only being used as a red herring, a cover-up, a way to give the appearance that something is being done."[32] Many suggested that they didn't expect the commission to ever actually get off the ground. "The key word is 'announced,'" said one, while another dismissed it as "just a ploy for CHOGM."[33]

It is clear from the foregoing that the creation of each of these institutions was prompted by external pressure for accountability. Although they did not actually address responsibility for atrocities, they were nontrivial exercises into which the Sri Lankan government poured significant resources. The 2013 implementation plan for the LLRC called for an expenditure of nearly 1.3 billion Sri Lankan rupees or approximately $7.2 million in today's dollars.[34] The following year, the government spent another Rs 400 million ($2.6 million) on the commission on disappearances.[35]

While these may not sound like a huge expenditures, it's worth noting that Sri Lanka budgeted only 5.4 billion rupees to its Ministry of Justice in 2013.[36] In other words, the government spent about one-third as much on a sham transitional justice process as it did on its entire court system. Additionally, Sri Lanka's expenditures on these institutions are on par with what other countries transitioning out of conflict or autocracy have spent on robust accountability mechanisms. For instance, in 1995, South Africa spent $18 million on its much-lauded Truth and Reconciliation Commission, representing 0.06 percent of the country's overall annual spending of $28 billion.[37] By contrast, Cambodia, which has a similarly sized economy and budget to Sri Lanka's, has dragged its feet and protested spending approximately $18.6 million over a ten-year period on its share of the expenses for the tribunal prosecuting Khmer Rouge leaders.

It was also clear at the time that the Sri Lankan government paid political costs to set up these institutions. The Rajapaksas' electoral strategy has always relied on their Sinhala-Buddhist "son of the soil" credentials and their ties to openly supremacist individuals and groups, including the militant monk outfit Bodu Bala Sena. But Sinhala-Buddhist supremacists objected strongly to the creation of any accountability institutions, however weak, on the grounds that they constituted an attack on the "war heroes."

The triumphant military were heroes to the Sinhalese public. Just six months after the war's end, Mahinda Rajapaksa called presidential elections approximately two years ahead of schedule. On the strength of the defeat of the LTTE, he won handily, polling at nearly 80 percent throughout most of the Sinhala-Buddhist south and west.[38] Many in the south had understood the military victory not only as a defeat of terror, but as a vindication of Sinhala-Buddhist supremacist ideology. The LTTE were viewed as an external incursion, the "invaders from the North" of militant Buddhist rhetoric.[39] Tamil victims of war crimes were therefore not legitimate subjects of the Sri Lankan state deserving of justice, but a defeated enemy. Most Sinhalese bought the official line that the campaign had been conducted with a "zero civilian casualty" profile. When pressed on the absurdity of the claim, some admitted that civilians died, but insisted that any deaths were "justified."[40]

As a Tamil activist put it in 2013, it was simply not an option to "point a finger at the army." It would "be deemed to be unpatriotic" by the Sinhalese.[41] In the 2010 election, when opposition candidate General Sarath Fonseka publicly accused Gotabaya Rajapaksa of ordering war crimes, it backfired spectacularly.[42] Many in the Sinhala-Buddhist south viewed him as a traitor who had sold out his own men. President Mahinda Rajapaksa was careful to guard against being similarly perceived himself, repeatedly assuring the military "we will not betray you."[43]

The political importance of loyalty to the troops reflected not only popular sentiment, but the defense establishment's increased power in the postwar period. By 2009, the military was a huge organization, more than a hundred times larger than the force of 3,500 with which it entered the war in 1983. As a former high-level commander cautioned, such a large force made it "difficult to convert to peacetime."[44] After the war, high-ranking members of the military invested heavily in the economy, and lower-ranking members were given incentives to open businesses. One Colombo entrepreneur spoke of losing his government contracts to an army-owned competitor and said that it was virtually impossible for small businesses to outcompete military companies.[45]

The expansion of the role of the military in postwar Sri Lanka was accompanied by a vicious crackdown on domestic civil society. Sri Lanka became one of the most dangerous places in the world to be a journalist. Sri Lankan NGOs were labeled "traitors," "terrorists," or "shills for foreign powers."[46] Rumors circulated that the regime had created a special unit of the police to investigate individuals suspected of providing human rights information to the UN and international NGOs.[47] The result was that domestic advocacy for accountability was almost completely absent, "with even civil and peace groups saying it's better to leave alone."[48]

Even in the event of regime change, one civil society leader argued in 2013, a future administration would also be reluctant to "jeopardize relations with the army."[49] But senior government officials' own alleged complicity in war crimes and ongoing abuses made the possibility of justice even more fraught. As another activist noted in 2013, predicting that the Rajapaksa administration would not budge on accountability, "they have a lot to lose."[50]

In fact, when the LLRC report was released, representatives of the hardline-Patriotic National Movement publicly questioned the competence of the commissioners Rajapaksa had appointed. Monk-led mobs disrupted workshops on its implementation.[51] One prominent former supporter, voicing a widely held opinion, described the government's creation of human rights institutions as "groveling at the feet of the foreigners" and "betrayal of those who fought to save [Sri Lanka] from terrorism."[52]

Yet despite the costs incurred to operate them, these institutions were treated as utterly inadequate by those members of the international community calling for action. In the case of the LLRC, the governments of the United States, the UK, and Canada all highlighted the lack of any real inquiry into violations of international humanitarian law.[53] The reception from international civil society was even more critical. Human Rights Watch observed that the report "disregard[ed] the worst abuses by government forces, rehash[ed] longstanding recommendations, and fail[ed] to advance accountability."[54] Amnesty International described it as simply "the latest in a long line of failed domestic mechanisms in Sri Lanka."[55]

The response to the army court of inquiry and the commission on disappearances was even harsher. International human rights advocates stated that the court of inquiry's findings "stretch[ed] credulity" and demonstrated that accountability would be "next to impossible" to achieve domestically.[56] During an official visit to Sri Lanka at which she was briefed on the work of the commission on disappearances, US Assistant Secretary of State for South and Central Asian Affairs Nisha Biswal decried the "lack of progress" on "issues of justice and accountability."[57]

These reactions show that the institutions Sri Lanka created in response to international pressure were wholly unsuccessful at satisfying those actors calling for accountability. And like Burma's government in the previous chapter, the Rajapaksa regime consistently signaled that it was not making a good faith effort to supply accountability. It denied all allegations of war crimes and rejected all international demands for justice. This began in the weeks immediately following the war's end, with President Rajapaksa giving an interview to *Time* in which he characterized accusations of war crimes as "propaganda."[58] A few months later, a government minister accused the UN special rapporteur for extrajudicial killings of being "at the heart of a terrorist media campaign against the Sri Lankan Government."[59]

This behavior only intensified as international pressure increased. When the UN Panel of Experts report came out, the regime lashed out at civil society members suspected of contributing and accused them of underhanded attempts at regime change.[60] As Kristine Höglund and Camilla Orjuela document, "an effort to collect one million signatures against the report was made and large demonstrations were staged against the UN report, where one of the slogans was 'Ban Ki-moon, we don't want you. We want our president.'"[61]

By 2013, the government was routinely throwing public tantrums in response to accountability pressure, even as it continued to unveil new institutions.

A prominent civil society leader put it starkly: "The official position is absolutely hostile and dismissive."[62] When High Commissioner Pillay arrived for her country visit, the government mounted a campaign to undermine her. One activist who was involved in her visit described this as "coordinated, pre-planned, deliberate government strategy" to "humiliate and discredit her."[63] The regime was equally vitriolic in response to the pressure surrounding the Commonwealth Heads of Government Meeting later that year. In the angry words of the communications minister, "we are a sovereign nation. You think someone can just make a demand from Sri Lanka?"[64] And in early 2014, when the US Assistant Secretary of State for South and Central Asian Affairs warned that "patience [wa]s wearing thin," the Sri Lankan government reacted furiously, accusing the international community of "setting the groundwork to hang our President" and refusing a visa to the US Ambassador for Global Women's Issues in retaliation.[65]

These actions indicate that Sri Lanka was actively resisting demands for justice. It is clear that international actors calling for accountability interpreted Sri Lanka's creation of these supposed accountability institutions as disingenuous. Following the release of the LLRC report, the members of the UN Panel of Experts argued that it "cast serious doubt on [Sri Lanka's] willingness to uncover what really happened in those fateful months."[66] Human Rights Watch dismissed the entire exercise as "playing for time."[67] International Crisis Group went further, decrying it as an attempt to "exonerate the government" and "roll[] back well-established principles of international law."[68] They spoke similarly about the army court of inquiry—"a transparent ploy to deflect a global push for a genuine international investigation"—and the commission on disappearances—"throwing bones to the international community."[69] In 2014, when Sri Lanka announced that it would not permit the investigators mandated by the Human Rights Council resolution to enter the country and proscribed sixteen Tamil diaspora organizations and more than four hundred individuals, local activists and international audiences understood these measures as an effort to control the flow of information to the international investigation.[70]

If the goal in setting up these ostensible domestic accountability institutions was silencing critics in the West and the international human rights community, they were a failure. But Sri Lanka's actions were received very differently elsewhere.

The withdrawal of aid that accompanied Western human rights pressure was met with a corresponding uptick in flows from alternative sources. China, which provided critical arms and support in the last stages of the war, had become Sri Lanka's single biggest aid donor by 2009, providing $1.2 billion out of $2.2 billion in total commitments.[71] As then-Foreign Secretary Palitha Kohona put it in an interview with the *New York Times*, Sri Lanka's "traditional donors" in the West had "receded into a very distant corner" to be replaced by China.[72]

Unlike its bilateral relationships with the West, which the Rajapaksa regime perceived as "no carrots and all sticks," Chinese aid and infrastructure loans came with no governance or reform conditions attached.[73] In Foreign Secretary Kohona's words, Chinese money was preferable because "Asians don't go around teaching each other how to behave."[74] The turn toward China also played into the broader regional dynamics of competition between China and India. The traditionally close relationship with India became strained in the postwar years, in part due to India's advocacy on behalf of Sri Lanka's Tamils. Rajapaksa exploited his resistance to Indian pressure on Tamil issues to shore up support among his Sinhala-Buddhist nationalist constituency. At the same time, he used Chinese loans to fund massive infrastructure projects in his southern support base, including an airport and deep-water port in his hometown of Hambantota.

The regime assiduously cultivated the relationship with China, for example, boycotting the Nobel Peace Prize ceremony for Chinese dissident Liu Xiaobo in 2010. In 2011, after the UN Panel of Experts report came out, the Chinese foreign minister spoke up on Sri Lanka's behalf, saying that China was "confident" in Sri Lanka's ability to address the matter internally and calling on the international community to refrain from "taking measures that could further complicate the issue."[75]

The staunch support of China and the diminishing dependence on Western donors allowed Sri Lanka some breathing room from accountability pressure. Furthermore, although the alleged deaths of more than forty thousand Tamil noncombatants during the final months of the war represented deliberate violence against civilians on a scale rarely matched, international reaction was relatively muted, possibly as a consequence of Sri Lanka's success in framing its fight against the LTTE as counterterrorism.[76] In the postwar period, while vocal about the unacceptability of war crimes going uninvestigated, Western governments were reluctant to take responsibility for ensuring accountability themselves. US Department of State spokeswoman Victoria Nuland outlined the US position in late 2011: "We've long said that it is better for Sri Lankans to take these issues themselves and address them fully . . . So let's see what they are willing to do going forward."[77]

This wait-and-see approach, despite the fact that no perpetrators of mass atrocities anywhere have ever prosecuted themselves, reflects the potentially high price of pursuing accountability. Because Sri Lanka is not a member of the International Criminal Court, there was no automatic international mechanism available to investigate the alleged atrocities. An international inquiry would instead require multilateral action, either through (1) a UN Security Council referral of the situation to the International Criminal Court, (2) the establishment of a specialized tribunal by the Security Council, or (3) the creation of an international investigation by either the Security Council or the Human Rights Council. Sri Lanka's close relationship with China, which strengthened as Western governments withdrew preferential trade and aid over human rights concerns, prevented action at the Security Council. That left the Human Rights Council as the primary site of contestation over accountability. Led by the United States, Western countries pushed for a strong resolution that would empanel an international investigation.

No state has a veto power on the Human Rights Council. Its forty-seven members are elected to three-year terms by the UN General Assembly and are distributed according to the regional blocks. The Western European and Others Group (WEOG) holds only seven seats. This means that resolutions, which pass by a simple majority, must secure the support of a broad coalition of states.

Exploiting these dynamics, the Rajapaksa regime mounted a vigorous campaign to block the Human Rights Council from mandating an international investigative body. Sri Lanka's diplomacy took aim at the non-Western council members. It had two components. The first was to talk up its "home-grown" institutions. The second was to characterize any criticism as illegitimate and to invoke developing world solidarity against Western oppression. These two strategies worked in tandem to provide peer states on the Human Rights Council cover for supporting Sri Lanka as well as a reason to do so.

The emphasis on a "home-grown" approach focused primarily on the LLRC. Speaking to the September 2011 session of the Human Rights Council, the head of Sri Lanka's delegation emphasized that the LLRC members were "highly regarded professionals" and said they "should be given time and space to come up with their findings and recommendations."[78] He echoed this call for time and space in March 2012, when he warned a ministerial-level audience about undermining an "effective ongoing domestic process." He went into significant detail aimed at demonstrating that the LLRC's hearings were conducted rigorously and transparently and stated that "Sri Lanka is best placed to successfully conclude a home grown process of reconciliation acceptable to, and benefitting all of its people."[79] He also highlighted the creation of the army court of inquiry, saying "Sri Lanka has taken clear and definite steps towards implementation of the recommendations of the [LLRC], barely two months after the report was made public."[80]

In 2013, when Sri Lanka was again up for consideration by the Human Rights Council, its representatives continued to hold up the "home-grown reconciliation mechanism" as sufficient to address accountability concerns.[81] They challenged the resolution before the council on the grounds that it would "undermine or devalue ongoing processes" (i.e., the implementation of the LLRC's recommendations) by suggesting that they were "somehow deficient."[82]

Following High Commissioner Pillay's critical report on her August 2013 country visit, the Sri Lankan ambassador to Geneva told the Human Rights Council that "multiple mechanisms to address accountability ha[d] been put in place and are in motion." He referred specifically to the recently announced commission on disappearances, claiming that "all reported cases of disappearances are being comprehensively investigated."[83] In the run-up to the March 2014 session, Sri Lanka issued a lengthy written reply to the high commissioner's report, which in addition to the LLRC, the army court of inquiry, and the commission on disappearances, also highlighted investigations into two 2006 massacres.[84]

Sri Lanka's efforts to foreground its domestic mechanisms were almost always accompanied by harsh criticism of Western accountability pressure as "a witch hunt" and a "systematic and organized campaign aimed at distorting and misinforming."[85] This began in 2011, when High Commissioner Pillay called for an international investigation into the allegations contained in the Panel of Experts report. Sri Lanka's ambassador to Geneva immediately denounced her "demonstrable lack of objectivity and impropriety."[86]

Shortly thereafter, his successor said of Amnesty International and other advocacy organizations that "it is evident that the real aim of those questioning the legitimacy of LLRC is to undermine the principle of State sovereignty."[87] Sovereignty would become a persistent theme of Sri Lanka's rhetoric. In 2012, with discussions about a resolution underway, the head of the delegation asked the members of the Human Rights Council if they would "permit a usurpation of an independent nation's prerogative to act in its people's paramount interests."[88] The ambassador explained Sri Lanka's strategy to the press: "Developing countries fear that such a decision would set a precedent giving an historic character to the Council permiting [sic] a powerful country, for reasons of its own, to reopen a dossier that has been closed to examine past violations."[89]

Sri Lanka's diplomats emphasized to their peer states that they could be next. "Today it is Sri Lanka," warned Minister Mahinda Samarasinghe in 2013. "Tomorrow, it may be any other country in this Council."[90] As the Human Rights Council debated the draft resolution in 2013, Sri Lanka's ambassador cautioned that it could "have an adverse impact on all developing countries."[91] He reiterated his warning in 2014, adding that the proposal to empanel an international inquiry was "highly intrusive in nature and . . . in breach of sovereignty of the Sri Lankan people and territorial integrity of Sri Lanka."[92]

Sri Lanka also advanced this rhetoric outside of Geneva. Speaking at the 2013 UN General Assembly in New York, President Rajapaksa decried the "relentless pursuit" of Sri Lanka as part of a "growing trend in the international arena, of interference by some, in the internal matters of developing countries, in the guise of security, and guardians of human rights."[93] As the March 2014 Human Rights

Council session approached, he reached out personally to the sub-Saharan African members, calling for developing world solidarity against neoimperialist human rights pressure.[94] In a statement to the press, he memorably characterized Western calls for an international inquiry as mean-spirited bullying, "like Cassius Clay playing against a schoolboy."[95]

In both 2012 and 2013, Colombo managed to stave off an international inquiry. The LLRC's report had been released just in time to muddy the waters for the March 2012 Human Rights Council session. The announcement of the army court of inquiry immediately preceding the session was another thumb on the scale. Discussing the court of inquiry with me in 2013, one member of Sri Lankan civil society agreed that while it was an attempt to "pull the wool over the eyes of some international actors," it was not aimed at those calling for accountability. Rather, it was targeted at still-undecided Human Rights Council members. If Sri Lanka could "pick off" some of these states in the run-up to the March 2012 session, it would improve the chances of defeating a resolution.[96]

With Sri Lanka's diplomats touting its "home-grown" mechanisms and challenging Western pressure, the majority of the Human Rights Council was disinclined to empanel an investigation. India's declaration that it would maintain a "policy of not interfering into the internal matters of a country" was particularly helpful as, in the words of one diaspora activist, "other countries look to India to signal how to respond" on Sri Lanka issues.[97] In the face of these dynamics, the United States, leading the push for accountability, backed down. Instead of pushing for an international investigation, it put on the table what it described as "a moderate and balanced resolution" calling on Sri Lanka to implement the recommendations of the LLRC despite its weakness on accountability.[98] The new language did not include any mention of the UN Panel of Experts report.

Despite an oral revision to give Sri Lanka final say over any "advice and technical assistance" provided by the UN, the Rajapaksa administration still fought the passage of the watered-down resolution. And although it passed (and was reiterated in 2013), the public debates in the Human Rights Council revealed how deeply the narratives of home-grown methods and Western interference had penetrated.[99] In their explanation of "no" votes in 2012, developing states emphasized that domestic mechanisms must take precedence over international (Uganda, Indonesia) and that "Sri Lanka's home-grown process should be prioritized" (Thailand). Many also argued that Sri Lanka must be given more time and space to implement the LLRC (Maldives, Kyrgyzstan) and that the resolution risked "undermin[ing] national efforts currently underway" (Cuba, on behalf of those voting against). Others criticized the "biased approach" of the international community (Ecuador, Bangladesh).

Similar dynamics prevailed during the March 2013 debate. Once again, the language of the resolution was weakened at the eleventh hour so that it simply "encourage[ed]" Sri Lanka to take action.[100] Once again, the "no" votes emphasized the "ongoing domestic reconciliation process" (Russia, on behalf of those voting against) and criticized the "biased" nature of Western calls for accountability (Venezuela, Belarus).

In the March 2014 debate following High Commissioner Pillay's formal presentation of her country visit report, member states again parroted the Sri Lankan rhetoric about "home-grown methods" and Western bias. Several criticized the high commissioner's "discriminatory approach" (Pakistan) and the "politicization" of the process (Venezuela). They highlighted concerns that the international investigation she called for would "undermine" the domestic process (Namibia, India, Indonesia). Following President Rajapaksa's diplomatic offensive, which called for developing world solidarity, at least two African states abandoned their plans to support the resolution mandating an international inquiry.[101]

But Sri Lanka's luck had run out. On March 27, with a plurality of twenty-three out of forty-seven votes in favor, the Human Rights Council passed resolution 25/1. It requested that the high commissioner "undertake a comprehensive investigation into alleged serious violations and abuses of human rights and related crimes by both parties in Sri Lanka during the period covered by the Lessons Learnt and Reconciliation Commission."[102]

The resolution was a loss for Sri Lanka, but the Rajapaksa government had successfully delayed any international action on accountability for five years and prevented a stronger international response. Even though many international actors were extremely critical, the "home-grown institutions" still became a focal point of international pressure on Sri Lanka, justifying first a "wait-and-see" approach and then the foregrounding of the LLRC in the UNHRC resolutions. Observing this shift from emphasis on the pursuit of a robust accountability mechanism, the Tamil diaspora newspaper *Tamil Guardian* forcefully argued that "the LLRC has for too long been the international community's fig leaf, used by governments across the world, including the US and the UK, to stall calls for accountability."[103]

As one Tamil activist lamented, the regime's ability to convince members of the international community to prioritize disingenuous domestic remedies was a huge success as a "time-buying activity."[104] And although an inquiry was ultimately empaneled, the delay was time the regime had to destroy evidence, bulldoze mass graves, intimidate and disappear witnesses, and appoint accused perpetrators to ambassadorial posts where they had diplomatic immunity.

The success of this strategy rested on swaying the audience of nonactivist states on the Human Rights Council. And while some of the states that parroted

Sri Lanka's rhetoric would likely always have been "no" votes, a number of them were demonstrably swing states. Indonesia, for example, sided with Sri Lanka to vote against the 2012 and 2013 resolutions, but abstained in 2014. Likewise Botswana, which abstained in 2012 and 2013, shifted to a "yes" vote in 2014. Others, such as Uruguay, Mexico, and Nigeria, that voted "yes" in 2012 and 2013 were explicit that they would not support the stronger language favored by the West. They emphasized the importance of the domestic mechanisms that Sri Lanka had set up. By creating institutions tangentially related to accountability and then emphasizing the primacy of domestic processes and sovereignty against Western interference, Sri Lanka was able to prevent many of its peer states from joining the Western push for robust action and to convince some of them to vote against even the weakened resolutions that passed in 2012 and 2013.

Sri Lanka's refusal to investigate and prosecute those responsible for mass atrocities has been a source of contention with the West since the alleged war crimes first came to light in 2009. Domestic political constraints made the provision of justice an extremely unappealing prospect for the postwar government. And resistance to international involvement, due in part to the complicity of members of the ruling regime in the alleged atrocities, made cooperation with an international accountability mechanism even less attractive. Nevertheless, in the face of sustained international pressure, the regime spent millions of dollars on a succession of weak accountability institutions, drawing invective from their staunchly nationalist constituency, which felt they were caving to international pressure. The reactions of international audiences demonstrate that the domestic mechanisms rolled out by Sri Lanka were unconvincing to the actors invested in demanding justice. Furthermore, Sri Lanka was openly antagonistic to international advocacy on war crimes and the skeptical response of activist states and international NGOs demonstrates that they understood Sri Lanka's behavior as bad faith.

However, peer states on the UN Human Rights Council had a very different reaction. Coupled with rhetoric portraying itself as "this poor third-world country" bullied by Western governments, Sri Lanka pointed to the creation of quasi-compliant institutions as evidence that it was acting domestically.[105] The strategy paid off. Even after the 2014 resolution authorizing an investigation, Sri Lanka's allies on the council continued to protest the move as "unwarranted, especially in the context where the country is implementing its own domestic processes" and a potentially "dangerous precedent[], which may adversely affect all our countries."[106]

The final days of Sri Lanka's civil war rank as some of the worst state-led violence against civilians in the twenty-first century. The politics of accountability for these atrocities are therefore important to understand in their own right. But the fact that international debates over postwar justice in Sri Lanka played out primarily in the UN Human Rights Council adds to the importance of the case. Because of the Human Rights Council's role as a "chamber of peer review," it is the venue in which human rights perpetrators most frequently engage in efforts to defend their behavior to an audience of fellow states.[107] It is therefore a likely site for observing the sorts of framing contests the theory anticipates.[108] As scholars of the Human Rights Council (and its predecessor organization, the UN Commission for Human Rights) have observed, "the plurality of weak states and their ability to employ organizational leverage to their advantage" means that outcomes antithetical to powerful states' preferences are highly possible and indeed common.[109] In other words, there's real benefit available to perpetrator states that win framing contests. The case of postwar Sri Lanka suggests that quasi-compliance can be a valuable strategy for accomplishing this and for influencing (and blocking) the formation of coalitions within the council.

CONCLUSION

It rained unusually hard in Hargeisa, Somaliland, in May 1997. When the flood-waters receded, there were bones on the ground—the broken skeletons of several hundred people who had been tied together, shot in the head, and dumped into shallow graves. They had lain undisturbed since the 1980s, victims of Somalia's brutal counterinsurgency campaign against the separatist Somali National Movement. Human rights groups estimate that dictator Siad Barre's security forces slaughtered more than fifty thousand unarmed civilians in their attempt to put down the rebellion. Survivors say the body count was closer to two hundred thousand.

Somaliland declared its independence from Somalia after Barre was overthrown in 1991. As Somalia descended into anarchy, Somaliland became a relatively peaceful multiparty democracy. Somaliland has never been recognized as a sovereign state; its 3.5 million inhabitants are still nominally citizens of Somalia. But for more than three decades, it has self-governed, printing currency and issuing passports, providing social services and security. And since 1997, a War Crimes Investigation Commission has worked to document the evidence of atrocities, gathering witness testimony and locating and preserving mass graves. The government in Hargeisa continues to push for international recognition. If it gets it, one of a newly independent Somaliland's first priorities will be to pursue justice for the Barre regime's crimes.

Somaliland's efforts, and their connection to its pursuit of statehood, reflect the ascendance of a global norm that atrocities must not go unpunished, and that the states where they occur have an obligation to hold the perpetrators accountable.

International human rights advocates, UN officials, and Western governments regularly add their voices to those of the victims of mass atrocities to call for justice. In the face of demands for accountability from domestic and/or international audiences, some postatrocity governments prosecute the perpetrators or cooperate with international tribunals, but many more do nothing. And the data presented in the last four chapters show that the question "was justice provided?" can't be answered with a simple yes or no. There's substantial variation in what both accountability and impunity look like.

Postatrocity governments' response to calls for justice depends on where those calls come from. They only pursue accountability when it improves the chances of regime survival. But some postatrocity governments whose domestic politics favor impunity nevertheless often create institutions that are ostensibly accountability seeking. I have explained this behavior as quasi-compliance; a calculated effort to do just enough to escape penalties for failing to comply with human rights norms.

The theory of quasi-compliance helps explain what initially appears to be puzzling behavior by repressive regimes in response to international pressure on all sorts of human rights issues: the creation of institutions that cost them dearly in terms of both resources and political capital but failed to silence international criticism. I explain this as a strategic response to the uncertainty surrounding enforcement of human rights norms.

Even the most human rights–engaged states are often reluctant to act decisively against abusers because of the effort and expense involved. This dynamic opens opportunities for states facing human rights pressure to try to do just enough to further discourage international action without actually complying with their obligations. Because this strategy is resource intensive and can pose political risks, I've argued that it will be likeliest where two conditions are met: (1) enforcement of the rule is inconsistent but not wholly absent, and (2) enforcement action would impose significant political or economic costs on the target state.

This argument fits into a broader literature on the unintended consequences of human rights pressure. While advocates maintain that naming and shaming is "still the human rights movement's best weapon," scholars like Jack Snyder have pointed out that it "has a built-in propensity to produce counterproductive backlash."[1] Rochelle Terman argues that the approach itself may produce as much resistance as the actual content of human rights norms, suggesting that "norm opposition emerges because, not in spite of, shaming."[2] In this vein, Leslie Vinjamuri documents the bizarre role that international accountability pressure played in bringing to power two ICC-accused politicians in Kenya's 2013 elections.[3] Even when pressure doesn't prompt overt backlash, it can still be profoundly counterproductive. Jelena Subotić, who examines cases in which there is low domestic demand for accountability for atrocities, shows that when the issue can be "hi-jacked" for domestic political purposes, international efforts to push for transitional justice "at best miss their mark and at worst produce perverse results."[4]

In line with this literature, my findings suggest that while external pressure *can* measurably impact repressive states' behavior, it *cannot* elicit compliance with international standards. The evidence presented in the previous chapters shows that international pressure is far more likely to prompt the creation of sham institutions than true fulfillment of human rights obligations.

In the context of accountability for mass atrocities, quasi-compliance often takes the form of underpowered commissions of inquiry. While these institutions may purport to seek accountability, they often preclude it. What's more, the inadequacy of these institutions is easily apparent to engaged international audiences. Thus, Human Rights Watch's response to the work of Burma's so-called independent commission of enquiry: "The commission appears to admit just enough to try to placate international opinion, which has overwhelmingly concluded that crimes against humanity and even genocide occurred, while shielding senior military commanders who planned and ordered atrocities."[5] Likewise, the International Commission of Jurists, upon Nepal's creation of a new commission of inquiry, immediately identified it as one more example of a known type: "instead of providing justice to victims and survivors, the commissions have effectively shielded perpetrators."[6]

Yet as Philip Alston notes, despite their often obviously disingenuous intent, "attempts to use commissions to avoid rather than advance accountability often succeed."[7] The previous chapter showed how states that are unwilling to pursue justice use these institutions as a coalition-blocking mechanism, essentially giving sympathetic peer states the political cover to act as veto points on multilateral efforts to enforce the accountability norm. And even if more engaged audiences remain critical, their advocacy may still be shaped by the presence of these institutions, whether that means calling on the quasi-compliant state to strengthen them or simply deciding to see how an obviously inadequate domestic process plays out before ramping up their criticism again.

Even temporarily defusing pressure can be a very valuable outcome for a post-atrocity government. But there are wider-ranging potential impacts of how quasi-compliance is received by international audiences, including measurable effects on the content of the obligation to provide accountability and the benchmarks for compliance. We can see these dynamics at play in the case of the Democratic Republic of the Congo discussed in chapter 5.

The limited prosecutions of sexual violence crimes in the Kivus are an instance in which behavior that doesn't look much like accountability appears to have been accepted as sufficient by many members of the international community. Even though these trials have failed to target high-level perpetrators, meet international fair trial standards, or provide justice to the victims, they have been welcomed as meaningful progress toward justice for mass atrocities. For the DRC, the benefits of being treated as compliant rather than intransigent are obvious: avoiding penalties for noncompliance and enjoying continued positive relationships with international organizations and donor governments.

Outside of the DRC, the implications are less clear. Contestation over quasi-compliant accountability behavior can send important signals about what behavior will be considered acceptable going forward. As Mona Lena Krook and Jacqui True point out, norms are not fixed targets, but "works-in-progress."[8] They are continually evolving as a result of the "constitutive force of contestatory practice."[9] And at times, norm violators are able to "establish a new sense of what is appropriate,"[10] effectively modifying the norm.

It does not strain credulity to think that a future postatrocity government might look to the DRC's example as evidence that a handful of prosecutions of low-ranking soldiers, accompanied by protestations of good faith and limited capacity, are an adequate accountability response to mass atrocity. This example suggests that what type of institution will be acceptable, who must be tried, for what crimes, and with what protections in place are all live issues for international audiences enforcing the obligation to provide accountability for mass atrocities.

Practically speaking, what has been required of states (i.e., what they have been pressured by international audiences to do) in the accountability context has varied enormously over time. In 1996, when the South African Truth and Reconciliation Commission began its work, it was heralded as a vindication of the rights of the victims of apartheid violence. By contrast, in 2014 Nepal met with immediate criticism from international human rights groups for proposing a similar truth and reconciliation commission that would allow the perpetrators of international crimes to receive amnesty in return for testifying.[11] Similarly, while in the 1980s the trials of a handful of high-level perpetrators were considered major progress in the fight against impunity, recent debates about postatrocity justice have emphasized the need to prosecute a "representative" set of crimes, i.e., ensuring that it's not only one type of perpetrator or victim who has their day in court.

And while some of this variation reflects the requirements of the obligation becoming more stringent over time, the progression is not smooth. Nicole Deitelhoff and Lisbeth Zimmermann argue that "the more norms involve positive duties (which demand proactive behavior from actors), the more contestation of their application is to be expected."[12] The obligation to provide accountability is exactly this type of norm, and this produces dynamics that are not captured by traditional accounts of norm life cycles.[13] Rather than a unidirectional "cascade" of a single standard, its development reflects Krook and True's characterization of "trajectories . . . fraught with contestation and reversals."[14] The result is that the substantive requirements that states will be pressured to comply with are in some sense a moving target and their exact contours may be indeterminate at any given moment.

Illustrating this fraught trajectory, South Africa continues to peddle the truth and reconciliation commission approach as an alternative to prosecutions, despite consistent messaging from international courts and human rights NGOs that amnesties are unlawful. In 2013 and 2014, South African officials met several times with members of the Sri Lankan government to discuss how they might implement such a mechanism. Similarly, following the revolutions in North Africa, Spanish diplomats encouraged the new government in Tunisia to follow Spain's example of letting the crimes of the past go in order to move forward.

It is not entirely clear what position these alternate models operate vis-à-vis the accountability norm. Per Alan Bloomfield and Shirley V. Scott, South Africa and Spain might be "norm antipreneurs," acting to "prevent the accumulation of precedents which would otherwise strengthen" the accountability norm.[15] Arguably, these models constitute an emerging practice, which, if it is not framed as noncompliance, would contribute to weakening the accountability norm.[16] Their proponents might even be acting intentionally to create what Clifford Bob calls "counter-norms."[17]

The impact of noncompliance is made more complex by the fact that "gold standard" compliance with the obligation to provide accountability for mass atrocity remains quite rare. Even in cases of extensive cooperation with the international community, the degree to which the obligation to prosecute those most responsible for the most serious crimes has been fully met has been low. It's therefore fair to say that while the legal obligation to try those most responsible for the more serious international crimes has remained constant for decades, all justice mechanisms, even those understood as fully compliant with the norm, fall somewhat short of this ideal.

For example, in the case of Cambodia discussed in chapter 3, despite a fully hybridized court set up by the United Nations at the invitation of the government to try Khmer Rouge crimes, the domestic and international constituencies have not been able to agree on who should be prosecuted. Efforts by the international staff to issue indictments of still-powerful individuals have been blocked by the Cambodian government. The difficulties of pursuing justice under these conditions led to the resignation of four international investigating judges in five years.

Nevertheless, Cambodia is treated as a case in which accountability has been provided, in part, perhaps because it sits in comparison to all the cases in which politics has prevented *any* action from being taken.

States look to past examples of international reaction to determine what they can get away with. As the examples above show, the set of behaviors that will be practically treated as "in compliance" with a given human rights obligation is likely larger than what the on-paper rule requires. Even where on-paper rules are clear, ambiguity can persist about what behavior will be treated as "good enough" and what behavior will be punished. Thus, the unevenness of enforcement in the international system not only creates uncertainty about the risks of noncompliance; it also creates uncertainty about what international human rights standards actually require.

Because acquiescence by international audiences to questionable behavior essentially certifies it as compliance, these dynamics in turn influence rules' development and life cycle through their effect on their clarity and content. This contributes to the indeterminacy of human rights obligations, providing fertile ground for future contestations over their meaning and the benchmarks for compliance. It also creates opportunities for strategic behavior, including the promotion of counternorms. This adds to the appeal of quasi-compliance as a strategy; there's always the chance that such an approach won't just be allowed to slide but will actually redefine compliance.

In 2016 and 2017, I spent several weeks in northeastern Sri Lanka, talking to members of the war-affected Tamil community about justice, memory, and reconciliation. These conversations took place on the porches of homes, in politicians' offices, at churches, outside temples, and amidst the makeshift roadside encampments where families of the disappeared sat protesting the government's inaction on transitional justice. Many were conducted with a wary eye for agents of the state, whose pervasive presence chills Tamils' free expression of their opinions about the postwar status quo and their hopes for the future.

But the people I met were eager to share their views, nearly all of which boiled down to a deep skepticism about the prospects for change. "The government is not serious" said one activist, referring to the promises Sri Lanka's new government had made to the UN Human Rights Council in 2015.[18] Others pointed to Sri Lanka's long history of window dressing accountability institutions. Some family members of the disappeared estimated that they had submitted information about their missing loved ones as many as fifty times to previous commissions, police stations, and government officials.[19] These experiences had left them exhausted and disheartened.

The survivors I spoke with saw very clearly the disconnect between Sri Lanka's assurances abroad and its actions at home. None seemed surprised that the government had failed to act on its transitional justice commitments. "How can those responsible prosecute themselves?" one activist asked rhetorically.[20] Even people who had been protesting in the road for months downplayed any expectation that the government would respond to their demands. Instead, they saw themselves as speaking to a different audience: Western policy makers and international organizations who might put pressure on Sri Lanka. "It has to have an effect" said one long-time human rights worker. "At least let the international community know what's happening."[21]

For victim communities like Sri Lanka's Tamils, who continue to suffer under the repressive rule of those who committed atrocities against them, the international community often feels like their only hope. And so their activism focuses on calls for international action: for sanctions, for UNHRC resolutions, for reductions in aid and trade. But more than anything else they seek attention, a place on the international agenda, and the designation of their persecutors as human rights abusers.

The people I speak with in northeast Sri Lanka are impassive when I ask for their consent to include what they tell me in academic publications. But when I tentatively suggest that I might also use some of it in a newspaper or magazine article, they brighten. They want more white people to know about them, one woman explained in 2017. In Sri Lanka, and elsewhere, I hear again and again: "Tell your government."

In the process of conducting and writing up the research for this book, I presented it often. On panels with names like "The Politics of Transitional Justice" and "The Future of R2P," I've spoken about the barriers to accountability for atrocities when repressive regimes remain in power. I explain that the fight for justice is often long and inconclusive, that perpetrators never prosecute themselves, and that the repeated failure to protect or avenge the victims of mass atrocities is a feature, not a bug, of the international system. In academic settings, I am often the only presenter speaking from experience as a human rights lawyer and activist. In practitioner settings, I am often the only one whose conclusions are drawn from years of research. Inevitably, the question is directed to me: "But what should we do?"

We: the victims and survivors, their advocates and allies.

Even though I'm expecting it, it's not a question that can be answered in a 90 second Q&A response. Mostly, I try to make clear that I understand why they're asking. And that my findings don't mean that we should abandon the pursuit of justice.

Here is what I wish I had time to tell them:

External pressure will never convince perpetrator regimes to prosecute their own. Never. Absent the threat of invasion, the stakes of international opprobrium cannot compete with the stakes of domestic politics. Under heavy international pressure, the most perpetrator regimes will do is create quasi-compliant institutions. But that doesn't mean naming and shaming tactics or "unrealistic" absolutist advocacy positions have no value. It's true they won't materially affect perpetrator regimes' disincentives to provide justice for mass atrocities. However, they can have powerful demonstration effects.

The value of making unrealistic demands becomes clear when we consider the consequences of not making them. Take the dilemma activists faced in 2017–2018 over whether to push for a Security Council referral of the Rohingya crisis to the ICC. Critics of the approach rightly pointed out that it was a nonstarter, given China's support for Burma and Russia's statements that it would veto any future ICC referrals. Even if one did miraculously pass, they added, it would be toothless and unlikely to materially increase the chances of prosecution of those most responsible for atrocities against the Rohingya.[22]

But, however flawed of a prospect it is, UN Security Council action is the primary mechanism that exists for pursuing accountability for atrocities committed by non-ICC member states.[23] Failing to pursue the option risked signaling to the Rohingya victims of Burmese atrocities that their suffering is less worthy of international concern than that of victims in Darfur, Syria, or Libya. Not only that, but abandoning the effort to get such an obviously qualifying case—one of truly horrific atrocities bearing the hallmarks of genocide—to the ICC would have downstream effects, potentially further undermining an already deficient and poorly entrenched system.

Unrealistic demands can also be part of an effective advocacy strategy aimed at third-party state audiences. Chapter 6 showed that repressive regimes can use their peer states as a shield against international censure. The success of these tactics relies on the fig leaf that quasi-compliance offers to spare third-party states the embarrassment of being associated with an unambiguous rights abuser. Even if they go unmet, loud and cohesive demands for international recognition of a genocide, for referral to the ICC, or for sanctions can increase third-party states' potential reputational consequences for supporting atrocity perpetrators.

This analysis is *not* analogous to the classic bargaining advice that it's strategically sound to make maximalist demands because you'll land at a compromise position. I am not suggesting that "unrealistic" asks like ICC referrals are an effective tactic through which to wring lesser concessions from the international community. They aren't. Rather, because of the complex context in which victims' pursuit of justice plays out, their demands have impacts on audiences other than those to whom they're addressed. They can therefore produce valuable results through indirect paths.

Because advocacy asks like Security Council action are unlikely to lead to justice directly, victims and their allies should pair these demands with other tactics. The evidence presented in this book shows that domestic support is a necessary precondition for robust accountability exercises. This is not something victims will have an easy time effecting themselves, particularly in contexts where they are a marginalized minority and the dominant group opposes transitional justice. However, they can push civil society allies from the majority community to take this up with their coethnics, they can ask international NGOs to pursue it in their advocacy, and they can lobby for Western governments to include education and sensitization about atrocities as a priority in their funding and capacity building for local civil society.

Also, having elite members of accountability-resistant communities acknowledge atrocities and the need for justice can be an important step toward transforming public attitudes. Those engaged in advocacy with Western governments can push those governments to more vocally support soft-liners in perpetrator-aligned postatrocity regimes. This may understandably be an unpalatable move for victims' representatives to make so is likely better left to their international allies, but we know from the study of transitional societies that it is usually in-group elites who are most able to effect change. International recognition of officials who have signaled a commitment to pursuing accountability can strengthen their position in internal power struggles. This can help ensure that justice doesn't fall off the agenda when international attention moves on.

Finally, even (or perhaps especially) in situations where domestic and international politics make the chances of justice advocacy's success very slim, victims and their allies can and should work to document atrocities and preserve evidence. This is no simple task when perpetrators remain in power. The state may surveil and intimidate victims and witnesses, restrict access to massacre sites, or even criminalize allegations of war crimes. In such contexts, evidence of atrocities can be extremely dangerous to collect and possess. But gathering it and keeping it safe—while working to chip away at international tolerance for impunity and pushing those actors who can affect domestic sentiment to commit to doing so—is one of the most effective ways to increase the chances that perpetrators will be held accountable for mass atrocities.

This is slow and frustrating work. But it's worth remembering that justice for atrocities is, in some sense, unnatural. Shifting conditions of impunity requires a herculean effort and weak institutions and absent or inconsistent political will at the international level do little to mitigate this. Nevertheless, victims and their allies have managed it, often after decades-long campaigns of what appeared to be futile efforts. The absence of an easy path to justice doesn't mean there's no way to get there from here.

I teach aspiring human rights advocates and activists. My job is to train them in international law and research methods, but I also try to help them think through what it means to do this work. We talk about critiques of the human rights movement, about positionality and the white savior complex, and about the personal challenges of a career in human rights. The question they ask most frequently is: "when does it stop affecting you?" What they mean is: When will they be able to read firsthand accounts of torture without curling their fingernails into their palms to protect them from phantom pliers? When will the shock and nausea be replaced with professional detachment?

I tell them: Never.

I often find myself talking to people about the worst thing that ever happened to them. Some of the worst things, in fact, that have ever happened to anyone. These conversations are hard. It's hard not to cry when the person you're speaking to breaks down in the middle of a story of unimaginable loss. It's hard not to feel you've done something unconscionable by asking her to relive it. It's hard not to feel weak and self-absorbed for struggling to get through the interaction when you're not the one who's survived a genocide. And it's hard to figure out how to carry it with you and return to your "normal" life. But it's hardest when the people you speak to have no hope.

The takeaway of this book is that justice for mass atrocities is rare and the political obstacles to achieving it are difficult to surmount. But those of us whose research lays bare how the odds are stacked against the victims can't leave it at that. Sometimes the prospect of justice is the only thing keeping people going after the horrors they've experienced. Taking that from them would be unconscionable. So, we have to think seriously about the potentially demoralizing impact of our findings and about what hope we can give in return.

Fortunately, it's not insignificant. Because it's only through understanding the barriers to change—their sources, their shape, and their weight—that we can craft effective strategies to shift them. Ultimately, that means that being clear-eyed and precise about the challenge is not a pessimistic position, but a more solid ground upon which to build a hopeful activism.

APPENDIX A

TABLE A.1 List of atrocity-producing events

1. North Korean dictatorship	2. Burmese civil war	3. Colombian Civil War	4. Military dictatorships (South Korea)	5. First Sudanese Civil War	6. Gaddafi regime (Libya)
7. Black September (Jordan)	8. Guatemalan Civil War	9. Idi Amin regime (Uganda)	10. Pakistan v. Bengals	11. Hutu rebellion and genocide (Burundi)	12. Pinochet regime (Chile)
13. Pakistan v. Baluchi separatists	14. Ethiopia vs. Eritrean rebels	15. Communist reprisals (Vietnam)	16. Indonesian occupation of East Timor	17. Hmong genocide (Laos)	18. Lebanese Civil War
19. Angolan Civil War	20. Khmer Rouge (Cambodia)	21. Dirty War (Argentina)	22. Red Terror (Ethiopia)	23. Khad killings (Afghanistan)	24. Sandinista rebellion (Nicaragua)
25. Ethiopia vs. TLF	26. Salvadoran Civil War	27. Mozambique Civil War	28. Soviet war in Afghanistan	29. Palmyra prison massacre	30. Garissa massacre
31. Suppression of Kurdish rebellion	32. Iran–Iraq War	33. Suppression of Hama uprising	34. Luwero War	35. Contra War	36. Habré regime
37. Peruvian Civil War	38. Matabeleland	39. Sri Lankan Civil War	40. Second Sudanese Civil War	41. Anti-Sikh pograms	42. Wagalla massacre
43. South Yemen Civil War	44. LRA	45. Sri Lanka vs. JVP II	46. Tiananmen Square massacre	47. Repression of 8/8/88 uprising	48. Somaliland massacres
49. Prison massacres	50. Mass killing of Hutus	51. al-Anfal	52. First Liberian Civil War	53. Nagorno–Karabakh War	54. Cédras regime
55. Croatian independence	56. Somalia Civil War	57. Sierra Leone Civil War	58. Algerian Civil War	59. Attacks on Marsh arabs	60. Bosnian Serbs
61. Tajikistan Civil War	62. Afghanistan Civil War	63. Abkhazia	64. Second Burundi Civil War	65. First Chechen War	66. Rwandan Civil War and genocide
67. Nepalese Civil War	68. Attacks on the refugee camps in Eastern DRC	69. Taliban rule	70. Kosovo	71. Second Congo War	72. East Timor referendum violence
73. Second Liberian Civil War	74. Ituri conflict	75. Second Chechen War	76. Jos riots	77. Gujarat violence	78. Darfur conflict
79. Kivu conflict	80. Andijan massacre	81. Kenyan election crisis	82. Boko Haram uprising	83. Plateau State communal violence	84. Second Ivorian Civil War
85. Libyan Civil War	86. Syrian civil war	87. Northern Mali conflict	88. Rakhine violence	89. Central African Republic	90. ISIS v. Iraq

APPENDIX B

This appendix provides additional discussion of the modeling approach, empirical results, and robustness checks underlying the statistical analysis presented at the end of chapter 4. As explained in the chapter, the role of these results is not to prove (or more properly, falsify) the theoretical argument, but to identify broad patterns meriting qualitative analysis and to motivate case selection. I strongly considered omitting the quantitative analysis from the book entirely (given disciplinary norms regarding causal identification), but a scholarly monograph is, in some sense, a memoir of the research process, and compiling and analyzing these data played a crucial role in shaping my thinking about post-atrocity governments' accountability behavior. I therefore include them in the interests of transparency about (1) what underlies the conclusions I come to in this book, and (2) the limitations on what these data can actually tell us.

Modeling Approach

The country-year version of the data set takes the former of time-series cross-sectional data with binary dependent variables (BTSCS data) and a mix of binary and continuous predictors. BTSCS data is common in international relations literature and is generally analyzed using logistic regression, which models the effects of changes in the predictor variables on the logit, or natural logarithm, of the odds of the outcome (the probability that the outcome occurs divided by the probability that it does not occur). The probability (π_i) that the outcome variable

(Y) takes a value of 1 can be written as the function of predictor variables x_i with coefficients β:

$$\pi_i = \frac{1}{1 + e^{-x_i\beta}}$$

I follow this convention, with some refinements due to the fact that ordinary logit models treat each observation's outcome as fully independent. This may not be a reasonable assumption in a time series data set like mine that includes repeated observations on the same cases. Failure to account for within-unit dependence can render a logit model inefficient. One way to deal with this problem is to estimate a fixed effects model, which controls for all time-invariant characteristics of the individual. This approach is not ideal for my data, given that I am interested in modeling not only within-unit changes over time but between-unit changes as well and a fixed effects model cannot estimate the effects of time-invariant factors (like the scale of the atrocity) or slowly changing time-variant factors (like a country's CINC score). Additionally, because positive values on my outcome variables are infrequent, a fixed effects approach would ignore the majority of the data. (Note the number of observations in the models reported in table B.1.) This is because units that always score 0 on the outcome variable will be treated as explained by the unit-specific unobservables and dropped from the analysis of the explanatory variables' impact.

The better option for this type of data is a random effects model, which is preferable in that it can estimate within-unit (time-variant) and between-unit (time-invariant) processes as well as the relationships between them. However, using random effects requires that the unit's error term not be correlated with the model's explanatory variables. Hausman tests comparing the fixed effects models with random effects models show that the random effects assumption is met for

TABLE B.1   Fixed effects models

	(1)	(2)	(3)
	DOMESTIC PROSECUTIONS	**TRUTH COMMISSIONS**	**INTERNATIONAL REFERRALS**
Dependency			
Perp in Power			
Polity			
Movement	2.41×10^{18}	0.95	4.53
	(1.415×10^{27})	(0.880)	(5.167)
Observations	362	248	148

SE (eform) in parentheses
***p<0.01, **p<0.05, *p<0.1

the models reported in tables B.2 and B.5 below, which means that the two approaches yield similar results.[1] I additionally control for within-unit unobservables by adding robust standard errors clustered on the atrocity-producing event.

Because accountability events, especially when disaggregated by type, are extremely rare, I also run "rare events logistic regressions" using ReLogit. This is a statistical software package developed to correct for small sample bias, particularly in data sets where "the number of observations is small (under a few thousand) and the events are rare (under 5% or so)" (King and Zeng 1999). With 2,469 observations and only sixty-three total events (~3 percent), my data set qualifies.[2] When ReLogit produces different estimates of a theoretical variable's effect or significance, I report it in the main regression tables as an alternate model.

Results and Robustness Checks

Table B.2 presents the main results showing that the presence of domestic demand, operationalized as the variable *Movement* has a strong positive effect on the likelihood that a postatrocity government initiates prosecutions (in either a domestic or international court) or a truth commission.

Control Variables

There are several control variables included here. First, I attempt to account for prior history. Because domestic prosecutions can follow the creation of international tribunals, I include a dichotomous variable (*Prior Int'l*) for whether an international court has prosecuted any individual in connection with the atrocity. Similarly, because trials may follow truth commissions or other earlier domestic institutions, I include a dichotomous variable (*Prior Domestic*) for whether any prior domestic mechanism exists. Finally, I code a count variable (*Country Count*) of the number of accountability mechanisms that have been put in place (for any atrocity) to capture any country-level effects.

I include a logged death count (*Scale*) to control for the scale of the atrocity and dummies to control for regional effects. Because it makes sense to expect that accountability must wait until an atrocity ends, I include a dichotomous variable (*Atrocity Ongoing*) indicating whether the atrocity-producing event in question has ended. Governments might also be reluctant to supply accountability for past abuses while engaged in activities that may themselves trigger calls for justice, so I add a variable (*Civil War*) indicating whether a civil war (using the intrastate wars identified in the Correlates of War list) involving government forces was ongoing

TABLE B.2 Determinants of accountability

	(1)	(2)	(3)
	MODEL 1	MODEL 2	MODEL 3
Movement	2.08***	2.34***	2.14***
	(0.417)	(0.464)	(0.494)
Polity			0.10**
			(0.049)
Scale			0.28*
			(0.149)
Atrocity Ongoing			0.07
			(0.670)
Civil War			0.14
			(0.573)
Prior Int'l		0.88	
		(0.795)	
Prior Domestic		0.01	
		(0.731)	
Country Count		−0.59	
		(0.441)	
Duration	No	Yes	Yes
N	2,469	2,469	2,234
Akaike Information Criterion (AIC)	277.093	278.8077	228.8941

Robust standard errors in parentheses
*** $p < 0.01$, ** $p < 0.05$, * $p < 0.1$

on the state's territory in that year. I also include a measure of regime type (*Polity*) using the Polity2 scores (scaled from −10 to 10) from the Polity IV project.[3]

Finally, it's plausible that time matters. Surviving in a state of impunity for twenty years may make the likelihood of experiencing an accountability event much less likely at year 21 than it was at year 1. I therefore include year dummies, a year counter, and a log transformation measuring the time elapsed since the beginning of the atrocity to permit checks of duration dependency.

As table B.2 shows, the effect of demand is robust to the inclusion of variables associated with prior history in model 2 and to the inclusion of time-invariant and time-variant controls in model 3. The coefficients on duration are not reported because the data do not exhibit duration dependency. The variable included in this model and the models of other outcome variables in subsequent sections is the simple duration count of years in the data set. Neither the log transformation nor the lowess function were significant in any model, nor did they improve the fit of any model.

The effect of demand is also robust to the inclusion of year dummies, none of which have a significant effect. Nor do any of the region dummies have a significant effect, nor do they improve the fit of the controlled models. (See table B.3)

The positive effect of *Polity* is significant and its inclusion improves the fit of the model. We might expect that domestic movements should have stronger effects in more democratic societies, so I test a model including a variable interacting *Movement* and *Polity* (table B.4). The interaction term is not significant,

TABLE B.3 Accountability with region dummies

	(1)
	FULL
Movement	2.14***
	(0.408)
Region = 1	0.47
	(0.451)
Region = 2	−0.63
	(0.526)
Region = 3	0.03
	(0.834)
Region = 4	0.24
	(0.500)
Observations	2,469

Robust standard errors in parentheses
***p<0.01, **p<0.05, *p<0.1

TABLE B.4 Interaction test

	(1)	(2)
	MODEL 1	**MODEL 2**
Movement	1.95***	1.85***
	(0.508)	(0.647)
Polity	0.06*	−0.00
	(0.039)	(0.050)
Polity × Movement		0.11
		(0.088)
N	2,234	2,234
Akaike Information Criterion (AIC)	227.4034	228.1919

Robust standard errors in parentheses
***p<0.01, **p<0.05, *p<0.1

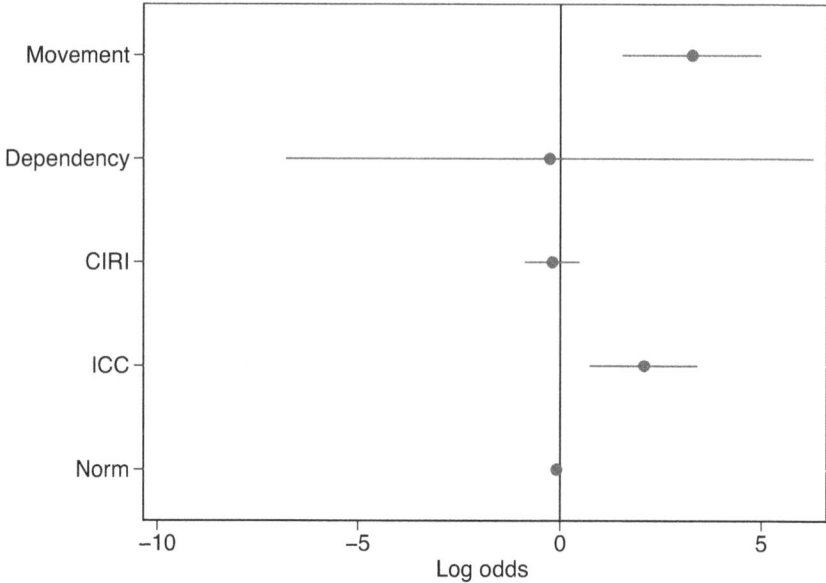

FIGURE B.1. Alternative explanations for accountability

suggesting that the positive effect of demand on the prospect of prosecutions is fairly constant across regime types.

Figure B.1 considers alternate explanations. To proxy for judicial capacity, I use the Cingranelli-Richards Human Rights Data Project's judicial independence indicator (*CIRI*), which comprises a discrete scale of 0 (not independent), 1 (partially independent), and 2 (generally independent). To test a straightforward story of norm entrenchment, I include as a simple proxy for the accountability norm's life cycle (*Norm*) a count of years since 1970 to allow a test of the hypothesis that as the norm becomes stronger, accountability becomes more likely. I also add a lagged dummy variable for ICC membership (*ICC*) to account for a potential corollary to the *Justice Cascade* story: the possibility that "good," law-abiding governments that have signed on to the Rome Statute and accepted the ICC's jurisdiction will be more likely to supply accountability.[4] (Alternately, they will be scared by the prospect of ICC prosecutions into taking action themselves.)

The insignificant result for judicial capacity is stable to an alternate specification that using the Political Risk Services Group's law and order index (*PRS*), which is scored on a continuous 0- to 6-point scale and is the additive result of two components assessing "the strength and impartiality of the legal system" and "popular observance of the law" each on a 0- to 3-point scale.[5] Likewise, the nonresults on the norm's life cycle are robust to (1) relaxing the monotonic assumption with a log transformation of the count of years elapsed, and (2) substitution with a post-1989 dummy (i.e., after the first set of Latin American transitional justice examples).

Turning to the determinants of quasi-compliant accountability behavior, figures B.2 and B.3 visually represent the relationship between dependency on Western aid and the likelihood that a postatrocity government will create quasi-compliant accountability institutions.

Table B.5 presents the results of the regression (model 1) used to generate this figure.

Dependency and *Polity* are both positively and significantly associated with quasi-compliance and robust to the inclusion of controls. The result on *Perp in Power* ties is less stable: it loses significance when controls are added (model 2) but regains it in the controlled ReLogit model (model 3). None of the region dummies had a significant impact (table B.6), so they are not included in the models. However, *Dependency* loses its significance when included in a model with all the region dummies (which drops a number of cases). When the empty categories are omitted (increasing the N), P > |z| = 0.054 in the random effects logit and 0.031 in the ReLogit (models 2 and 3 of table B.6, respectively).

The significance of the *Polity* variable in models 1 and 3 of table B.5 indicates that the likelihood of quasi-compliance increases with level of democracy. When we break up Polity scores into regime type coding we see that quasi-compliant mechanisms are almost never implemented under autocracy (1 in 894 autocracy

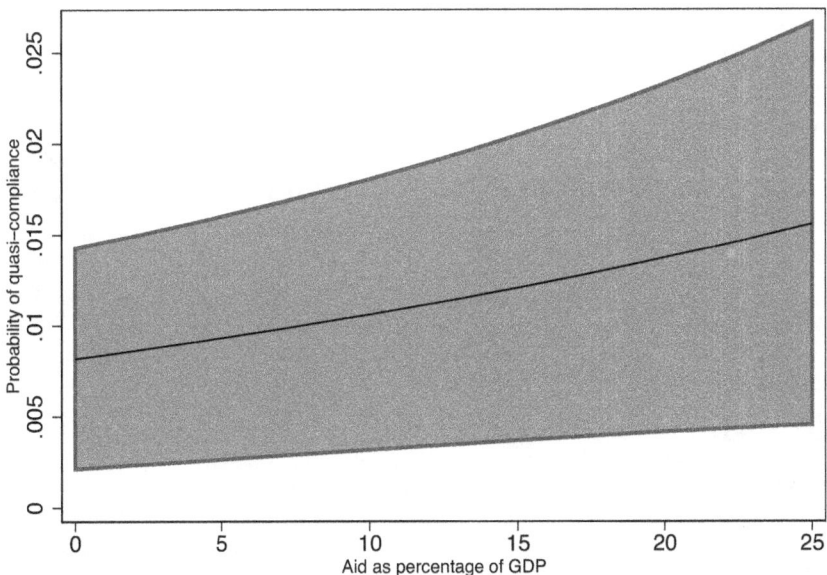

FIGURE B.2. Effects of dependency on quasi-compliance, predictive margins

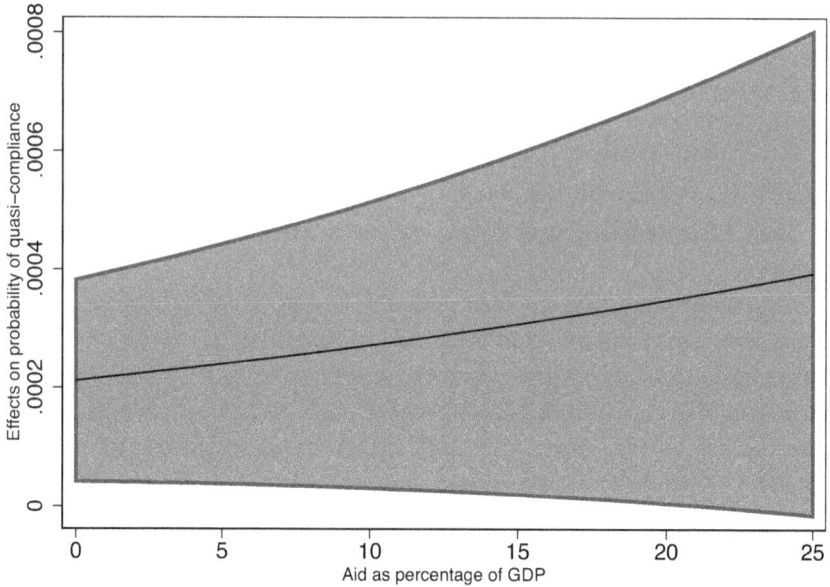

FIGURE B.3. Effects of dependency on quasi-compliance, average marginal effects

TABLE B.5 Determinants of quasi-compliance

	(1)	(2)	(3)
	MODEL 1	**MODEL 2**	**MODEL 3**
Dependency	2.65***	2.18**	3.16***
	(0.858)	(1.033)	(1.219)
Perp in Power	1.76***	1.36	1.54**
	(0.598)	(0.863)	(0.600)
Polity	0.19***	0.20***	0.19***
	(0.052)	(0.043)	(0.033)
Scale		0.04	0.01
		(0.161)	(0.138)
Atrocity Ongoing		0.19	0.70
		(0.716)	(0.575)
Civil War		0.06	0.18
		(0.519)	(0.450)
Duration	No	Yes	Yes
ReLogit	No	No	Yes
N	1,824	1,824	1,824
Akaike Information Criterion (AIC)		255.2446	260.3128

Robust standard errors in parentheses
***p<0.01, **p<0.05, *p<0.1

TABLE B.6 Quasi-compliance with region dummies

	(1)	(2)	(3)
	MODEL 1	MODEL 2	MODEL 3
Dependency	7.47	7.11*	15.23**
	(13.940)	(7.234)	(19.271)
Perp in Power	6.38***	6.03***	6.32***
	(3.529)	(3.275)	(2.702)
Polity	1.21***	1.22***	1.20***
	(0.067)	(0.060)	(0.042)
Region = 1	1.87		
	(1.451)		
Region = 2	1.25		
	(1.016)		
Region = 3	0.40		
	(0.529)		
Region = 4, omitted	—		
Africa		2.93*	2.25
		(1.707)	(1.197)
Asia		1.92	2.39*
		(1.476)	(1.239)
Observations	1,732	1,824	1,824

SE (eform) in parentheses
***$p<0.01$, **$p<0.05$, *$p<0.1$

years), but are fairly evenly spread between democracies and nondemocracies (16/820 and 18/755, respectively). But, as figure B.4 shows, an interaction of regime type with dependency is not significant, suggesting that the effect of dependency is relatively constant across different regime types. Nor are the effects of dependency markedly different when perpetrators are in power than when they aren't (figure B.5).

As noted in chapter 4, an alternate measure of aid dependency, *ODA GNI*, returns very similar results to those reported above, suggesting that the result is not sensitive to the coding of *Dependency* (table B.7).

By contrast, substituting aid in absolute terms using *Total Aid* returns very different results.

This makes sense. We would not expect these results to run in the same direction as those for *Dependency* because total aid flows reflect very different dynamics: for instance, the size of the recipient state and potentially its standing in the international community. In fact, the effects for *Total Aid* are small and negative.

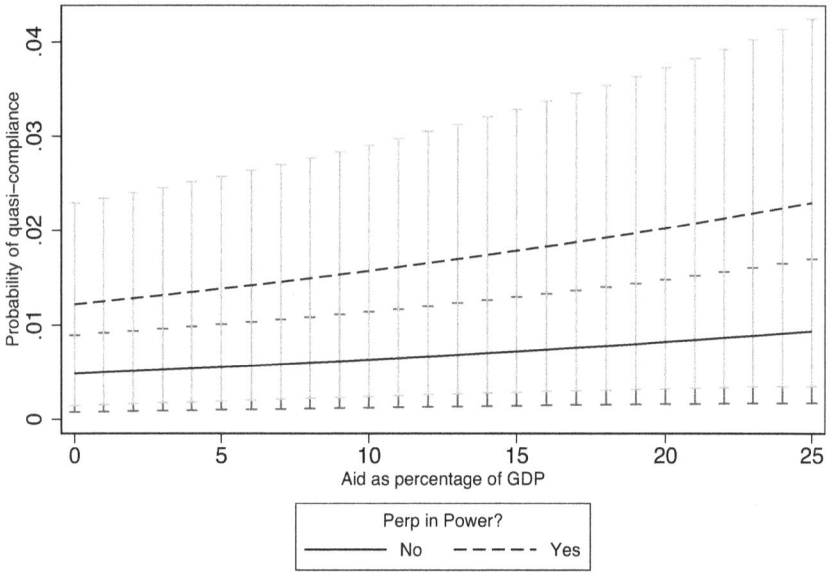

FIGURE B.4. Conditional effects of dependency given perpetrator ties

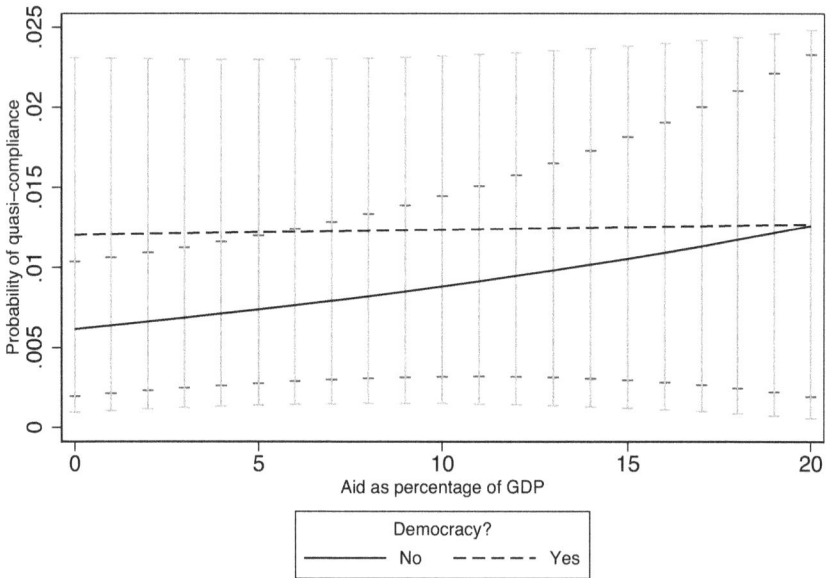

FIGURE B.5. Conditional effects of dependency given regime type

TABLE B.7 Determinants of quasi-compliance with alternate dependency coding

	(1)	(2)	(3)	(4)
	MODEL 1	MODEL 2	MODEL 3	MODEL 4
ODA GNI	1.01***	1.02***	1.01**	1.02**
	(0.004)	(0.007)	(0.005)	(0.007)
Perp in Power	5.77***	7.14***	3.77	4.54**
	(3.461)	(3.154)	(3.236)	(2.745)
Polity	1.21***	1.21***	1.22***	1.20***
	(0.062)	(0.040)	(0.050)	(0.039)
Scale			1.04	1.02
			(0.170)	(0.143)
Atrocity Ongoing			1.22	2.05
			(0.861)	(1.188)
Civil War			1.05	1.18
			(0.541)	(0.528)
Duration	No	No	Yes	Yes
ReLogit	No	Yes	No	Yes
Observations	1,777	1,777	1,777	1,777

Robust SE (eform) in parentheses
***$p<0.01$, **$p<0.05$, *$p<0.1$

TABLE B.8 Effects of total aid on quasi-compliant accountability responses

	(1)	(2)	(3)	(4)
	MODEL 1	MODEL 2	MODEL 3	MODEL 4
Total Aid	1.00**	1.00**	1.00**	1.00*
	(0.001)	(0.000)	(0.001)	(0.000)
Perp in Power	5.57**	7.62***	3.84	4.75**
	(3.795)	(3.777)	(3.361)	(2.887)
Polity	1.26***	1.26***	1.29***	1.26***
	(0.070)	(0.052)	(0.060)	(0.046)
Scale			1.05	1.01
			(0.182)	(0.149)
Atrocity Ongoing			0.94	1.51
			(0.642)	(0.849)
Civil War			1.09	1.32
			(0.546)	(0.575)
Duration	No	No	Yes	Yes
ReLogit	No	Yes	No	Yes
Observations	2,142	2,142	2,142	2,142

Robust SE (eform) in parentheses
***$p<0.01$, **$p<0.05$, *$p<0.1$

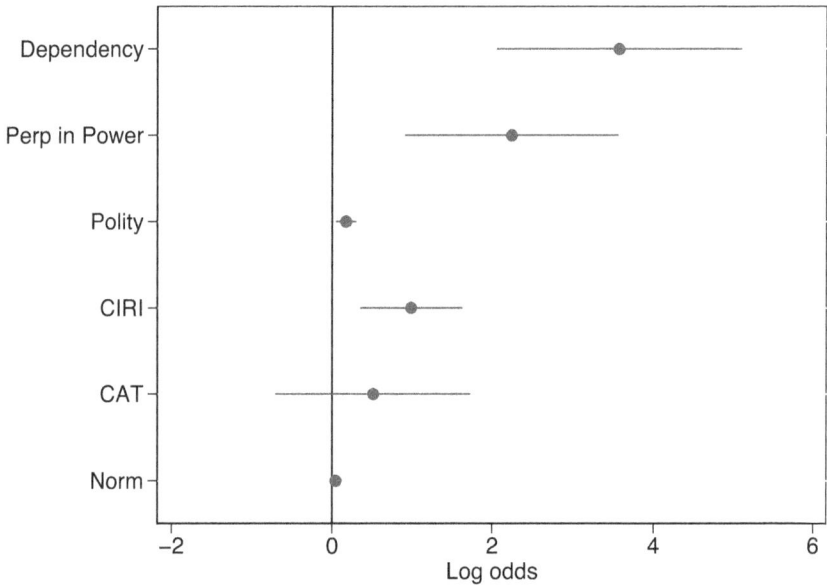

FIGURE B.6.   Determinants of quasi-compliance, testing alternate explanations

Figure B.6 supports the conclusion in chapter 4 that dependency outperforms alternate explanations for quasi-compliant accountability behavior.

Because the key expectation of my argument is that postatrocity governments create quasi-compliant institutions when they feel vulnerable to international enforcement, I check that the results are not tied to particular conceptualization of the theoretical variable of vulnerability. I therefore replicate the models using the Composite Index of National Capabilities from the Correlates of War National Material Capabilities dataset (v4.0) (*CINC*). Because a state's *CINC* score is a rough measure of its power in the international system, we would expect the effect to run in the opposite direction of *Dependency*, that is, the higher a postatrocity state's *CINC* score, the less likely it should be to select quasi-compliance. Predictably, the impact of *CINC*, as shown in table B.9, is negative and significant.

The other variables in the model and the controls perform similarly to the way they do when included alongside *Dependency* (table B.5). The same is true for variables associated with alternate explanations (figure B.7).

I run two final tests on samples based on possible scope conditions on the theory. First, because the theory suggests that low domestic demand may be a scope condition on quasi-compliance, I drop the country-years in which domestic movements were actively demanding justice. The results for the new sample (figure B.8) are similar to those reported above.

TABLE B.9 Determinants of quasi-compliance, alternate vulnerability proxy

	(1)	(2)
	MODEL 1	MODEL 2
CINC	0.62***	0.62***
	(0.098)	(0.101)
Perp in Power	4.98***	4.51**
	(2.980)	(2.832)
Polity	1.26***	1.26***
	(0.077)	(0.063)
Scale		1.07
		(0.170)
Atrocity Ongoing		1.18
		(0.768)
Civil War		1.35
		(0.878)
Duration	No	Yes
Observations	1,757	1,757

Robust SE (eform) in parentheses
*** p<0.01, ** p<0.05, * p<0.1

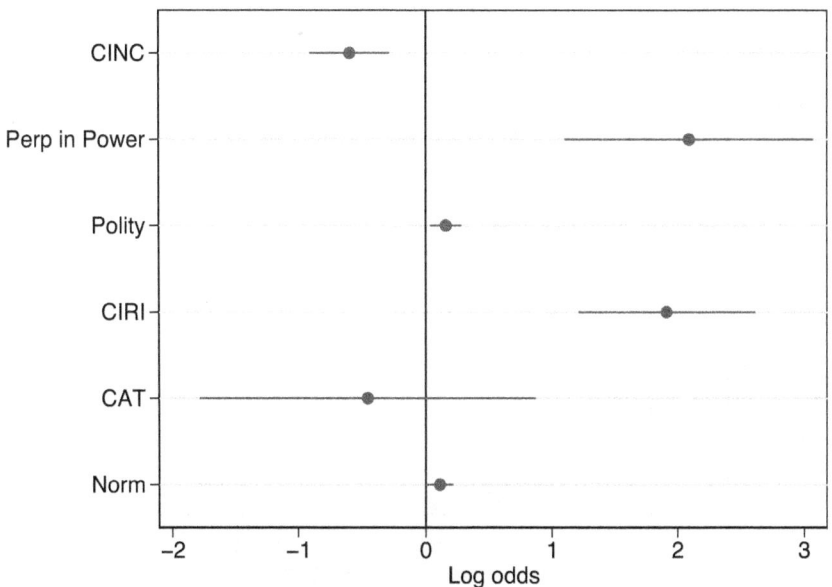

FIGURE B.7. Quasi-compliance alternative explanations with *CINC*

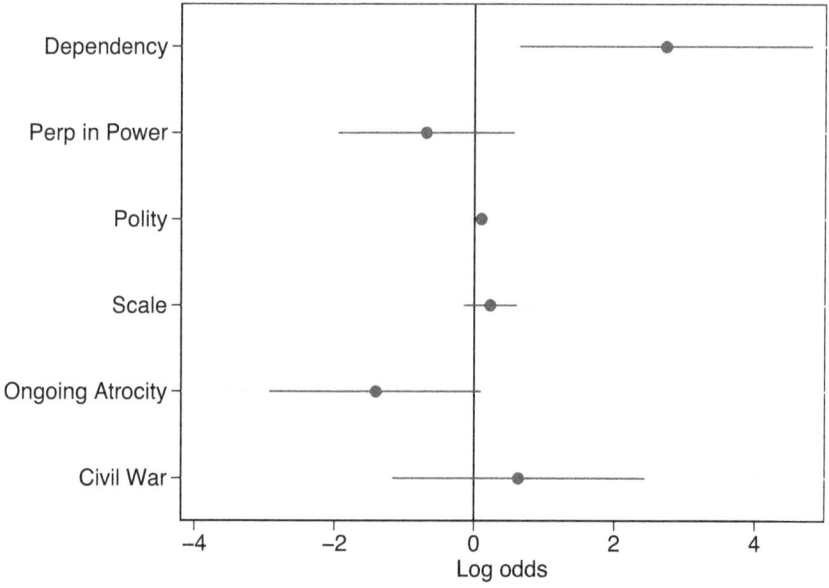

FIGURE B.8. Quasi-compliance in the absence of domestic demand

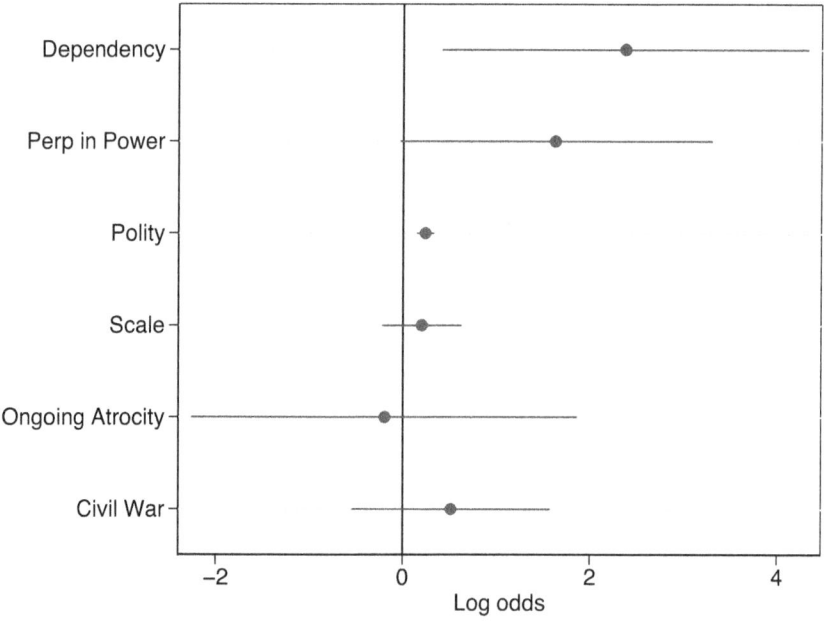

FIGURE B.9. Quasi-compliance post-1989

Among this subset of cases, *Dependency* remains positively and significantly associated with quasi-compliant accountability strategies. *Perp in Power*, however, is not significant, and appears to have a slight negative effect. *Polity* also loses significance, reflecting the correlation between more democratic regime types and the presence of justice movements.

Second, the theory predicts that quasi-compliance will be undertaken in response to international pressure for accountability. But this type of pressure was extremely rare before the 1990s. I therefore run the analysis on a new sample, restricted to the post-1989 period. The effects of the covariates do not change significantly (figure B.9).

Notes

INTRODUCTION

1. Dave Zirin, "Crack Down on Footballers," *Aljazeera*, April 15, 2011.
2. Sharmila Devi, "Medical Community Urged to Defend Bahraini Doctors," *The Lancet* 378, no. 9799 (October 8, 2011): 1287.
3. Human Rights Watch, *Bahrain's Human Rights Crisis* (July 5, 2011).
4. "Bahrain Trials Bear Marks of 'Political Persecution,' Says UN Human Rights Office," *UN News*, June 24, 2011.
5. Human Rights First, *Despite National Dialogue Crackdown Continues in Bahrain* (July 14, 2011).
6. International Crisis Group, *Popular Protest in North Africa and the Middle East (VIII): Bahrain's Rocky Road to Reform* (July 28, 2011).
7. Kingdom of Bahrain, Royal Order no. 28/2011, Art. 1.
8. "Interview with the Foreign Minister of Bahrain," *Al-Arabiya*, November 27, 2011, cited in Mohamed S Helal, "Two Seas Apart: An Account of the Establishment, Operation and Impact of the Bahrain Independent Commission of Inquiry (BICI)," *European Journal of International Law* 30, no. 3 (December 11, 2019): 903–27.
9. "Daily Press Briefing by Mark C. Toner," US Department of State, June 29, 2011; Human Rights Watch, *Bahrain's Human Rights Crisis*.
10. *Report of The Bahrain Independent Commission of Inquiry* (Manama, Bahrain: November 23, 2011).
11. Kenneth Katzman, *Bahrain: Unrest, Security, and U.S. Policy*, US Congressional Research Service Report 95-1013 (May 23, 2019).
12. The National Commission of the Kingdom of Bahrain, "The National Commission Assigned to Follow-up the BICI Recommendations," March 21, 2012.
13. *Report of The Bahrain Independent Commission of Inquiry.*
14. Human Rights Watch, *Bahrain: Vital Reform Commitments Unmet* (March 28, 2012).
15. Americans for Democracy & Human Rights in Bahrain, *Fundamentally Flawed: Bahrain's Prisoners and Detainees Rights Commission* (September 2, 2015).
16. *Behind the Rhetoric: Human Rights Abuses in Bahrain Continue Unabated* (London: Amnesty International, 2015).
17. Cairo Institute for Human Rights Studies, "United Nations Member States Jointly Call on Bahrain to End Rights Violations," June 28, 2012.
18. *Implementation of the Bahrain Independent Commission of Inquiry Report* (Tom Lantos Human Rights Commission, 2012) (testimony of Michael H. Posner).
19. Jawad Fairooz, "State Terrorism: Revoking the Nationality of Citizens in Bahrain: An Affected Person's Perspective," in *The World's Stateless 2020: Deprivation of Nationality* (Institute on Statelessness and Inclusion, March 2020).
20. Human Rights Watch, *Bahrain: Arrest Powers Restored to Abusive Agency* (January 31, 2017).
21. In earlier work, I have called this behavior "human rights half measures." See Kate Cronin-Furman, "Human Rights Half Measures: Avoiding Accountability in Post-War Sri Lanka," *World Politics* 72, no. 1 (2020): 121–63.

22. Hussain Abdulla, "Clueless of Clever? Bahrain's Disregard for the Bahrain Independent Commission of Inquiry," *Huffington Post*, January 25, 2014.

23. "Amnesty: UK 'Utterly Disingenuous' about Human Rights in Bahrain," *The Guardian*, November 21, 2016.

24. Mohamed S. Helal, "Two Seas Apart: An Account of the Establishment, Operation and Impact of the Bahrain Independent Commission of Inquiry (BICI)," *European Journal of International Law* 30, no. 3 (December 11, 2019): 903–27.

25. PBS, "Save Darfur Coalition," *Worse Than War* (blog), March 8, 2010.

26. Amnesty International, "Sudan: Humanitarian Crisis in Darfur caused by Sudan Government's Failures," press release, November 27, 2003.

27. Human Rights Watch, "Darfur Destroyed: Ethnic Cleansing by Government and Militia Forces in Western Sudan," press release, May 7, 2004.

28. Darfur Genocide Accountability Act of 2005, 109th Congress, H.R. 1424.

29. European Union, "Declaration by the Presidency on behalf of the European Union on the report by the International Commission of Inquiry on Darfur" February 7, 2005.

30. "Death in the Ghost House," *Der Spiegel*, August 2, 2004.

31. Human Rights Watch, *Lack of Conviction: The Special Criminal Court on the Events in Darfur* (2006).

32. *Report of the International Commission of Inquiry on Darfur to the United Nations Secretary-General* (Geneva: United Nations, January 25, 2005).

33. Omar al-Bashir finally lost power in 2019 after nearly thirty years as Sudan's president. In 2020, Sudan's new government signaled that it might be willing to send him to the Hague to face trial and engaged in talks with an ICC delegation about a possible transfer. At the time of writing, Bashir was on trial in Sudan over charges relating to the 1989 coup in which he took power.

34. Gary Jonathan Bass, *Stay the Hand of Vengeance: The Politics of War Crimes Tribunals* (Princeton University Press, 2000); Kathryn Sikkink, *The Justice Cascade: How Human Rights Prosecutions Are Changing World Politics*, The Norton Series in World Politics (Norton, 2011).

1. THE POLITICS OF PRESSURE

1. Jess Kelly, "Trump's 'Favorite Dictator' Imprisoned My Husband—To Test Joe Biden," *New York Times*, November 25, 2020, sec. Opinion.

2. Margaret E. Keck and Kathryn Sikkink, *Activists Beyond Borders* (Cornell University Press, 1998).

3. Human Rights Watch, *Egypt: Restrictions on Civic Work Underscored* (April 16, 2021).

4. Emilie Marie Hafner-Burton and James Ron, "Seeing Double: Human Rights Impact Through Qualitative and Quantitative Eyes," *World Politics* 61, no. 2 (2009): 373.

5. See, e.g., Jack Snyder, *Human Rights for Pragmatists: Social Power in Modern Times* (Princeton, NJ: Princeton University Press, forthcoming 2022); Beth A. Simmons, *Mobilizing for Human Rights: International Law in Domestic Politics* (Cambridge University Press, 2009).

6. Amanda M. Murdie and David R. Davis, "Shaming and Blaming: Using Events Data to Assess the Impact of Human Rights INGOs," *International Studies Quarterly* 56, no. 1 (2012): 1–16; James C. Franklin, "Shame on You: The Impact of Human Rights Criticism on Political Repression in Latin America," *International Studies Quarterly* 52, no. 1 (2008): 187–211.

7. Cullen S. Hendrix and W. H. Wong, "When Is the Pen Truly Mighty? Regime Type and the Efficacy of Naming and Shaming in Curbing Human Rights Abuses," *British Journal of Political Science* 43, no. 3 (2013): 651–72.

8. Rochelle Terman and Erik Voeten, "The Relational Politics of Shame: Evidence from the Universal Periodic Review," *Review of International Organizations* 13, no. 1 (March 1, 2018): 1–23.

9. Emilie M. Hafner-Burton, "Sticks and Stones: Naming and Shaming the Human Rights Enforcement Problem." *International Organization* 62, no. 4 (2008): 689–716.

10. Jacqueline H. R. DeMeritt and Courtenay R. Conrad, "Repression Substitution: Shifting Human Rights Violations in Response to UN Naming and Shaming," *Civil Wars* 21, no. 1 (January 2, 2019): 128–52.

11. Caroline L. Payne and M. Rodwan Abouharb, "The International Covenant on Civil and Political Rights and the Strategic Shift to Forced Disappearance," *Journal of Human Rights* 15, no. 2 (April 2, 2016): 163–88.

12. Darius Rejali, *Torture and Democracy* (Princeton University Press, 2007).

13. Kristin M. Bakke, Neil J. Mitchell, and Hannah M. Smidt, "When States Crack Down on Human Rights Defenders," *International Studies Quarterly* 64, no. 1 (March 1, 2020): 85–96.

14. Emilie M. Hafner-Burton and Kiyoteru Tsutsui, "Human Rights in a Globalizing World: The Paradox of Empty Promises," *American Journal of Sociology* 110, no. 5 (2005): 1373–1411.

15. Sonia Cardenas, *Conflict and Compliance: State Responses to International Human Rights Pressure* (University of Pennsylvania Press, 2007); James Raymond Vreeland, "Political Institutions and Human Rights: Why Dictatorships Enter into the United Nations Convention Against Torture," *International Organization* 62, no. 1 (January 2008): 65–101; Oona A. Hathaway, "Do Human Rights Treaties Make a Difference?" *Yale Law Journal* 111 (May 18, 2002); Oona A. Hathaway, "Why Do Countries Commit to Human Rights Treaties?" *Journal of Conflict Resolution* 51, no. 4 (August 1, 2007): 588–621; Todd Landman, "The Political Science of Human Rights," *British Journal of Political Science* 35, no. 3 (2005): 549–72; Jay Goodliffe and Darren G. Hawkins, "Explaining Commitment: States and the Convention against Torture," *Journal of Politics* 68, no. 2 (2006): 358–71; Eric Neumayer, "Do International Human Rights Treaties Improve Respect for Human Rights?" *Journal of Conflict Resolution* 49, no. 6 (2005): 925–53.

16. Hafner-Burton and Tsutsui, "Human Rights in a Globalizing World"; Xinyuan Dai, "Why Comply? The Domestic Constituency Mechanism," *International Organization* 59, no. 2 (2005): 363–98.

17. Heather Smith-Cannoy, *Insincere Commitments: Human Rights Treaties, Abusive States, and Citizen Activism* (Georgetown University Press, 2012), 15.

18. Thomas Risse, Stephen C. Ropp, and Kathryn Sikkink, eds., *The Power of Human Rights: International Norms and Domestic Change*, Cambridge Studies in International Relations (Cambridge: Cambridge University Press, 1999).

19. Beth A. Simmons, "From Ratification to Compliance: Quantitative Evidence on the Spiral Model," in *The Persistent Power of Human Rights: From Commitment to Compliance*, Cambridge Studies in International Relations, ed. Thomas Risse, Stephen C. Ropp, and Kathryn Sikkink (Cambridge: Cambridge University Press, 2013), 43–59.

20. Ronald B. Mitchell, "Compliance Theory: Compliance, Effectiveness, and Behaviour Change in International Environmental Law," in *The Oxford Handbook of International Environmental Law*, 1st ed., ed. Daniel Bodansky, Jutta Brunnée, and Ellen Hey (Oxford University Press, 2008); Lisa Martin, "Against Compliance," in *Interdisciplinary Perspectives on International Law and International Relations: The State of the Art*, ed. Jeffrey L. Dunoff and Mark A. Pollack (Cambridge: Cambridge University Press, 2012).

21. Cardenas, *Conflict and Compliance*, 8.

22. James D. Morrow, "When Do States Follow the Laws of War?" *American Political Science Review* 101, no. 3 (August 2007): 559–72; Cardenas, *Conflict and Compliance*;

Courtney Hillebrecht, "Rethinking Compliance: The Challenges and Prospects of Measuring Compliance with International Human Rights Tribunals," *Journal of Human Rights Practice* 1, no. 3 (November 1, 2009): 362–79.

23. Jennifer M. Dixon, "Rhetorical Adaptation and Resistance to International Norms," *Perspectives on Politics* 15, no. 1 (March 2017): 84; Judith G. Kelley, "Assessing the Complex Evolution of Norms: The Rise of International Election Monitoring," *International Organization* 62, no. 2 (2008): 221–55; Nitza Berkovitch and Neve Gordon, "Differentiated Decoupling and Human Rights," *Social Problems* 63, no. 4 (2016): 499–512.

24. Alexander Cooley and Matthew Schaaf, "Grounding the Backlash: Regional Security Treaties, Counternorms, and Human Rights in Eurasia," in *Human Rights Futures*, ed. Stephen Hopgood, Jack Snyder, and Leslie Vinjamuri (Cambridge: Cambridge University Press, 2017), 166.

25. Saskia Nauenberg Dunkell, "From Global Norms to National Politics: Decoupling Transitional Justice in Colombia," *Peacebuilding* 9, no. 2 (2021): 203.

26. Jelena Subotić, *Hijacked Justice: Dealing with the Past in the Balkans* (Ithaca, NY: Cornell University Press, 2009), 171.

27. Leslie Vinjamuri, "Human Rights Backlash," in *Human Rights Futures*, ed. Stephen Hopgood, Jack Snyder, and Leslie Vinjamuri (Cambridge: Cambridge University Press, 2017), 114–34.

28. This episode is known as the Tampa affair and is considered a defining moment in modern Australian history.

29. Penelope Mathew, "Australian Refugee Protection in the Wake of the Tampa," *American Journal of International Law* 96, no. 3 (2002): 661–76.

30. Convention relating to the Status of Refugees, Geneva, July 25, 1951, *United Nations Treaty Series*, vol. 189, p. 137, Art. 33(1).

31. Convention relating to the Status of Refugees, Art. 31(1).

32. Zoltán I. Búzás, "Evading International Law: How Agents Comply with the Letter of the Law but Violate Its Purpose," *European Journal of International Relations* 23, no. 4 (December 1, 2017): 857–83; see also Zoltán I. Búzás, "Racism and Antiracism in the Liberal International Order," *International Organization* 75, no. 2 (ed 2021): 440–63.

33. Búzás, "Evading International Law," 862.

34. Dixon, "Rhetorical Adaptation and Resistance to International Norms," 86.

35. Dixon, "Rhetorical Adaptation and Resistance to International Norms," 84.

36. Gerald Hill, *The People's Law Dictionary* (New York: MJF, 2002).

37. *Black's Law Dictionary*, 9th ed. (2009), s.v. "quasi-contract," available at Westlaw.

38. Abram Chayes and Antonia Handler Chayes, "On Compliance," *International Organization* 47, no. 2 (1993): 175–205.

39. Wayne Sandholtz and Kendall W. Stiles, *International Norms and Cycles of Change* (Oxford: Oxford University Press, 2009), 323; see also Wayne Sandholtz, *Prohibiting Plunder: How Norms Change* (New York: Oxford University Press, 2007).

40. My discussion of the strategic value of ambiguity here owes an enormous debt to Tonya Putnam's thinking on the subject, some of which is captured in her 2020 International Organization article on international legal obligations. Tonya L. Putnam, "Mingling and Strategic Augmentation of International Legal Obligations," *International Organization* 74, no. 1 (January 13, 2020): 31–64.

41. Mona Lena Krook and Jacqui True, "Rethinking the Life Cycles of International Norms: The United Nations and the Global Promotion of Gender Equality," *European Journal of International Relations* 18, no. 1 (March 1, 2012): 105.

42. Búzás, "Evading International Law," 860.

43. Búzás, "Evading International Law," 860.

44. Cardenas, *Conflict and Compliance.*

45. Subotić, *Hijacked Justice*, 171.

46. The compensation scheme for families of victims of the crackdown alone was budgeted at approximately USD 6.2 million. "Bahrain Making Reforms Progress," *Gulf Daily News*, November 22, 2012. See also Bahrain Independent Commission of Inquiry (BICI), *Implementation by the Government of Bahrain of the Recommendations by the Bahrain Independent Commission of Inquiry* (Bahrain: 2011); Kenneth Katzman, *Bahrain: Unrest, Security, and U.S. Policy*, US Congressional Research Service Report 95-1013 (May 23, 2019).

47. The categories of "likely targets for punishment" and "worst offenders" will not overlap completely because some states remain protected from enforcement by international power dynamics.

48. Chapter 6 provides a detailed case study of how this played out during UN Human Rights Council debates about accountability for atrocities committed at the end of Sri Lanka's civil war.

49. Ronald R. Krebs and Patrick Thaddeus Jackson, "Twisting Tongues and Twisting Arms: The Power of Political Rhetoric," *European Journal of International Relations* 13, no. 1 (March 1, 2007): 35-66. See also Frank Schimmelfennig, "The Community Trap: Liberal Norms, Rhetorical Action, and the Eastern Enlargement of the European Union," *International Organization* 55, no. 1 (2001): 47-80; Margarita H. Petrova, "Rhetorical Entrapment and Normative Enticement: How the United Kingdom Turned from Spoiler into Champion of the Cluster Munition Ban," *International Studies Quarterly* 60, no. 3 (September 2016): 387-99.

50. Michael Barnett, "Culture, Strategy and Foreign Policy Change: Israel's Road to Oslo," *European Journal of International Relations* 5, no. 1 (March 1, 1999): 5-36.

51. Rodger A. Payne, "Persuasion, Frames and Norm Construction," *European Journal of International Relations* 7, no. 1 (March 2001): 37-61.

52. Martha Finnemore, "Legitimacy, Hypocrisy, and the Social Structure of Unipolarity: Why Being a Unipole Isn't All It's Cracked Up to Be," *World Politics* 61, no. 1 (January 2009): 58-85. Stephen D. Krasner, *Sovereignty: Organized Hypocrisy* (Princeton University Press, 1999).

53. Finnemore, "Legitimacy, Hypocrisy, and the Social Structure of Unipolarity"; Marc Lynch, "Lie to Me: Sanctions on Iraq, Moral Argument and the International Politics of Hypocrisy," in *Moral Limit and Possibility in World Politics*, ed. Richard M. Price, Cambridge Studies in International Relations (Cambridge: Cambridge University Press, 2008), 165-96.

54. Jon Elster, "Deliberation and Constitution Making," in *Deliberative Democracy*, ed. Jon Elster, Cambridge Studies in the Theory of Democracy (Cambridge: Cambridge University Press, 1998), 97-122.

55. Lynch, "Lie to Me."

2. THE OBLIGATION TO SEEK JUSTICE

1. Universal jurisdiction is the principle that any country's courts may prosecute serious international crimes like genocide and torture, regardless of where the crime was committed.

2. Human Rights Watch, *Decision on the Hissene Habre Case and the African Union Doc. Assembly/Au/3 (Vii)* (August 2, 2006).

3. UN Committee against Torture, 36th sess., "Communication No. 181/2001: Committee against Torture" (Geneva: UN, May 2006).

4. Questions relating to the Obligation to Prosecute or Extradite (*Belgium v Senegal*), 2012 ICJ 422 (July 20) (judgment).

5. *Ministère Public v Hissein Habré*, Extraordinary African Chambers, judgment of May 30, 2016.

6. Library of Congress, "The United Nations Rome Statute of the International Criminal Court," 2001, https://www.loc.gov/item/lcwaN0018822/.

7. For example, Adam Bower, "Contesting the International Criminal Court: Bashir, Kenyatta, and the Status of the Nonimpunity Norm in World Politics," *Journal of Global Security Studies* 4, no. 1 (January 1, 2019): 88–104; Kathryn Sikkink, *The Justice Cascade: How Human Rights Prosecutions Are Changing World Politics*, The Norton Series in World Politics (Norton, 2011); Jelena Subotić, "Bargaining Justice: A Theory of Transitional Justice Compliance," in *Transitional Justice Theories*, ed. Susanne Buckley-Zistel et al. (London: Routledge, 2013); Louise Mallinder, "Amnesties' Challenge to the Global Accountability Norm? Interpreting Regional and International Trends in Amnesty Enactment," *SSRN Electronic Journal*, 2012.

8. Martha Finnemore and Kathryn Sikkink, "International Norm Dynamics and Political Change," *International Organization* 52, no. 4 (1998): 891. Michelle Jurkovich offers a useful elaboration of this definition: "norms have three essential component parts: (1) a moral sense of 'oughtness' . . . (2) a defined actor 'of a given identity'; and (3) a specific behavior or action expected of that given actor. A norm must also meet the condition that these three component parts are collectively shared within a particular society (distinguishing a norm from an individual's private belief) and that these component parts are sufficiently specific such that it is possible for a violator to be identified." Michelle Jurkovich, "What Isn't a Norm? Redefining the Conceptual Boundaries of 'Norms' in the Human Rights Literature," *International Studies Review* 22, no. 3 (September 1, 2020): 693–711.

9. The fact that the obligation to prosecute existed on paper long before anyone considered it binding reflects the fact that, as Michelle Jurkovich explains, "laws and norms are not the same thing, and the existence of one does not necessarily imply the existence of the other." Jurkovich, "What Isn't a Norm?" 704. We have good examples in the international system where strong norms are codified into weak law (e.g., Sarah V. Percy, "Mercenaries: Strong Norm, Weak Law," *International Organization* 61, no. 2 [April 2007]: 367–97) and conversely, where clear legal rules exist, despite the erosion of the underlying norm (e.g., Rosemary Foot, "Torture: The Struggle over a Peremptory Norm in a Counter-Terrorist Era," *International Relations* 20, no. 2 [June 1, 2006]: 131–51). In the case of the accountability norm, however, this distinction is muddied a bit by the fact that the sense of "oughtness" is almost always framed by advocates and activists through an appeal to international law. I therefore talk about the accountability norm in terms of "perception of a binding legal obligation" throughout this chapter and the rest of the book.

10. International Law Commission. *Historical Survey of the Question of International Criminal Jurisdiction—Memorandum submitted by the Secretary-General*, A/CN.4/7/Rev.1 (April 1949).

11. The simultaneously occurring trials of Japanese war criminals at the International Military Tribunal for the Far East are less frequently emphasized in histories of international justice.

12. Ruti G. Teitel, *Humanity's Law* (New York: Oxford University Press, 2011).

13. Kevin Jon Heller, *The Nuremberg Military Tribunals and the Origins of International Criminal Law* (New York: Oxford University Press, 2011).

14. Gary Jonathan Bass, *Stay the Hand of Vengeance: The Politics of War Crimes Tribunals*, first paperback printing, with a new afterword, 2002, Princeton Studies in International History and Politics (Princeton, NJ: Princeton University Press, 2002).

15. William Schabas, *Unimaginable Atrocities: Justice, Politics, and Rights at the War Crimes Tribunals* (New York: Oxford University Press, 2012).

16. Schabas, *Unimaginable Atrocities*, 53.

17. Schabas, *Unimaginable Atrocities*, 58.

18. Art. IV reads: "Persons committing genocide or any of the other acts enumerated in article III shall be punished, whether they are constitutionally responsible rulers, public officials or private individuals." UN General Assembly, Convention on the Prevention and Punishment of the Crime of Genocide, December 9, 1948, *United Nations Treaty Series*, vol. 78, p. 277.

19. Because General Assembly resolutions tend to reflect the opinion of states about existing law, rather than "making" new law, it is likely that consensus on the existence of this obligation significantly predated the passage of GA Resolution 2840.

20. These numbers are deeply contested; see discussion in chapter 4.

21. Out of eleven hits from the 1950s, six report on international lawmaking in response to Nazi crimes, and five deal with the applicability of international criminal law to aggression by North Korea and the USSR. Of the five hits in 1960s, four relate to Nazi crimes and one editorializes about possible UN war crimes. Of eight hits in the 1970s, there are two for international lawmaking, three for terrorism, one for Pakistani conduct in Bangladesh, one for Vietnamese treatment of ethnic minorities, and one for US involvement in Vietnam (characterizing it as illegal aggression). And of six hits in the 1980s, one celebrates the fortieth anniversary of the Genocide Convention, three discuss terrorists, and two suggest the applicability of international criminal law to the Iran hostage crisis.

22. "A Few Candidates for the Dock," *Chicago Daily Tribune*, December 23, 1961; "World Jurists Want Trial of Pak POWs," *Times of India*, September 7, 1972; "Letter to the Editor: Vietnamese Atrocities Are Like Nazis'," *Chicago Tribune*, June 30, 1979.

23. Eric Bourne, "Opinion: The Nuremberg Precedent," *Christian Science Monitor*, October 9, 1992; Ian Waddell, "A Force to Reckon With: How and Why an International Court Would Help Keep Peace," *Vancouver Sun*, October 10, 1992; Arlen Specter, "Get On With the War Crimes Trials," *Washington Post*, November 9, 1993.

24. The right to an effective remedy is codified in Art. 2(3) of the International Covenant on Civil and Political Rights, Art. 14 of the Convention against Torture, among other core international human rights treaties. In 2005, the United Nations General Assembly adopted the "Basic Principles and Guidelines on the Right to a Remedy and Reparation for Victims of Gross Violations of International Human Rights Law and Serious Violations of International Humanitarian Law," A/RES/60/147.

25. Tai-Heng Cheng, "The Universal Declaration of Human Rights at Sixty: Is It Still Right for the United States," *Cornell International Law Journal* 41, no. 2 (July 1, 2008): 251.

26. Robert Blitt, "Who Will Watch the Watchdogs? Human Rights Nongovernmental Organizations and the Case for Regulation," *Buffalo Human Rights Law Review* 10, no. 1 (September 1, 2004): 261.

27. *Velásquez Rodríguez* case, Inter-Am.Ct.H.R. (Ser. C) No. 4 (1988).

28. Per the International Center for Transitional Justice, the phrase originated with American academics who "coined the term to describe the different ways that countries had approached the problems of new regimes coming to power faced with massive violations by their predecessors." International Center for Transitional Justice, "What is Transitional Justice?" https://www.ictj.org/about/transitional-justice.

29. In fact, when the Sandinistas came to power in Nicaragua in 1979, they commenced more than six thousand criminal trials of Somoza officials for regime abuses, but these prosecutions never made it into the transitional justice story. See chapter 3 for further discussion.

30. Naomi Roht-Arriaza, "State Responsibility to Investigate and Prosecute Grave Human Rights Violations in International Law," *California Law Review* 78, no. 2 (1990): 451.

31. Diane F. Orentlicher, "Settling Accounts: The Duty to Prosecute Human Rights Violations of a Prior Regime," *Yale Law Journal* 100, no. 8 (1991): 2537–2615.

32. Diane F. Orentlicher, "Settling Accounts Revisited: Reconciling Global Norms with Local Agency," *International Journal of Transitional Justice* 1 (2007): 10–22, 13.

33. This is the standard for establishing the existence of a customary international legal rule, as articulated by the ICJ. International Court of Justice, *North Sea Continental Shelf* judgment, ICJ Reports 1969, 3.

34. Because human rights are particularly difficult to enforce, international judges and legal scholars have found that even in the presence of regular violations, *opinio juris* may be sufficient to establish the existence of a legal obligation. (See, e.g., ICJ, *North Sea Continental Shelf* judgment). Thus, even if a state did not provide accountability for atrocities within its territory, pressuring other states to provide accountability for their own abuses would suggest a belief that the obligation was binding.

35. Hurst Hannum, "International Law and Cambodian Genocide: The Sounds of Silence," *Human Rights Quarterly* 11, no. 1 (1989): 82–138; Stephen P. Marks, "Forgetting 'The Policies and Practicies of the The Past': Impunity in Cambodia," *Fletcher Forum of World Affairs* 18, no. 2 (1994): 17–43. See chapter 2 for a discussion of how and why Khmer Rouge officials were eventually prosecuted.

36. Human Rights Watch, *World Report: 1992.*

37. Human Rights Watch, *World Report: 1989.*

38. Aryeh Neier, "What Should Be Done about the Guilty?" *New York Review of Books*, February 1, 1990.

39. Africa Watch, *Evil Days: 30 Years of War and Famine in Ethiopia*, (September 1, 1991). (Although the regional watch bodies were united under the name Human Rights Watch in 1988, reports were still attributed to Africa Watch, Americas Watch, Asia Watch, Helsinki Watch, and Middle East Watch in the early 1990s).

40. Africa Watch, *Somalia: Beyond the Warlords: The Need for a Verdict on Human Rights Abuses*, (March 1, 1993).

41. Theo van Boven, *Study concerning the Right to Restitution, Compensation and Rehabilitation for Victims of Gross Violations of Human Rights and Fundamental Freedoms*, Doc. No. E/CN.4/Sub.2/1993/8, July 2, 1993.

42. See Galina Nelaeva's discussion of "Historical analogies in the establishment of the ICTY" in "Establishment of the International Criminal Tribunal in the Former Yugoslavia (ICTY): Dealing with the 'War Raging at the Heart of Europe,'" *Romanian Journal of European Affairs* 11 (2011): 100.

43. *Prosecutor v. Tadić* (decision on jurisdiction), IT-94-1, International Criminal Tribunal for the former Yugoslavia (ICTY), August 10, 1995; *Prosecutor v. Kanyabashi* (decision on jurisdiction), ICTR-96-15-A, International Criminal Tribunal for Rwanda, June 18, 1997.

44. Aryeh Neier, *War Crimes: Brutality, Genocide, Terror, and the Struggle for Justice*, 1st ed. (New York: Times Books, 1998).

45. International Commission on Intervention and State Sovereignty, *The Responsibility to Protect: Report of the International Commission on Intervention and State Sovereignty* (2001).

46. L. Joinet, *Question of the Impunity of Perpetrators of Violations of Human Rights (Civil and Political Rights)*, Doc. No. E/CN.4/Sub.2/1996/18, June 29, 1996.

47. Americas Watch, *Human Rights in Guatemala: No Neutrals Allowed* (November 23, 1982); Americas Watch, *Creating a Desolation and Calling it Peace: May 1983 Supplement to the Report of Human Rights in Guatemala* (May 1, 1983).

48. It is interesting that during this period human rights organizations reliably called for the prosecution and punishment of current officials implicated in torture. See, e.g., the 1990 Middle East Watch report *Human Rights in Iraq* or Amnesty International's 1990 Senegal report *Torture: The Casamance Case.*

49. Africa Watch, *"Mengistu Has Decided to Burn Us Like Wood": Bombing of Civilians and Civilian Targets by the Air Force* (July 24, 1990).

50. Africa Watch, *A Government at War with Its Own People: Testimonies about the Killings and the Conflict in the North in Somalia* (January 31, 1990).

51. Africa Watch, *Liberia: A Human Rights Disaster: Violations of the Laws of War by All Parties to the Conflict* (October 26, 1990).

52. Africa Watch, *Beyond the Rhetoric: Continuing Human Rights Abuses in Rwanda* (1993).

53. Jemera Rone, 'Abd Allāh Aḥmad Naʻīm, and Africa Watch Committee, *War in South Sudan: The Civilian Toll: Africa Watch Condemns Abuses by All Sides in the Conflict in South Sudan* (Washington, DC: Africa Watch, 1993).

54. Human Rights Watch, Bloodshed in the Caucasus: Indiscriminate Bombing & Shelling by Azerbaijani Forces in Nagorno-Karabakh (July 1, 1993).

55. George Black, *Genocide in Iraq: The Anfal Campaign against the Kurds*, Middle East Watch Report (New York: Human Rights Watch, 1993).

56. Human Rights Watch, *Three Months of War in Chechnya* (February 1995).

57. Dinah PoKempner et al., eds., *Cambodia at War* (New York: Human Rights Watch, 1995); Human Rights Watch, *"Attacked by All Sides" Civilians and the War in Eastern Zaire* (March 1, 1997), A901.

58. Carlos Nino, "The Duty to Punish Past Abuses of Human Rights Put into Context: The Case of Argentina," *Yale Law Journal* 100, no. 8 (January 1, 1991).

59. David Scheffer, *All the Missing Souls: A Personal History of the War Crimes Tribunals*, Human Rights and Crimes against Humanity (Princeton, NJ: Princeton University Press, 2013).

60. David Bosco, *Rough Justice: The International Criminal Court in a World of Power Politics* (Oxford University Press, 2013).

61. Michael Scharf, "Getting Serious About an International Criminal Court," *Pace International Law Review* 103 (1997).

62. Nicole Deitelhoff, "The Discursive Process of Legalization: Charting Islands of Persuasion in the ICC Case," *International Organization* 63, no. 1 (January 2009): 33–65.

63. Library of Congress, "The United Nations Rome Statute of the International Criminal Court." Finnemore and Sikkink describe the entrenchment phase of norm life cycles as one in which "norms acquire a taken-for-granted quality and are no longer a matter of broad public debate" (Martha Finnemore and Kathryn Sikkink, "International Norm Dynamics and Political Change," 895).

64. Scheffer, *All the Missing Souls*.

65. Neier, *War Crimes*, 250.

66. Library of Congress, "The United Nations Rome Statute," Preamble.

67. Juan E. Méndez, "Accountability for Past Abuses," *Human Rights Quarterly* 19, no. 2 (1997): 259. The article was first released as a working paper in 1996 before its publication in 1997.

68. Méndez, "Accountability for Past Abuses," 261.

69. *Kurt v. Turkey*, Appl. No. 15/1997/799/1002, Council of Europe: European Court of Human Rights, May 25, 1998.

70. International Criminal Tribunal for the Prosecution of Persons Responsible for Serious Violations of International Humanitarian Law Committed in the Territory of the Former Yugoslavia since 1991 (ICTY), *Prosecutor v. Anto Furundžija*, Case No. IT-95-17/1-T, judgment of the trial chamber, December 10, 1998.

71. Michal Ben-Josef Hirsch and Jennifer M. Dixon, "Conceptualizing and Assessing Norm Strength in International Relations," *European Journal of International Relations* 27, no. 2 (June 2021): 524.

72. The reliability with which international actors call for accountability doesn't just reflect their virtuous adherence to international human rights norms. Focusing on post hoc justice for mass atrocities is much, much easier than responding to them while they're still occurring, a fact that has likely contributed to the entrenchment of the accountability norm.

73. Beth A. Simmons and Hyeran Jo, "Measuring Norms and Normative Contestation: The Case of International Criminal Law," *Journal of Global Security Studies* 4, no. 1 (January 1, 2019): 19.

74. Rosemary Nagy, "Transitional Justice as Global Project: Critical Reflections," *Third World Quarterly* 29, no. 2 (2008): 275–89, 276.

75. Ben-Josef Hirsch and Dixon, "Conceptualizing and Assessing Norm Strength in International Relations."

76. Ben-Josef Hirsch and Dixon, "Conceptualizing and Assessing Norm Strength in International Relations," 524, 526.

77. Bower, "Contesting the International Criminal Court."

3. VICTIMS AND PERPETRATORS

1. Human Rights Watch, *"Bullets Were Falling Like Rain": The Andijan Massacre, May 13, 2005* (June 2005).

2. Edward Kissi, *Revolution and Genocide in Ethiopia and Cambodia* (Lexington Books, 2006), 80.

3. Kissi, *Revolution and Genocide in Ethiopia and Cambodia*, 89.

4. Rene Lefort, *Ethiopia: An Heretical Revolution* (London: Zed Books, 1983), 202.

5. Bahru Zewde, *A History of Modern Ethiopia, 1855–1991* (Athens: Ohio University Press, 2002), 247.

6. Lefort, *Ethiopia*, 238.

7. A. Waal and Africa Watch, *Evil Days: 30 Years of War and Famine in Ethiopia* (1991), 109.

8. Ben Parker, *Ethiopia: Breaking New Ground* (Oxfam, 1995), 27.

9. Waal and Africa Watch, *Evil Days*.

10. Messay Kebede, *Ideology and Elite Conflicts: Autopsy of the Ethiopian Revolution* (Lexington Books, 2011), 309.

11. Edmond Joseph Keller, *Revolutionary Ethiopia: From Empire to People's Republic* (Bloomington: Indiana University Press, 1991), 125.

12. Kjetil Tronvoll, Charles Schaefer, and Girmachew Alemu Aneme, "The 'Red Terror' Trials," in *The Ethiopian Red Terror Trials: Transitional Justice Challenged*, ed. Kjetil Tronvoll, Charles Schaefer, and Girmachew Alemu Aneme, (Rochester, UK: Boydell & Brewer, 2009), 1–16.

13. Tronvoll, Schaefer, and Aneme, "The 'Red Terror' Trials," 5–6.

14. Kjetil Tronvoll, Charles Schaefer, and Girmachew Alemu Aneme, eds., *The Ethiopian Red Terror Trials: Transitional Justice Challenged* (Rochester, UK: Boydell & Brewer, 2009), 95.

15. "Ethiopia: Proclamation Establishing the Office of the Special Prosecutor," Proclamation No. 22/1992, August 8, 1992, https://www.usip.org/sites/default/files/resources/Ethiopia-Charter.pdf; Office of the Special Prosecutor, "The Special Prosecution Process of War Criminals and Human Rights Violators in Ethiopia," February 1994, https://www.usip.org/sites/default/files/Ethiopia-SPODossier-2.pdf.

16. Commission on Human Rights, "Letter Dated 28 January 1994 from the Permanent Representative of the Transitional Government of Ethiopia to the United Nations Office at Geneva addressed to the Assistant Secretary-General for Human Rights," E/CN.4/1994/103.

17. Commission d'Enquête Nationale du Ministère Tchadien de la Justice, *Les crimes et détournements de l'ex-Président Habré et de ses complices*, Éditions L'Harmattan, 1993.

18. Neil J. Kritz, ed., *Transitional Justice: How Emerging Democracies Reckon with Former Regimes*, vol. 3, *Laws, Rulings, and Reports* (Washington, DC: United States Institute of Peace, 1995), 48–50.

19. The victims of Habré regime crimes have dedicated years to meticulously documenting the torture they suffered, advocating for the prosecution of those responsible. Their activism, and international advocacy on their behalf, eventually led to Habré's conviction by the hybrid international crimes tribunal described in chapter 2. Chad's cooperation with this court was uneven. Ultimately, the government's reluctance to surrender former officials for transfer to Senegal led to a rushed prosecution and conviction in 2015 of twenty Habré-era security agents on charges that had been filed more than a decade earlier. Although victims cheered the result, as of this writing, the government had not executed its court-ordered obligations to provide compensation.

20. For example, "7,000 Will Face Trial in Nicaragua," *New York Times*, December 10, 1979.

21. National Service of Gacaca Jurisdictions, *Summary of the Report Presented at the Closing of Gacaca Court Activities* (Kigali, Rwanda: National Service of Gacaca Jurisdictions, 2012).

22. Gregory Warner, "Rwanda Honors Dead, Celebrates Progress, 20 Years after the Genocide," *NPR*, April 7, 2014.

23. For further discussion of the Kagame regime's use of transitional justice for rule legitimation, see, e.g., Cyanne E. Loyle and Christian Davenport, "Transitional Injustice: Subverting Justice in Transition and Postconflict Societies," *Journal of Human Rights* 15, no. 1 (January 2, 2016): 126–49; Timothy Longman, *Memory and Justice in Post-Genocide Rwanda* (Cambridge: Cambridge University Press, 2017).

24. Truth, Justice, and Reconciliation Commission, Public Hearing Transcripts—North Eastern—Wagalla Massacre (Nairobi), May 17–18, 2011; June 2–10, 2011; June 14–16, 2011; June 24, 2011, https://digitalcommons.law.seattleu.edu/tjrc-core.

25. Associated Press, "Kenya: Official Apology for Past Wrongs," March 27, 2015; Oliver Mathenge, "No Answers or Justice on 1984 Wagalla Massacre as Moi Exits," *The Star*, February 10, 2020.

26. Brian Concannon, "Beyond Complementarity: The International Criminal Court and National Prosecutions, A View from Haiti," *Columbia Human Rights Law Review* 32, no. 1 (October 1, 2000): 201–50.

27. Joanna R. Quinn, "Haiti's Failed Truth Commission: Lessons in Transitional Justice," *Journal of Human Rights* 8, no. 3 (September 4, 2009): 265–281, 276.

28. Quinn, "Haiti's Failed Truth Commission," 276.

29. John Ryle, "An African Nuremberg," *New Yorker*, September 24, 1995.

30. Girmachew Alemu Aneme, "Apology and Trials: The Case of the Red Terror Trials in Ethiopia," *African Human Rights Law Journal* 6, no. 1 (January 1, 2006): 64–84, 78.

31. Aneme, "Apology and Trials," 78.

32. Jeremy Sarkin, "Transitional Justice and the Prosecution Model: The Experience of Ethiopia," *Law Democracy and Development* 3, no. 2 (1999): 253–66, 261.

33. Sarkin, "Transitional Justice and the Prosecution Model," 257–58.

34. Aneme, "Apology and Trials," 79.

35. Julie V. Mayfield, "The Prosecution of War Crimes and Respect for Human Rights: Ethiopia's Balancing Act Notes and Comments," *Emory International Law Review* 9, no. 2 (1995): 553–94.

36. James C. McKinley Jr., "Ethiopia Tries Former Rulers In 70's Deaths," *New York Times*, April 23, 1996, sec. World, https://www.nytimes.com/1996/04/23/world/ethiopia -tries-former-rulers-in-70-s-deaths.html.

37. Ryle, "An African Nuremberg," 61.

38. Ryle, "An African Nuremberg," 58.

39. Firew Tiba, "The Trial of Mengistu and other Derg Members for Genocide, Torture, and Summary Execution in Ethiopia," in *Prosecuting International Crimes in Africa*, ed. C. Murungu and J. Biegon (Pretoria, South Africa: Pretoria University Press, 2011), 174–75.

40. Tronvoll, Schaefer, and Aneme, eds., *The Ethiopian Red Terror Trials*, 92.

41. Tronvoll, Schaefer, and Aneme, eds., *The Ethiopian Red Terror Trials*, 94.

42. Tronvoll, Schaefer, and Aneme, eds., *The Ethiopian Red Terror Trials*, 92.

43. Lydia Polgreen, "A Master Plan Drawn in Blood," *New York Times*, April 2, 2006.

44. "Liberia leader defiant till the end," *BBC News*, August 11, 2003.

45. Ofeibea Quist-Arcton, "Nigeria Seizes Wanted Warlord Charles Taylor at Border," *NPR*, March 29, 2006, https://www.npr.org/templates/story/story.php?storyId=5308409.

46. Karl Dönitz, the German admiral who succeeded Adolf Hitler as the German head of state, was convicted of crimes against the peace and war crimes at Nuremberg in 1946. Slobodan Milošević was prosecuted by the International Criminal Tribunal for the former Yugoslavia on war crimes, crimes against humanity, and genocide charges, but died before the trial came to verdict.

47. See, e.g., Josephine Volqvartz, "ICC Under Fire Over Uganda Probe," *CNN*, 2005. The debate about the effects of ICC intervention on the prospects for peace in conflict-affected situations remains extremely vigorous. See, e.g., Mark Kersten, *Justice in Conflict: The Effects of the International Criminal Court's Interventions on Ending Wars and Building Peace* (Oxford University Press, 2016); Alyssa K. Prorok, 2017, "The (In)compatibility of Peace and Justice? The International Criminal Court and Civil Conflict Termination," *International Organization* 71, no. 2: 213–43.

48. For a discussion of states' strategic use of self-referrals, see Oumar Ba, *States of Justice: The Politics of the International Criminal Court* (Cambridge: Cambridge University Press, 2020).

49. For example, Mac McClelland, "I Can Find an Indicted Warlord. So Why Isn't He in The Hague?" *Mother Jones*, September/October 2011.

50. "Congo 'Terminator' turns himself in to US embassy," *Reuters*, March 18, 2013, https://www.abc.net.au/news/2013-03-19/congo-terminator-turns-himself-in-to-us -embassy/4580810. The ICC ultimately sentenced Ntaganda to thirty years' imprisonment on November 7, 2019.

51. For a discussion of similar dynamics at the ad hoc tribunals, see Victor Peskin, *International Justice in Rwanda and the Balkans: Virtual Trials and the Struggle for State Cooperation* (Cambridge: Cambridge University Press, 2008).

52. Sidney Leclercq, "Injustice through Transitional Justice? Subversion Strategies in Burundi's Peace Process and Postconflict Developments," *International Journal of Transitional Justice* 11, no. 3 (November 1, 2017): 525–44.

53. Thomas Hammarberg, "How the Khmer Rouge Tribunal was Agreed," *Magazine of Documentation Center of Cambodia*, 2001, http://d.dccam.org/Tribunal/Analysis/How _Khmer_Rouge_Tribunal.htm.

54. Hammarberg, "How the Khmer Rouge Tribunal was Agreed."

55. *Report of the Group of Experts for Cambodia Established Pursuant to General Assembly Resolution 52/135* (Geneva, Switzerland: United Nations, 1999).

56. Hammarberg, "How the Khmer Rouge Tribunal was Agreed."

57. John D. Ciorciari and Anne Heindel, *Hybrid Justice: The Extraordinary Chambers in the Courts of Cambodia*, Law, Meaning, and Violence (Ann Arbor: University of Michigan Press, 2014), 29.

58. Human Rights Watch, *Serious Flaws: Why the U.N. General Assembly Should Require Changes to the Draft Khmer Rouge Tribunal Agreement* (April 30, 2003).

59. Ciorciari and Heindel, *Hybrid Justice*, 35, 39.

4. WHAT HAPPENS AFTER MASS ATROCITIES

1. "Actors Demand Genocide Trial," *Reuters*, May 23, 2012.

2. October 1977 in *La Prensa*, placed by Las Madres de la Plaza de Mayo.

3. For example, Kathryn Sikkink, *The Justice Cascade: How Human Rights Prosecutions Are Changing World Politics*, The Norton Series in World Politics (New York: Norton, 2011).

4. For example, Leslie Vinjamuri and Jack Snyder, "Law and Politics in Transitional Justice," *Annual Review of Political Science* 18, no. 1 (May 11, 2015): 303–27.

5. Alex J. Bellamy, *Mass Atrocities and Armed Conflict: Links, Distinctions, and Implications for the Responsibility to Prevent* (Stanley Foundation, 2011); Benjamin A. Valentino, *Final Solutions: Mass Killing and Genocide in the 20th Century* (Cornell University Press, 2013).

6. B. Coghlan, et al., *Mortality in the Democratic Republic of the Congo; an Ongoing Crisis* (International Rescue Committee, 2007). For a discussion of the flaws with dominant approaches to excess mortality estimation, see Michael Spagat and Stijn van Weezel, "Half a Million Excess Deaths in the Iraq War: Terms and Conditions May Apply," *Research & Politics* 4, no. 4 (October 2017).

7. "ICC to Investigate Reports of Viagra-Fueled Gang-Rapes in Libya," *CNN*, May 18, 2011.

8. Serajur Rahman, "Letter: Mujib's Confusion on Bangladeshi Deaths," *The Guardian*, May 23, 2011.

9. See "Limitations" discussion at p. 46 of Michael Van Rooyen, et al., *"Now, the World Is without Me": An Investigation of Sexual Violence in Eastern Democratic Republic of Congo* (Cambridge, MA: Harvard Humanitarian Initiative and Oxfam America, 2010).

10. For a fuller discussion of these issues, see, e.g., Patrick Ball, "On the Quantification of Horror: Field Notes on Statistical Analysis of Human Rights Violations," in *Repression and Mobilization*, ed. Christian Davenport, Hank Johnston, and Carol Mueller (Minneapolis: University of Minnesota Press, 2005); Ann Marie Clark and Kathryn Sikkink, "Information Effects and Human Rights Data: Is the Good News about Increased Human Rights Information Bad News for Human Rights Measures?" *Human Rights Quarterly* 35, no. 3 (August 2013): 539–68; Dara K. Cohen, "Rape Reporting During War: Why the Numbers Don't Mean What You Think They Do," *Foreign Affairs*, August 1, 2011.

11. I omit the Darfur conflict because the scale of the violations is simply astronomical, and the Russia–Georgia conflict because it is a case of unlawful territorial aggression rather than mass atrocities.

12. See table A.1 in appendix A for a list of these events.

13. Nineteen countries experienced multiple mass atrocities during the time period covered. Afghanistan and the Democratic Republic of the Congo proved most lethal, each with four separate mass atrocity–producing events. Nine more countries experienced three such events: Burundi, Burma, Ethiopia, Iran, Iraq, Kenya, Nigeria, Sudan, and Uganda.

14. Note that this does not sum to ninety because many events involved both types of perpetrators.

15. For instance, the Nuremberg tribunal's failure to allow cross-examination of witnesses would today be considered a breach. At the time, however, they were consistent with fair trial standards and practices.

16. "Summary of Contributions to Date by Donors: As at 30 June 2021" (Cambodia, 2021), https://www.eccc.gov.kh/sites/default/files/06-Fund_contributions.pdf.

17. This appears in the quantitative results reported in Appendix B as a dichotomous variable labeled *Movement*. Although there might appear to be endogeneity concerns with regard to this variable because the same conditions that predict accountability outcomes could foster the presence of domestic movements (or even reverse causation, as movements might arise while mechanisms are being debated), justice movements generally preexist action on accountability by many years.

18. This is a blunt instrument and does not capture changes in the strength of movements, which we might expect to see vary with changes in the repressiveness of postatrocity regimes or with any number of other political and economic indicators.

19. To measure regime type, I used the Polity2 variable (scaled from −10 to 10) from the Polity IV data set. Autocracy defined as polity < −5, democracy as polity > 5.

20. This appears in the quantitative results reported in Appendix B as a dichotomous variable, labeled *Perp in Power*.

21. Jeremy Keenan, "General Mohamed Toufik Mediene: 'God of Algeria,'" *Aljazeera*, September 29, 2010.

22. But postatrocity governments comprising significant numbers of low-ranked perpetrators of past atrocities are likely to also be resistant to providing accountability, so this is worth coding and testing in the future.

23. The two predictor variables *Movement* and *Perp in Power* are negatively correlated (−0.2499).

24. I therefore do not include the resistance variable in the statistical models reported in Appendix B.

25. This association, reported in appendix B, table B.2, is robust to the inclusion of both time-variant and -invariant controls, as well as variables associated with the alternative explanations discussed below.

26. Judicial (and general state) capacity is notoriously hard to proxy and has multiple available meanings. We might invoke judicial capacity to talk about anything from the quality of courtroom technology to corruption among court officers. But for my purposes, the critical dimensions are resources (a judiciary that is barely managing to process day-to-day cases will not be able to undertake a complicated war crimes prosecution effort) and independence from the executive.

27. See appendix B, figure B.1.

28. See appendix B, figure B.1.

29. See appendix B, figure B.1.

30. As explained in chapter 2, the ICC's jurisdiction is "complementary" to its member states', which means that the primary obligation to pursue accountability for mass atrocities belongs to the territorial state in which they occur. For a thorough discussion of the theory underlying the court's complementary jurisdiction and its effects in practice, see Sarah M. H. Nouwen, *Complementarity in the Line of Fire: The Catalysing Effect of the International Criminal Court in Uganda and Sudan* (Cambridge: Cambridge University Press, 2013).

31. This variable is labeled *Dependency* in the results reported in appendix B and is measured using ratio of aid from Development Assistance Committee (DAC) sources to the postatrocity state's gross domestic product (GDP) in each year (lagged). Aid data are from the Organization for Economic Cooperation and Development (OECD) Query Wizard for International Development Statistics and GDP from the World Bank's World

Development Indicators. In 2000 postatrocity years in the data set for which these data were available, the mean value of *Dependency* was 0.056 with a standard deviation of 0.091. The highest value on this variable occurred in Liberia in 2009, when aid disbursements were equivalent to more than 99% of the country's GDP.

32. Standard deviation of 10.17.

33. Standard deviation of 9.07. Standard deviation 2.15.

34. See appendix B, tables B.5 and B.7 for this comparison.

35. See appendix B, table B.8.

36. *Dependency* retains its significance and substantive effect when included in a model with controls and proxies for alternate explanations. See appendix B, figure B.4.

37. The results are similar if we instead conceptualize vulnerability in terms of relative military power in the international system. See appendix B, table B.9.

38. See appendix B, table B.5.

39. See appendix B, figure B.4.

5. DOING JUST ENOUGH?

1. See, e.g., "UN Head of Refugee Agency: Rohingya Crisis 'among the Worst I've Ever Seen,'" *Channel 4 News*, September 27, 2017; "Myanmar Must Give Rohingya 'Pathway to Citizenship'—U.N. Investigator," *Reuters*, June 26, 2019, sec. APAC; International Rescue Committee (IRC), "Rohingya Crisis: IRC on What Is Needed One Year In," August 25, 2018.

2. Amnesty International, "Myanmar: Scorched-Earth Campaign Fuels Ethnic Cleansing of Rohingya from Rakhine State," September 14, 2017.

3. United Nations High Commissioner for Human Rights, "Human Rights Council 36th Session: Opening Statement," 2017, http://www.ohchr.org/EN/NewsEvents/Pages/DisplayNews.aspx?NewsID=22041.

4. Shayna Bauchner, "Burma Bars UN Rights Expert," Human Rights Watch, December 21, 2017.

5. I'm pretty sure you can't write a book touching on international law without referencing my law school human rights professor Louis Henkin's famous maxim that "almost all nations observe almost all principles of international law and almost all of their obligations almost all of the time." Invoking the Henkin rule here is not to say, however, that there aren't significant differences in the level of international attention across cases. This is less a function of international NGO interest, however, than patterns of media coverage that reflect global power dynamics in predictable and troubling ways.

6. An additional source of uncertainty stems from the fact, as noted in chapter 2, states can use accountability pressure as a substitute for action to stop mass atrocities while they are occurring.

7. Sometimes, international opinion coalesces to demand justice for mass atrocities, even where a postatrocity government has pursued a quasi-compliant strategy. (This is what happened in the example described in the Introduction, in which the Security Council referred the Darfur situation to the International Criminal Court, despite Sudan's efforts to defuse international pressure with a commission of inquiry and a military court.)

8. I have been involved in research and advocacy on atrocities in the Democratic Republic of the Congo since 2001. In July and August 2014, I spent two weeks in Goma conducting semistructured interviews with domestic and international actors involved in the prosecution of sexual violence crimes, some of which are quoted in the following pages.

9. Séverine Autesserre, *Peaceland: Conflict Resolution and the Everyday Politics of International Intervention* (New York: Cambridge University Press, 2014).

10. MONUSCO interview, August 8, 2014.

11. Eve Ensler, "Women Left for Dead—and the Man Who's Saving Them," *Glamour*, July 31, 2007.

12. For example, in 2013, Congo's GDP was approximately USD 30 billion, and it received more than USD 2.5 billion in development aid.

13. Milli Lake, "Organizing Hypocrisy: Providing Legal Accountability for Human Rights Violations in Areas of Limited Statehood," *International Studies Quarterly* 58, no. 3 (September 2014): 515–26.

14. UN peacekeepers have been deployed in North Kivu since 1999, originally as MONUC, which was renamed MONUSCO in 2010.

15. A 2013 law granted some jurisdiction over international crimes to Congo's civilian courts; however, it remains unclear whether this extends to cases where the perpetrators are members of the military.

16. United Nations Joint Human Rights Office, *Progress and Obstacles in the Fight Against Impunity for Sexual Violence in the Democratic Republic of the Congo* (2014).

17. United Nations Joint Human Rights Office, *Progress and Obstacles*.

18. UNDP interview, Goma, Democratic Republic of the Congo, August 5, 2014.

19. Mark Townsend, "Revealed: How the World Turned Its Back on Rape Victims of Congo," *The Guardian*, June 13, 2015; see also Human Rights Watch, *Justice on Trial: Lessons from the Minova Rape Case in the Democratic Republic of Congo* (October 1, 2015).

20. Defense attorney interview, Goma, Democratic Republic of the Congo, August 7, 2014.

21. At $3 per page, plus a $20 authorization fee. Defense attorney interview, Goma, Democratic Republic of the Congo, August 7, 2014.

22. Milli Lake, "Building the Rule of War: Postconflict Institutions and the Micro-Dynamics of Conflict in Eastern DR Congo," *International Organization* 71, no. 2 (2017): 281–315.

23. Amnesty International USA, "New Mass Rapes in DRC Are Result of Horrific Failure of Justice," June 24, 2011.

24. Lake, "Organizing Hypocrisy."

25. Human Rights Watch, "Etats Généraux of the Justice System in the Democratic Republic of Congo," April 27, 2015.

26. In September and October 2017, I wrote pieces for (respectively) *Foreign Policy* and *Slate*, arguing that what was happening to the Rohingya likely met the definition of genocide. Since then, I have remained tangentially involved in advocacy on this issue and have kept in contact with activists working on it. The account in the following pages is constructed from my own recollections and email and WhatsApp records, verified with, and cited to, publicly available contemporaneous media and NGO reporting.

27. Amnesty International, *Myanmar: The Rohingya Minority: Fundamental Rights Denied* (May 18, 2004).

28. Human Rights Watch, *All You Can Do Is Pray* (April 22, 2013); Francis Wade and Paul French, *Myanmar's Enemy Within: Buddhist Violence and the Making of a Muslim "Other"* (London: Zed Books, 2017).

29. United States Holocaust Memorial Museum and Simon-Skjodt Center for the Prevention of Genocide, *"They Want Us All to Go Away": Early Warning Signs of Genocide in Burma* (2015).

30. Allard K. Lowenstein, "Persecution of the Rohingya Muslims: Is Genocide Occurring in Myanmar's Rakhine State? A Legal Analysis," International Human Rights Clinic, Yale Law School, 2015.

31. International State Crime Initiative, "Countdown to Annihilation: Genocide in Myanmar," Queen Mary University of London, 2015.

32. Office of the High Commission for Human Rights, *Flash Report: Interviews with Rohingyas fleeing from Myanmar since 9 October 2016* (2017).

33. Kate Cronin-Furman, "The Word 'Genocide' Is Overused, but It Applies to What's Happening to the Rohingya," *Slate*, October 31, 2017.

34. Benjamin Westcott, "Myanmar's Military Clears Itself over Alleged Rohingya Atrocities," *CNN*, November 14, 2017.

35. Amnesty International, "Myanmar: Military Attempts to Whitewash Crimes against Humanity Targeting Rohingya," November 13, 2017; Human Rights Watch, "Burma: Army Report Whitewashes Ethnic Cleansing," November 14, 2017.

36. Human Rights Watch, "Burma: Army Report Whitewashes Ethnic Cleansing."

37. Human Rights Watch, "Burma: Army Investigation Denies Atrocities," May 24, 2017.

38. Jonah Fisher, "Myanmar's Rohingya: Truth, Lies and Aung San Suu Kyi," *BBC News*, January 27, 2017, sec. Asia; Maung Zarni, Natalie Brinham, and Alice Cowley, "An Evolution of Rohingya Persecution in Myanmar: From Strategic Embrace to Genocide," Middle East Institute, April 20, 2017.

39. Shoon Naing and Antoni Slodkowski, "Myanmar Police 'Set Up' Reuters Reporters in Sting—Police Witness," *Reuters*, sec. Media and Telecoms, April 20, 2018.

40. "Police Pressured Reuters Journalists to Bury Report on Inn Din Massacre, Says Wa Lone," *Myanmar Now*, July 17, 2018.

41. Hannah Beech and Saw Nang, "As Signs of a Mass Grave Emerge, Myanmar Cracks Down," *New York Times*, sec. World, December 19, 2017.

42. Adam Taylor, "In a First, Burmese Military Admits That Soldiers Killed Rohingya Found in Mass Grave," *Washington Post*, January 10, 2018.

43. Taylor, "In a First."

44. Thu Thus Aung, "Muslim Insurgents Say 10 Rohingya Found in Myanmar Grave Were 'Innocent Civilians,'" *Jakarta Globe*, January 14, 2018.

45. Simon Lewis, "Myanmar Admission Soldiers Killed Rohingya 'an Important Step': U.S. Envoy," *Reuters*, January 11, 2018, sec. APAC; Hannah Beech and Saw Nang, "Reuters Reporters Are Charged in Myanmar with Obtaining State Secrets," *New York Times*, January 10, 2018, sec. World.

46. Wa Lone, Kyaw Soe Oo, Simon Lewis, and Antoni Slodkowski, "Massacre in Myanmar: One Grave for 10 Rohingya Men," *Reuters*, February 2, 2018.

47. "Staff of Reuters, with Notable Contributions from Wa Lone and Kyaw Soe Oo," Pulitzer Prize in International Reporting, 2019.

48. "Reuters Report on Myanmar Massacre Brings Calls for Independent Probe," *Reuters*, February 9, 2018, sec. Cyclical Consumer Goods.

49. "Myanmar Rejects Report Detailing Killing of Rohingya Muslims in Rakhine State," *Radio Free Asia*, February 9, 2019.

50. "Myanmar Says Soldiers, Police Facing Action over Village Killings," *Reuters*, February 11, 2018, sec. Emerging Markets.

51. "Statement by His Excellency U Kyaw Tin, Union Minister for International Cooperation of the Republic of the Union of Myanmar at the High-Level Segment of 37th Session of Human Rights Council" (Geneva: Human Rights Council, February 27, 2018).

52. "Statement by His Excellency U Kyaw Tin."

53. "Seven Myanmar Soldiers Sentenced to 10 Years for Rohingya Massacre," *Reuters*, April 10, 2018, sec. Media and Telecoms.

54. For example, "Rohingya Crisis: Myanmar Army Admits Killings," *BBC News*, January 10, 2018, sec. Asia; Taylor, "In a First."

55. Amnesty International, "'We Will Destroy Everything': Military Responsibility for Crimes Against Humanity in Rakhine State, Myanmar," 2018.

56. "Rohingya Massacre: Myanmar Grants Soldiers Early Release," *BBC News*, May 27, 2019, sec. Asia; Shoon Naing and Simon Lewis, "Exclusive: Myanmar Soldiers Jailed for Rohingya Killings Freed after Less than a Year," *Reuters*, May 27, 2019, sec. APAC.

57. "Statement by Mr. Marzuki Darusman, Chairperson of the Independent International Fact-Finding Mission on Myanmar, at the 37th Session of the Human Rights Council" (Geneva: Human Rights Council, March 12, 2018).

58. Param-Preet Singh, "Myanmar's Proposed Rakhine Commission Latest Sham," Human Rights Watch, June 3, 2018.

59. International Commission of Jurists, "Myanmar: New Commission of Inquiry Cannot Deliver Justice or Accountability, International Response Required," September 7, 2018.

60. International Commission of Jurists, "Myanmar: New Commission of Inquiry."

61. Richard Weir, "Don't Expect Much from Latest Myanmar Commission," Human Rights Watch, August 17, 2018.

62. Weir, "Don't Expect Much."

63. "Report of the Independent International Fact-Finding Mission on Myanmar" (Geneva: Human Rights Council, September 12, 2018).

64. "U Zaw Htay, Spokesman of the Office of the President: The Questions Have Been Raised as to the Reasons for the Removal of the Facebook Accounts and Pages associated with Tatmadaw," *The Global, New Light of Myanmar*, August 29, 2018.

65. Letter from the Permanent Mission of the Republic of the Republic of the Union of Myanmar to the United Nations, New York to the President of the Security Council, August 22, 2019.

66. "Genocide Threat for Myanmar's Rohingya Greater than Ever, Investigators Warn Human Rights Council," *UN News*, September 16, 2019; "Statement by Permanent Representative of Myanmar H. E. Mr. Kyaw Moe Tun at General Debate on Report of IIM," September 10, 2019, https://www.myanmargeneva.org/wp-content/uploads/2019/09/Statement-on-report-of-IIM.pdf.

67. "Statement by Permanent Representative of Myanmar H.E. Mr. Kyaw Moe Tun at General Debate on Report of IIM."

68. "Statement by Permanent Representative of Myanmar H.E. Mr. Kyaw Moe Tun at the Interactive Dialogue with the Special Rapporteur on Situation of Human Rights in Myanmar at the 42nd Session of Human Rights Council," September 16, 2019, https://www.myanmargeneva.org/wp-content/uploads/2019/09/Statement-by-PR-ID-with-SR-42nd-HRC-16-Sept-19.pdf.

69. "Statement by Permanent Representative of Myanmar H.E. Mr. Kyaw Moe Tun at General Debate on Report of IIM," September 10, 2019, https://www.myanmargeneva.org/wp-content/uploads/2019/09/Statement-on-report-of-IIM.pdf; "Statement by Permanent Representative of Myanmar H.E. Mr. Kyaw Moe Tun at the Interactive Dialogue with the Special Rapporteur on Situation of Human Rights in Myanmar at the 42nd Session of Human Rights Council."

70. United Nations, "Independent Investigative Mechanism for Myanmar, Terms of Reference," January 21, 2019.

71. Tatmadaw True News Information Team, "Court-Martial underway in Connection with Finding of Court of Inquiry," August 31, 2019, https://cincds.gov.mm/node/4266.

72. Foster Klug, "AP Finds Evidence for Graves, Rohingya Massacre in Myanmar," *AP News*, February 1, 2018.

73. "Myanmar Government Denies AP Report of Rohingya Mass Graves," *AP News*, February 3, 2018.

74. Application of the Convention on the Prevention and Punishment of the Crime of Genocide (The Gambia v. Myanmar), [2019] ICJ Verbatim Record 2019/19 at 18

(Dec. 11, 2019), https://www.icj-cij.org/public/files/case-related/178/178-20191211-ORA -01-00-BI.pdf

75. Global Justice Center, "Myanmar's Independent Commission of Enquiry: Structural Issues and Flawed Findings," February 2020.

76. Human Rights Watch, "Myanmar: Government Rohingya Report Falls Short," January 22, 2020, https://www.hrw.org/news/2020/01/22/myanmar-government-rohingya -report-falls-short.

77. "Application of the Convention on the Prevention and Punishment of the Crime of Genocide" (International Court of Justice, January 23, 2020), https://www.icj-cij.org /public/files/case-related/178/178-20200123-ORD-01-00-EN.pdf.

78. "Myanmar President Orders Officials to Preserve Evidence of Rakhine Atrocities," *The Irrawaddy*, April 9, 2020, https://www.irrawaddy.com/news/burma/myanmar-presi dent-orders-officials-preserve-evidence-rakhine-atrocities.html.

79. Param-Preet Singh, "What Myanmar Is and Is Not Doing to Protect Rohingyas from Genocide," *Just Security*, July 23, 2020.

80. "Myanmar Finds Troops Guilty in Rohingya Atrocities Court-Martial," *Aljazeera*, June 30, 2020.

81. "Myanmar Army Says It Has Convicted Three Troops For 2017 Massacre of Rohingya," *Radio Free Asia*, June 30, 2020.

82. Shibani Mahtani and and Wai Moe, "A Year after the Assault on the Rohingya, Myanmar's Generals Are Unapologetic," *Washington Post*, August 21, 2018.

83. Philip Alston, *Report of the Special Rapporteur on Extrajudicial, Summary or Arbitrary Executions* (Geneva: United Nations, May 2, 2008), para. 51.

84. Human Rights Watch, *Myanmar's Investigative Commissions: A History of Shielding Abusers* (September 2018), https://www.hrw.org/sites/default/files/supporting_resour ces/201809myanmar_commissions.pdf.

85. "Myanmar Army Says It Has Convicted Three Troops For 2017 Massacre of Rohingya"; Human Rights Watch, "Myanmar: Court Martial Latest Accountability Sham," July 3, 2020.

86. See Annex to United Nations Joint Human Rights Office 2014.

87. "Myanmar Rejects UN 'Genocide' Accusations," *Aljazeera*, August 29, 2018.

88. Bauchner, "Burma Bars UN Rights Expert."

89. "Myanmar Rejects UN Accusation of 'Genocide' against Rohingya," *BBC News*, August 29, 2018.

6. CHOOSING YOUR AUDIENCE

1. See the varied (and heavily contested) estimates reported in International Truth and Justice Project, "Death Tolls in Sri Lanka's 2009 War," https://sangam.org/wp-content /uploads/2021/03/ITJP-Death-Toll-in-Sri-Lanka.pdf.

2. This fieldwork was conducted in July–August 2013, October–November 2013, February–March 2014, January 2015, July–August 2016, and July 2017. This research, and much of the analysis presented in this chapter, was previously reported in a 2020 *World Politics* article. See Kate Cronin-Furman, "Human Rights Half Measures: Avoiding Accountability in Post-War Sri Lanka," *World Politics* 72, no. 1 (2020): 121–63.

3. Sarah Elizabeth Parkinson, "Organizing Rebellion: Rethinking High-Risk Mobilization and Social Networks in War," *American Political Science Review* 107, no. 3 (August 2013): 418–32.

4. Lee Ann Fujii, "Shades of Truth and Lies: Interpreting Testimonies of War and Violence," *Journal of Peace Research* 47, no. 2 (March 1, 2010): 231–41.

5. Most of these interviews are cited with a brief description of the interviewee, location, and date. Where there were heightened concerns about an individual's safety or

where an individual requested additional confidentiality measures for another reason, I use modified citation formats that omit some or all of this information.

6. There are numerous citations to both Sri Lankan and international media below. In many instances, I use these to provide a publicly available source to confirm information I received off the record. All such citations have been triangulated from multiple sources.

7. Marzuki Darusman, Steven Ratner, and Yasmin Sooka, *Report of the Secretary General's Panel of Experts on Accountability in Sri Lanka*, March 31, 2011, https://reliefweb .int/sites/reliefweb.int/files/resources/POE_Report_Full.pdf.

8. A statistical analysis conducted in late 2018 revealed that at least five hundred people were forcibly disappeared between May 17 and May 19, 2009, alone. Patrick Ball and Frances Harrison, "How Many People Disappeared on 17–19 May 2009 in Sri Lanka?" International Truth and Justice Project: Human Rights Sata Analysis Group, December 12, 2018.

9. Kate Cronin-Furman, "How to Get Away with Mass Murder: Denying Mass Atrocities in Sri Lanka and Syria," *War on the Rocks*, May 18, 2017, https://warontherocks .com/2017/05/how-to-get-away-with-mass-murder-denying-mass-atrocities-in-sri -lanka-and-syria/.

10. United Nations Human Rights Council, "A/HRC/S-11/1: Assistance to Sri Lanka in the promotion and protection of human rights," May 27, 2009.

11. US Department of State, *Report to Congress on Incidents during the Recent War in Sri Lanka*, October 22, 2009, https://reliefweb.int/sites/reliefweb.int/files/resources/479 2D63B35FAD909492576580005B2E2-Full_Report.pdf.

12. Daniel Nasaw, "Sri Lanka Blasts US Report on Human Rights Abuses," *The Guardian*, October 22, 2009, https://www.theguardian.com/world/2009/oct/22/sri-lanka-state -department-report.

13. Sri Lanka Ministry of Foreign Affairs, "GOSL Reaction on US State Department Report to the US Congress on Sri Lanka," October 22, 2009.

14. US Department of State, Bureau of Public Affairs, *2013 Investment Climate—Sri Lanka*, April 19, 2013.

15. International Alert, "Dynamics and Trends of Foreign Aid in Sri Lanka," August 2013, https://www.international-alert.org/wp-content/uploads/2021/08/Sri-Lanka -Aid-Effectiveness-EN-2013.pdf.

16. Darusman, Ratner, and Sooka, *Report of the Secretary-General's Panel of Experts.*

17. Sri Lanka Ministry of External Affairs, "Statement on the Appointment of the Sri Lanka Panel of Experts by the Secretary General of the United Nations," June 23, 2010.

18. Author interview with civil society member, Colombo, Sri Lanka, August 5, 2013.

19. Confidential interview.

20. Sharika Thiranagama, "Claiming the State: Postwar Reconciliation in Sri Lanka," *Humanity: An International Journal of Human Rights, Humanitarianism, and Development* 4, no. 1 (2013): 93–116.

21. Author interview with civil society member, Colombo, Sri Lanka, August 5, 2013.

22. Author interview with human rights activist.

23. Amnesty International, *When Will They Get Justice? Failures of Sri Lanka's Lessons Learnt and Reconciliation Commission* (September 7, 2011).

24. Confidential interview.

25. Author interview with civil society member, Colombo, Sri Lanka, August 14, 2013.

26. Confidential interview.

27. Commission of Inquiry on Lessons Learnt and Reconciliation, *Final Report*, November 15, 2011, http://slembassyusa.org/downloads/LLRC-REPORT.pdf.

28. "Sri Lanka Rejects Demand for International Probe into War Crimes," Press Trust of India, December 14, 2011, https://www.ndtv.com/world-news/sri-lankan-president-mahinda-rajapaksa-rejects-demand-for-probe-into-war-crimes-541324.

29. Sri Lanka Army Media Unit, "Army Commander-Appointed Court of Inquiry Probing into LLRC Report Observations in Progress," February 16, 2012, https://www.army.lk/news/army-commander-appointed-court-inquiry-probing-llrc-report-observations-progress-0#.

30. Sri Lanka Army Media Unit, "LLRC Observations Cleared; Army Commander Hands Over Court of Inquiry Report to Secretary Defence," April 10, 2013, https://www.army.lk/news/llrc-observations-cleared-army-commander-hands-over-court-inquiry-report-secretary-defence.

31. Mahinda Rajapaksa, "Proclamations & c., by the President." *Gazette of the Democratic Socialist Republic of Sri Lanka*, no. 1823/42. August 15, 2013, http://old.satp.org/satporgtp/countries/shrilanka/document/papers/PCI.pdf. This commission was formally known as the Presidential Commission of Inquiry into Complaints of Abductions and Disappearances.

32. Author interview with civil society member, Colombo, Sri Lanka, October 30, 2013.

33. Author interview with civil society member, Colombo, Sri Lanka, August 8, 2013; author interview with civil society member, Colombo, Sri Lanka, August 14, 2013.

34. Mahinda Rajapaksa, "Budget Speech: 2013," November 8, 2012, https://issuu.com/lpsl/docs/budget_speech_2013_sri_lanka (or video up on youtube here: https://www.youtube.com/watch?v=yrL-Ti8-kIc).

35. "Rs. 400 m Spent on Foreign Advisors for Domestic HR Inquiry," *Sunday Times*, February 15, 2015, http://www.sundaytimes.lk/150215/columns/rs-400-m-spent-on-foreign-advisors-for-domestic-hr-inquiry-135809.html.

36. Appropriations Bill, 2013, https://www.parliament.lk/files/pdf/budget/appropriation_2013_bill.pdf.

37. Republic of South Africa, Department of Finance, "Budget Review 15 March 1995," http://www.treasury.gov.za/documents/national%20budget/Budget%20Review%201995.pdf.

38. In the Tamil-majority Northern Province, he lost by large margins.

39. William McGowan, "Buddhists Behaving Badly," *Foreign Affairs*, August 2, 2012, https://www.foreignaffairs.com/articles/asia/2012-08-02/buddhists-behaving-badly.

40. Author's field notes, Colombo, Sri Lanka, 2013; author's field notes, Southern Province, Sri Lanka, 2014.

41. Author interview with Tamil activist.

42. Not only did Fonseka lose the election, he was also thrown in prison for years, first on fraud charges, then on charges that his allegations against Gotabaya Rajapaksa threatened national security.

43. Sri Lanka Army, "Second National Victory Day Anniversary Celebrations Honour Invaluable Ranaviru Sacrifices," May 27, 2011, https://www.army.lk/news/second-national-victory-day-anniversary-celebrations-honour-invaluable-ranaviru-sacrifices.

44. Author interview with former army commander, Colombo, Sri Lanka, August 14, 2013.

45. Author interview with Sinhalese businessman, Colombo, Sri Lanka, August 6, 2013.

46. "Sri Lanka and Human Rights: Never a Good Time," *The Economist*, March 21, 2014.

47. Author's field notes, Colombo, Sri Lanka, March 2014.

48. Frances Harrison, *Still Counting the Dead: Survivors of Sri Lanka's Hidden War* (London: Granta Books, 2013).

49. Author interview with civil society member, Colombo, Sri Lanka, August 8, 2013.

50. Author interview with civil society member, Colombo, Sri Lanka, August 14, 2013.

51. "Buddhist Monk Led Mob Sabotages Meetings Again, This Time on LLRC in Batticaloa," *Colombo Telegraph*, July 31, 2013.

52. S. L. Gunasekara, "Betrayal Most Foul," *Daily Mirror*, September 24, 2013, http://www.dailymirror.lk/article/betrayal-most-foul-35936.html.

53. US Department of State, "Daily Press Briefing—December 19, 2011," https://2009-2017.state.gov/r/pa/prs/dpb/2011/12/178982.htm; UK Foreign and Commonwealth Office, "Foreign Office Minister Responds to Report on the Conflict in Sri Lanka," January 12, 2012, https://www.gov.uk/government/news/foreign-office-minister-responds-to-report-on-the-conflict-in-sri-lanka; Foreign Affairs Media Relations Office (Canada), "LLRC Report: Decisive Action Now Required," January 12, 2012, https://srilankabrief.blogspot.com/2012/01/llrc-report-decisive-action-now.html?m=0.

54. Human Rights Watch, "Sri Lanka: Report Fails to Advance Accountability," December 16, 2011, https://www.hrw.org/news/2011/12/16/sri-lanka-report-fails-advance-accountability.

55. Amnesty International, *When Will They Get Justice?*

56. Yasmin Sooka, "The Empty Findings of Sri Lanka's Military Court of Inquiry," *Groundviews*, April 11, 2013, https://groundviews.org/2013/04/11/the-empty-findings-of-sri-lankas-military-court-of-inquiry/; International Crisis Group, "Sri Lanka's Authoritarian Turn: The Need for International Action," February 20, 2013, https://www.crisisgroup.org/asia/south-asia/sri-lanka/sri-lanka-s-authoritarian-turn-need-international-action.

57. Nisha Desai Biswal, "Press Conference on Status of Human Rights in Sri Lanka," February 2, 2014, https://2009-2017.state.gov/p/sca/rls/rmks/2014/221143.htm.

58. Jyoti Thottam, "The Man Who Tamed the Tamil Tigers," *Time*, July 13, 2009, http://content.time.com/time/world/article/0,8599,1910095,00.html.

59. Rajiva Wijesinha, "Arbitrary Execution by Philip Alston," *Daily News*, September 2, 2009, http://archives.dailynews.lk/2009/09/02/fea03.asp.

60. Author interview with civil society member, Colombo, Sri Lanka, August 8, 2013

61. Kristine Höglund and Camilla Orjuela, "Friction and the Pursuit of Justice in Post-War Sri Lanka," *Peacebuilding* 1, no. 3 (September 1, 2013): 300–316.

62. Author interview with civil society member, Colombo, Sri Lanka, August 8, 2013

63. Author interview with civil society member, Colombo, Sri Lanka, October 30, 2013.

64. "CHOGM: Sri Lanka's Mahinda Rajapaksa Hits Out at Critics," *BBC News*, November 14, 2013, https://www.bbc.com/news/world-asia-24936948.

65. "War Crimes Attempt on MR," *Colombo Gazette*, January 29, 2014; Shihar Aneez and Ranga Sirilal, "US: Sri Lanka Refuses Visa for State Dept Official after War Crimes Accusations," *Reuters*, February 4, 2014, https://www.reuters.com/article/us-srilanka-rights-usa/us-sri-lanka-refuses-visa-for-state-dept-official-after-war-crime-accusations-idUSBREA131EW20140204.

66. Marzuki Darusman, Steven Ratner, and Yasmin Sooka, "Revisiting Sri Lanka's Bloody War," *New York Times*, March 2, 2012.

67. Human Rights Watch, "Sri Lanka: Report Fails to Advance Accountability," December 16, 2011, https://www.hrw.org/news/2011/12/16/sri-lanka-report-fails-advance-accountability.

68. International Crisis Group, "Statement on the Report of Sri Lanka's Lessons Learnt and Reconciliation Commission," December 22, 2011, https://www.crisisgroup.org/asia

/south-asia/sri-lanka/statement-report-sri-lankas-lessons-learnt-and-reconciliation
-commission.

69. Human Rights Watch, "Sri Lanka: Army Inquiry a Delaying Tactic," February 15, 2012; Human Rights Watch, "Sri Lanka: No Justice in Aid Worker Massacre," July 31, 2013.

70. Author's field notes, Geneva, Switzerland, March 2014.

71. See Table 4.1 of Sri Lankan Ministry of Finance & Planning, Department of External Resources, Performance Report 2009, http://www.erd.gov.lk/images/pdf/performance_report_2009.pdf. With US military assistance curtailed and India refusing to supply offensive weaponry, Chinese arms sales to Sri Lanka increased "sevenfold" from 2006 to 2008. Nilanthi Samaranayake, "Are Sri Lanka's Relations with China Deepening? An Analysis of Economic, Military, and Diplomatic Data," *Asian Security* 7, no.2 (2011): 119–46. Contemporaneous reports also suggested that Pakistan's increase of military assistance loans, arms sales, and training to Sri Lanka's Air Force were the direct result of Chinese pressure. Brahma Chellaney, "China Fuels Sri Lankan War," *Japan Times*, March 4, 2009, https://www.japantimes.co.jp/opinion/2009/03/04/commentary/china-fuels-sri-lankan-war;

72. Somini Sengupta, "Take Aid from China and Take a Pass on Human Rights," *New York Times*, March 9, 2008.

73. US Senate Committee on Foreign Relations, "Sri Lanka: Recharting US Strategy after the War," 111th Congress: First Session, December 7, 2009, https://www.foreign.senate.gov/imo/media/doc/SRI.pdf.

74. Sengupta, "Take Aid from China."

75. "China Backs Sri Lanka," *Daily Mirror*, May 1, 2011.

76. Compare, for instance, the robust international response to another widely reported mass killing event of 2009: the stadium massacre in Conakry, Guinea. After security forces killed more than 150 civilians at an opposition rally, foreign governments instituted targeted sanctions against members of the Guinean regime and international and regional organizations sprang into action to demand accountability and protection of civilians. See also Suthaharan Nadarajah, "The Tamil Proscriptions: Identities, Legitimacies, and Situated Practices," *Terrorism and Political Violence* 30, no. 2 (March 4, 2018): 278–97.

77. US Department of State, "Daily Press Briefing—December 19, 2011."

78. Mahinda Samarasinghe, Statement of Sri Lanka, UNHRC, 18th Regular Session, September 12, 2011.

79. Mahinda Samarasinghe, Statement of Sri Lanka: High Level Segment, UNHRC, 19th Regular Session, February 27, 2012.

80. Samarasinghe, Statement of Sri Lanka, February 27, 2012.

81. Ravinatha Aryasinha, Statement of Sri Lanka, UNHRC, 23rd Regular Session, May 27, 2013.

82. Mahinda Samarasinghe, Statement of Sri Lanka, UNHRC, 22nd Regular Session, March 21, 2013.

83. Ravinatha Aryasinha, Statement of Sri Lanka, UNHRC, 24th Regular Session, September 25, 2013.

84. Permanent Mission of Sri Lanka to the UN Office at Geneva, Comments received from the Permanent Mission of Sri Lanka, A/HRC/25/G/9, February 24, 2014, http://ap.ohchr.org/Documents/E/HRC/c_gov/A_HRC_25_G_9_AEV.doc.

85. "Vested Groups' Intention of Interfering in Sri Lanka's Internal Affairs Exposed," *Asian Tribune*, March 6, 2012; Mahinda Samarasinghe, Statement of Sri Lanka, UNHRC, 19th Regular Session, March 22, 2012.

86. Kshenuka Senewiratne, Statement of Sri Lanka on the Statement of the High Commissioner for Human Rights Navanethem Pillay, UNHRC, 17th Regular Session, May 30, 2011.

87. Tamara Kunanayakam, "Response to Media Queries on the Amnesty International Report on the LLRC," September 10, 2011, http://www.lankamission.org/human-rights -humanitarian-affairs/591-sri-lanka-ambas sador-tamara-kunanayakam-responds-to -media-queries-on-the-ai-report-on-the-llrc-2.html.

88. Samarasinghe, Statement of Sri Lanka, March 22, 2012.

89. "'UNHRC Battle Will Be Fought to the Very Last Minute': Ambassador Tamara Kunanayakam," *Daily FT*, March 10, 2012, https://www.ft.lk/opinion/unhrc-battle-will -be-fought-to-the-very-last-minute-ambassador-tamara-kunanayakam/14-75948.

90. Samarasinghe, Statement of Sri Lanka, March 21, 2013.

91. Ravinatha Aryasinha, Intervention at the Informal Meeting on the Draft Resolution on "Promoting Reconciliation and Accountability in Sri Lanka," UNHRC, 22nd Regular Session, March 8, 2013.

92. Ravinatha Aryasinha, Intervention at the First Informal Meeting Called by the Sponsors of the Draft Resolution on Sri Lanka, UNHRC, 25th Regular Session, March 7, 2014.

93. Mahinda Rajapaksa, Address by His Excellency the President Mahinda Rajapaksa at the Sixty-Eighth Session of the United Nations General Assembly, September 24, 2013, https://gadebate.un.org/sites/default/files/gastatements/68/LK_en.pdf.

94. Author's field notes, Geneva, Switzerland, March 2014.

95. Shihar Aneez, "Sri Lanka's President Denounces US Plan for Rights Resolution," *Reuters*, February 28, 2014, https://uk.reuters.com/article/srilanka-president/sri-lankas -president-denounces-u-s-plan-for-rights-resolution-idINDEEA1R0AI20140228.

96. Author interview with civil society member, Colombo, Sri Lanka, August 8, 2013.

97. Vinay Kumar, "UNHRC Resolution: Govt. to Keep in Mind Implications," *The Hindu*, March 15, 2012, https://www.thehindu.com/news/national/unhrc-resolution -govt-to-keep-in-mind-implications/article2995433.ece; author interview with Tamil diaspora activist.

98. US Delegation to the Human Rights Council, Statement by Ambassador Eileen Chamberlain Donahoe: Introduction of Draft Resolution L.2 on Promoting Reconciliation and Accountability in Sri Lanka, UNHRC, 19th Regular Session, March 22, 2012, https://geneva.usmission.gov/2012/03/22/sri-lank.

99. Information on member votes and statements cited in this section are from the author's notes, either from attending the relevant UNHRC session or watching the UN Web TV telecast.

100. UN Human Rights Council, A/HRC/RES/22/1: Promoting Reconciliation and Accountability in Sri Lanka, March 21, 2013, http://ap.ohchr.org/documents/dpage_e .aspx?si=A/HRC/RES/22/1.

101. Author's field notes, Geneva, Switzerland, March 2014.

102. UN Human Rights Council, A/HRC/RES/25/1: Promoting Reconciliation and Accountability in Sri Lanka. March 27, 2014, http://ap.ohchr.org/documents/dpage_e .aspx?si=A/HRC/RES/25/1.

103. "No More Excuses, It Is Time to Act," *Tamil Guardian*, December 17, 2011, https:// www.tamilguardian.com/content/no-more-excuses-it-time-act.

104. Author interview with Tamil activist.

105. "New UN rights probe intensifies pressure on Sri Lanka," *Associated Press*, June 30, 2014, https://www.dawn.com/news/1116084.

106. Like Minded Group, Joint Statement, September 26, 2014, http://www.lankaweb .com/news/items/2014/09/26/like-minded-group-joint-statement-says-the-intrusive -mandate-given-to-the-ohchr-by-res-251-to-carry-out-investigations-on-sri-lanka-is -unwarranted.

107. Kofi Annan, "Secretary-General's Address to the Commission on Human Rights," April 7, 2005, https://www.un.org/sg/en/content/sg/statement/2005-04-07/secretary -generals-address-commission-human-rights.

108. M. Joel Voss, "Contesting Sexual Orientation and Gender Identity at the UN Human Rights Council," *Human Rights Review* 19, no. 1 (2018): 1–22, at 4.

109. James H. Lebovic and Erik Voeten, "The Politics of Shame: The Condemnation of Country Human Rights Practices in the UNCHR," *International Studies Quarterly* 50, no. 4 (December 1, 2006): 861–88.

CONCLUSION

1. Aryeh Neier, "'Naming and Shaming': Still the Human Rights Movement's Best Weapon," OpenGlobalRights, July 11, 2018; Jack Snyder, "Backlash against Naming and Shaming: The Politics of Status and Emotion," *British Journal of Politics and International Relations* 22, no. 4 (November 1, 2020): 644–53, 645.

2. Rochelle Terman, "Rewarding Resistance: Theorizing Defiance to International Norms," 2017, http://rochelleterman.com/wp-content/uploads/2014/08/4b_Defiance.pdf.

3. Leslie Vinjamuri, "Human Rights Backlash," in *Human Rights Futures*, ed. Stephen Hopgood, Jack Snyder, and Leslie Vinjamuri (Cambridge: Cambridge University Press, 2017), 114–34.

4. Jelena Subotić, *Hijacked Justice: Dealing with the Past in the Balkans* (Cornell University Press, 2009), 37.

5. Human Rights Watch, "Myanmar: Government Rohingya Report Falls Short," January 22, 2020, https://www.hrw.org/news/2020/01/22/myanmar-government-rohingya -report-falls-short.

6. "Nepal: Commissions of Inquiry Don't Address Need for Accountability," *International Commission of Jurists* (blog), June 28, 2012, https://www.icj.org/nepal-toothless -commissions-of-inquiry-do-not-address-urgent-need-for-accountability-icj-report/.

7. Philip Alston, *Report of the Special Rapporteur on Extrajudicial, Summary or Arbitrary Executions* (Geneva: United Nations, May 2, 2008), para 20.

8. Mona Lena Krook and Jacqui True, "Rethinking the Life Cycles of International Norms: The United Nations and the Global Promotion of Gender Equality," *European Journal of International Relations* 18, no. 1 (March 1, 2012): 103–27.

9. Hannes Hansen-Magnusson and Antje Vetterlein, eds., *The Routledge Handbook on Responsibility in International Relations* (Abingdon, UK: Routledge, 2021).

10. Regina Heller, Martin Kahl, and Daniela Pisoiu, "The 'Dark' Side of Normative Argumentation—The Case of Counterterrorism Policy," *Global Constitutionalism* 1, no. 2 (July 2012): 278–312.

11. Amnesty International, "Nepal: Fix Flawed Truth and Reconciliation Act," July 9, 2014.

12. Nicole Deitelhoff and Lisbeth Zimmermann, "Things We Lost in the Fire: How Different Types of Contestation Affect the Robustness of International Norms," *International Studies Review* 22, no. 1 (March 1, 2020): 51–76.

13. See, e.g., Martha Finnemore and Kathryn Sikkink, "International Norm Dynamics and Political Change," *International Organization* 52, no. 4 (1998): 887–917.

14. Kathryn Sikkink, *The Justice Cascade: How Human Rights Prosecutions Are Changing World Politics*, The Norton Series in World Politics (Norton, 2011); Krook and True, "Rethinking the Life Cycles of International Norms," 106.

15. Alan Bloomfield and Shirley V. Scott, "Norm Entrepreneurs and Antipreneurs," in *Norm Antipreneurs and the Politics of Resistance to Global Normative Change* (Routledge, 2016), 234.

16. Diana Panke and Ulrich Petersohn, "Why International Norms Disappear Sometimes," *European Journal of International Relations* 18, no. 4 (December 2012): 719–42.

17. See, e.g., Clifford Bob, *The Global Right Wing and the Clash of World Politics* (Cambridge University Press, 2012).

18. Activist interview, Trincomalee, Sri Lanka, July 2017.

19. Author's field notes, July 2017. For a fuller discussion of these survivors' experiences, see my coauthored article with Roxani Krystalli: Kate Cronin-Furman and Roxani Krystalli, "The Things They Carry: Victims' Documentation of Forced Disappearance in Colombia and Sri Lanka," *European Journal of International Relations* 27, no. 1 (March 1, 2021): 79–101.

20. Activist interview, Mullaitivu, Sri Lanka, July 2017.

21. Activist Interview, Vavuniya, Sri Lanka, July 2017.

22. Note that the ICC investigation currently proceeding into crimes against the Rohingya is based on the court's jurisdiction over Bangladesh (a member state) and is strictly limited to conduct committed at least in part on Bangladeshi territory.

23. Either in the form of an ICC referral or the even less likely prospect of the creation of a new ad hoc tribunal.

APPENDICES

1. $p = 0.1715$ and 0.5143, respectively.

2. Gary King and Langche Zeng, "Logistic Regression in Rare Events Data," *Political Analysis* 9 No. 2 (2001): 137–163.

3. "Intra-State War Data v4.1," The Correlates of War Project, https://correlatesofwar.org/data-sets.

4. Kathryn Sikkink, *The Justice Cascade: How Human Rights Prosecutions Are Changing World Politics* (Norton, 2011).

5. The PRS Group, "*ICRG* Methodology," https://www.prsgroup.com/wp-content/uploads/2014/08/icrgmethodology.pdf.

www.ingramcontent.com/pod-product-compliance
Lightning Source LLC
Chambersburg PA
CBHW020333071125
35095CB00043B/2400